THEORIES IN COUNSELING AND THERAPY
An Experiential Approach

JEFFREY A. KOTTLER

California State University–Fullerton

ALLYN AND BACON

Boston ■ London ■ Toronto ■ Sydney ■ Tokyo ■ Singapore

90.00

Executive Editor: *Virginia Lanigan*
Editorial Assistant: *Erin Liedel*
Marketing Manager: *Kathleen Morgan*
Editorial-Production Service: *Omegatype Typography, Inc.*
Composition and Prepress Buyer: *Linda Cox*
Manufacturing Buyer: *Julie McNeill*
Cover Administrator: *Kristina Mose-Libon*
Electronic Composition: *Omegatype Typography, Inc.*

Library of Congress Cataloging-in-Publication Data

Kottler, Jeffrey A.
 Theories in counseling and therapy : an experiential approach/Jeffrey A. Kottler.
  p. cm.
 Includes bibliographical references and index.
 ISBN 0-205-32473-8 (alk. paper)
 1. Counseling. 2. Psychotherapy. I. Title.

 BF637.C6 K685 2002
 158'.3-dc21

2001022111

Printed in the United States of America

10 9 8 7 6 5 4 3 2   06 05 04 03

CONTENTS

CHAPTER SEVEN

What Is Learned Can Be Unlearned:
Behavioral Approaches   137

CHAPTER EIGHT

All in the Family: Systemic Approaches   159

CHAPTER NINE

Problems and Solutions: Brief Approaches   191

PREFACE

■ ■ ■ ■ ■ ▬▬▬▬▬▬▬▬▬▬▬▬▬▬▬▬▬▬▬▬▬▬▬▬▬▬▬▬

This is a text for a *very* challenging course—not only for students but also for the instructor. There is so much material to cover, so many complex and confusing ideas to review, that most people involved in the experience often feel overwhelmed and bewildered. Names start to sound the same. Various theories all run together. Rather than feeling excited and stimulated by the wonderful theoretical background of the field, both students and faculty often keep their heads to the ground, grimly marching toward the distant goal of conceptual mastery. It's the theory-of-the-week club, and every seven days force the abandonment of one set of ideas for the next ones waiting around the corner.

This text will not only supply the background material that is needed for a first course on theory in counseling and therapy but it will also provide a structure for the experience that will keep things fun, stimulating, and personally meaningful. Similar to any experiential approach to a subject, the emphasis throughout this book is on applying concepts to your personal life and professional activities. This not only will keep you actively involved in the learning process but also will help you to develop ways for synthesizing the material in a personally meaningful way.

Who This Text Is For

This is a text for both undergraduate and graduate classes in psychology, counseling, social work, human services, family therapy, and related helping professions. It draws on theories from all these disciplines, as well as contributions from medicine, education, philosophy, and the social sciences. It is intended to be the primary text for courses such as Theories of Counseling, Theory and Practice of Psychotherapy, and Theory and Application, and is also suitable for a number of other courses that introduce students to the conceptual background of helping.

Because of its experiential format, this text is especially well suited to instructors whose teaching style involves lots of class discussions, interactive exercises, and demonstrations. Lectures and readings can carry even the most eager students only so far. At some point, they must have opportunities for more active learning structures.

This text is designed to help you as students to personalize and integrate what you learn. It speaks as a trusted companion who not only whispers in your ear the important things you will need to know but also advises you on the best ways to use these ideas in your life and work.

Structure of the Book

The book is divided into three main parts, an introductory section that gives you the background you need to understand the theories that follow, a middle section composed of several chapters that discuss the main theory "families," and a final section that synthesizes and applies what has been learned.

Throughout the text are series of experiential activities that include (1) reflective exercises, (2) class activities, (3) field studies, (4) homework assignments, and (5) personal applications. These are not the sorts of projects that you would want to skip in order to get to the real meat of things—they are the central focus of this text. When this course is over, you should be able to understand the major conceptual ideas of the field, be able to talk about them intelligently, and apply them in your life and work.

The Way Things Are Organized

There is considerable debate in the field about the best way to classify theories or to organize them according to their essential features. To make matters more complex, there is the practical problem of squeezing all the major models currently in use into a semester-long course format. Although there are perhaps hundreds of different theories favored by practicing counselors and therapists, only about two dozen of the models would be considered mainstream. The challenge is how to organize all of these different theories into reasonably sized packages that you can digest in a single sitting.

Instructors of this course have their own strong opinions about which theories should be featured and which ones should be excluded. That is one of the beauties of this field—so much is up to interpretation based on your own understanding of the literature and your own experiences as a clinician.

I think one of the best parts of your education as a practitioner involves being exposed to divergent viewpoints and then forming your own ideas based on research and practice. So, be prepared to hear considerable disagreement among your instructors (and textbook authors) about some of the ideas presented here. The good news is that most of us have reached consensus about the basic ideas in the field, and that will form your professional foundation.

As I mentioned, this text is organized with central ideas integrated into broad families rather than discrete and separate theories. I have done this for several reasons. For one, if each theory had its own chapter, you would feel even more overwhelmed with all the material to master; instead, I have managed to cover the principal approaches in eight chapters, each one including conceptual frameworks that share some common ancestors and basic ideas. For instance, it is common in texts for theories such as reality therapy (William Glasser), rational emotive behavior therapy (Albert Ellis), cognitive therapy (Aaron Beck), multimodal therapy (Arnold Lazarus), and Adlerian therapy (Alfred Adler) to each have their own chapter. Unfortunately, that means adding five chapters to the text, and this is only one family of ideas! What I have done instead is group these theories together as cognitive approaches because they all emphasize, to one extent or another, the importance of internal thinking processes on subsequent perceptions and actions. This, of course, is a gross simplification. Reality therapists and Adlerian therapists, in particular, might very well take exception to this decision.

Contents of the Book

In the first three chapters, the stage is set for the main acts that follow. The book begins with a very personal introduction to the subject of theory, reviewing the processes and experiences that you might reasonably expect to encounter during this journey. As you will soon learn, in order for therapy to work well, clients must be inducted into appropriate roles. They must learn what to expect, how to behave, and how to get the most from their experience. The same holds true for your role as a student of theory.

In Chapter 2, the context for the ways that practitioners use theories in their work is described. Some of the major trends in the profession are highlighted, with an emphasis on the realities of contemporary practice. Chapter 3 talks about the distinctly individualized aspects of theory development and application. Each practitioner develops an approach to helping that closely matches his or her own client populations, personality, values, philosophy of life, and preferences. Furthermore, you will be expected not only to integrate a therapeutic approach into your work but also to combine it with a number of other theories about how people learn, develop, and grow. This first section ends by providing a particular set of lenses through which to look critically at each model you will study. Flexibility and fluidity are extremely crucial in order for you to adapt theories to fit the unique cultural backgrounds of each client you will see.

In Chapter 4, the psychoanalytic family of theories is covered. Although hardly a cohesive, high-functioning group of siblings (more like feuding cousins), these frameworks do share a common heritage that emerged from Sigmund Freud's original work. The Vienna Psychoanalytic Society was at one time composed of the likes of Alfred Adler, Carl Jung, and others who went on to found their own schools of thought. Other related theories developed by Melanie Klein, Erich Fromm, and Wilhelm Reich are mentioned, as are a number of contemporary revisions proposed by so-called self-psychologists or ego theorists. The briefer forms of psychoanalytic treatment that are becoming increasingly common are presented in a later chapter on brief therapies.

The humanistic family of theories in Chapter 5 is just as diverse. Naturally, Carl Rogers and his client-centered approach are covered. But so are existential theory and Gestalt therapy, which are often afforded their own separate chapters. As different as these three theories might be, they share a core set of beliefs about the nature of human beings. They all value a particular kind of helping relationship that is genuine, authentic, and caring.

As I've already mentioned, Chapter 6 on cognitive approaches contains not only the standard entries of cognitive therapy and rational emotive behavior therapy but also contains integrative approaches such as multimodal therapy and Adlerian therapy that have some cognitive features. Reality therapy is also included here because of recent convergences in Glasser's work with that of other cognitive theorists (such integration between different theories is occurring with increasing regularity).

In comparison to the other theoretical families, Chapter 7 on behavioral approaches is fairly homogeneous. The basic tenets of behavioral theory are introduced, along with the generic interventions that have now become part of standard practice for most practitioners. Thus, the methods of relaxation training, systematic desensitization, behavioral contracting, and assertiveness training will be familiar to you.

Chapter 8 on systemic theories is somewhat unusual in a book such as this. This is mostly because there is not usually enough space available and these theories are typically covered in a separate course on family therapy. Nevertheless, I believe that systemic thinking has become so important to our field that you should have early and repeated exposure to the ideas. This is particularly the case because they are so different from those theories that were devised from an individual person's perspective. In addition to traditional family therapies, there is also an introduction to constructivist and narrative therapies that are becoming increasingly influential.

Chapters 9 and 10 are others that are not usually included in a theories text (perhaps you can tell that I rather enjoy conceiving of this material in the most contemporary, cutting-edge way possible). Chapter 9 on models of brief therapy describes the changing landscape of our profession, showing how more and more we will be expected to make a difference in people's lives in briefer periods of time. The most prominent models of brief therapy are presented, including Ericksonian hypnotherapy, strategic therapy, problem-solving therapy, solution-focused therapy, single-session therapy, eye movement and desensitization reprocessing, and a generic model that combines the best features of all.

Chapter 10 continues the discussion of cutting-edge approaches by reviewing those theories that are considered out of the mainstream. This is not to say that they are flaky or unscientific, just that they are rather innovative. (In time, many of them will become mainstream just as others will become obsolete.) The most important of these cutting-edge approaches is feminist theory, but various expressive therapies that employ music, drama, art, movement, exercise, and spiritual methods are also included.

The final section of the book helps integrate what was learned. Chapter 11 compares and contrasts the theories that have been covered and Chapter 12 encourages an introspective, critical process of personalizing the material.

Use of Terms

Use of the terms *therapist* and *therapy* is meant to refer generically to the work not only of psychologists, social workers, and family therapists but also to the work of school and agency counselors, psychiatric nurses, mental health workers, and other professional helpers.

ACKNOWLEDGMENTS

In a book such as this, serving as reviewer is a huge assignment. I am most grateful for the assistance of the following individuals who offered constructive feedback on the manuscript: Alfiee M. Breland, Michigan State University; R. L. Harbach, University of Nevada, Las Vegas; Byron Hargrove, Seton Hall University; Cynthia R. Kalodner, West Virginia University; Ronald S. Kiyuna, California State University—Fresno; Senez Rodriguez-Charbonier, Grand Valley State University.

I also wish to thank Virginia Lanigan, acquisitions editor at Allyn and Bacon, for her flexibility and support throughout the writing of this book. Much of it was written at a difficult time in a very remote place (Iceland).

ABOUT THE AUTHOR

Jeffrey A. Kottler has authored over forty-five books in the field for therapists, counselors, teachers, and the public, including *Compassionate Therapy: Working with Difficult Clients* (1992), *On Being a Therapist* (1993), *Beyond Blame* (1994), *The Language of Tears* (1996), *What You Never Learned in Graduate School* (1997), *Travel That Can Change Your Life* (1997), *Doing Good: Passion and Commitment for Helping Others* (2000), *Nuts and Bolts of Helping* (2000), and *Learning Group Leadership: An Experiential Approach* (2001).

Jeffrey has worked as a teacher, counselor, and therapist in a preschool, middle school, mental health center, crisis center, university, community college, and private practice. He has served as a Fulbright Scholar and Senior Lecturer in Peru (1980) and Iceland (2000), as well as teaching theory and practice throughout Australia and Asia.

Jeffrey is the chair of the counseling department at California State University–Fullerton.

CHAPTER 1

A PERSONAL INTRODUCTION TO THEORY

Throughout my training as a counselor and therapist, theory was the scourge of my life. I wanted to help people. I wanted to learn practical stuff that I could use immediately to make a difference in others' lives. Just as importantly, I hoped that much of what I was learning I could use to improve my personal relationships. I had visions that once I became proficient in the basic skills I could get people to like me more, understand better why people act the ways they do, and be more effective in my daily interactions.

Although theory could be useful in reaching these goals, I was impatient; often I couldn't see a clear connection between what I was learning in school and what I was expected to do in my work and in my life. When reading class assignments, I often found it difficult to concentrate on the words. All the names seemed to run together. And I couldn't figure out the point of learning so many different theories when they all seemed to contradict one another.

I was a very impressionable student, eager to learn as much as I could and motivated to impress my teachers. Each instructor would present a particular theory that he or she believed was The Answer. Research would be supplied to support the particular choice. Case examples of miracle cures further impressed me with how superior this theory was to all others. In no time, I was convinced that I had finally found The Truth.

My moment of revelation would last about as long as it took to arrive at my next class in which the instructor would be equally persuasive. An alternative theory would be presented that directly refuted the premises of the previous one. Naturally, I would resist attempts to convert me to the enemy camp, but I soon found myself a True Believer of another theory.

I won't bore you with the lengthy journey I have traveled down the road to theory enlightenment. When you consider that there are over 400 distinctly different theories that have been catalogued (Karasu, 1986), you can appreciate just how long it would take to sample all of them. Even if you narrow the choices to the dozen most popular approaches, you would still need a few lifetimes to do them justice.

I'm not exaggerating when I say that, at one time or another, I have followed the tenets of at least a dozen or more of the theories contained in this book. I loved them all! And I found they all worked most of the time.

You might wonder that if a theory was so helpful to me and my clients, why on earth would I have ever abandoned it in favor of others? You could chalk it up to my fickle nature, or my desire for novelty, or need for approval from supervisors, but I'd prefer to think I was always searching for a better, more efficient, more powerful means by which to promote lasting change in those I was assigned to help.

■ ■ ■ ■ ■ ▬▬▬▬▬▬▬▬▬▬▬▬▬▬▬▬▬▬▬▬▬▬▬▬

FOR PERSONAL REFLECTION OR CLASS ACTIVITY

Either in a journal or with a small group of peers, talk about the reactions you have to the author's confession. How does it compare with what you have experienced thus far in your training? Talk about your own journey toward theory development, including your major points of confusion and frustration.

SO MANY CHOICES, SO LITTLE TIME

I started with psychoanalytic theory because that was the approach taken by the first therapist I saw while I was a college student. I had been heartbroken by a girlfriend, so depressed I could barely get out of bed. I visited the counseling center on campus in a last, desperate effort to prevent myself from dropping out of school. The therapist was so understanding, so responsive—the mother I'd always wanted. We spent a lot of time talking about my childhood and how those experiences shaped the problems I was encountering in the present. After reading the collected works of Freud and many of his disciples, I decided to follow in the footsteps of my therapist and become a psychoanalytic therapist.

My first job as a crisis intervention counselor was quite at odds with the theory to which I had decided to devote my life. Here I was in a situation trying to help people who were overdosing on drugs or trying to kill themselves. Even if I could get them to pay attention for more than a minute at a time, they had very little interest in their dreams, unconscious, or repressed impulses; all they wanted was a little relief from their suffering—and they wanted it immediately.

I became a behaviorist within days of starting my job. I usually had only one session, or maybe two—sometimes just a brief phone call—in which to offer help. I learned rather quickly to program specific treatment goals, identify effective reinforcers, and help people to set up some kind of self-management program to deal with their problems. Then I'd refer them to a support group.

I read everything I could get my hands on about behavioral theory. I loved its specificity and concreteness. I felt so grateful for the structure that it offered, especially for a beginner like me who was trying to make sense of this mysterious process that everyone explained so differently. Moreover, I liked the way I could define specific goals and then measure the extent to which my efforts were helpful.

When I began graduate school, my advisor was a rational emotive therapist, so that's what I became next. I desperately wanted his approval, and because he believed that behavioral theory was so limited, I couldn't help but agree with him. Once he demonstrated the theory in action by helping me to work through a long-standing family problem in a single hour, I was truly blown away. I went to workshops on cognitive approaches and did my best to become an expert, even volunteering to be a client on stage during demonstrations. Just as convincing was how effective the approach seemed to be with the clients I was beginning to see as part of my training.

If we had more time together, I could elaborate further about how many theories I have followed during my career. From rational emotive theory, I adopted the client-centered approach and then Gestalt therapy and existential therapy. I loved each of them—loved them all!

In later years as I progressed through a master's and doctoral program, and worked in a dozen different jobs, I became a full-fledged, card-carrying, transpersonal, strategic, and constructivist practitioner. I have attended workshops on a dozen other conceptual approaches, finding all of them useful with my clients.

At one point, you can imagine the confusion that settled in. You are probably feeling much the same thing right now. All of these theories seem so different, yet they all seem to work well. How can this possibly be true? To make matters worse, at times all the theories sound the same—it's hard to keep them separate and remember where one ends and the other begins.

■ ■ ■ ■ ■

FOR PERSONAL REFLECTION

You must already have some hunches about how it is possible that so many different approaches to helping can be effective with some people some of the time. On your own, or in conversation with classmates, think about what you believe the most common elements might be.

Like most experienced practitioners, I tried to integrate the best features of each theory I studied. I borrowed a little here, changed a few ideas there, and combined the parts I liked most into a framework that seemed to work best with my personality and style, as well as with my clients. Since beginning this synthesis over thirty years ago, I am still making refinements in my theory in light of new ideas that emerge, new research that is published, and new experiences I accumulate with my clients. The changes have been so vast that clients I have seen ten years ago would hardly recognize my work today. Rather than apologizing for this evolution, I am proud and delighted by the ever-changing nature of this profession. You will be too—once you overcome some of your confusion, uncertainty, doubts, and fears.

FOR A FIELD STUDY

Approach several practitioners who are doing what you hope to do someday. Ask them about the evolution of their conceptual development. Rather than keeping the conversation solely on an intellectual level, as if their theories were selected purely based on logical choices, inquire about the personal motives and factors that influenced their development. Find out what the critical incidents were that shaped their ideas about how therapy works best.

HOW TO GET THE MOST FROM THIS CLASS AND TEXT

The main challenge of this course is that there is so much material to learn and so little time in which to learn it. Furthermore, you will be learning theories not only to understand their roots, to pass an exam, or to write a paper, but also to *apply* them effectively. Very soon you will be sitting opposite people who look to you for relief from their pain. They want you to explain what is wrong with them. They expect you to make their problems go away. They demand to know what you are going to do and how you are going to do it. And you had better have some answers—not only in addressing their concerns but also in delivering what you promise. Unless you have mastered a theory to make sense of what is happening and organize your interventions, not only won't you help people but also you can actually make things a lot worse.

I will do my best to "sell" each of the theories in this text. I will be as persuasive as I can to convince you why a theory is so wonderful, how much it offers, and all the neat stuff it provides in the way of guidance. Then, in the very next chapter, I will present *another* theory that sounds just as good. Then another, and another.

My recommendation is to treat each of the theories as valuable and important. Assume that every prominent approach is popular because many experienced professionals have found it effective. Know that current research has failed to support the superiority of any one of these theories over all the rest (although some are better than others for some situations and issues). That is not to say that you will *like* each of them; on the contrary, some will immediately attract you and others will strike you as silly or irrelevant or not at all representative of your experience. That is very good news actually because it will make your job so much easier in narrowing down the options to those that fit best with your interests, specialty, personality, and desired job setting.

As you read this text, I would like to offer the following advice about approaching this subject:

1. *Think critically about what you read.* Don't take my word for what is presented. Compare the ideas to your own experience. But don't argue with me or your instructor; argue with yourself.
2. *Talk about the concepts with family members and friends.* Take it home with you. Don't just compartmentalize what you are learning; if you do, you may end up leaving loved ones behind.
3. *Keep up with your reading.* This is not the sort of course in which you can wait until the last minute to prepare for a test or assignment.
4. *Form a study group with classmates.* It is important for you to find and create opportunities to talk about what you are learning and to apply ideas to your work and life.
5. *Do the exercises and activities.* Throughout the text there are numerous "time-outs" for reflection, field studies, class activities, and homework assignments. If your goal is to make this stuff part of you, you must make an effort to personalize the concepts.
6. *Manage your frustration and stress levels.* There is far too much content in this book for any one human being to master in a lifetime, much less in a single semester. Be patient and realistic with yourself about what you can do.
7. *Understand that you have the rest of your career to study a few of these theories in depth.* For now, your job is to get the basics down so that you have a working background in which to apply one or two theories with reasonable effectiveness.
8. *Make learning an active process.* Take responsibility for applying what you read and do in class to your daily life.

■ ■ ■ ■ ■

FOR PERSONAL APPLICATION

You may have glossed over one of the pieces of advice I offered to you. In item 2, I mentioned that it is a good idea to get your family, friends, and loved ones involved in your educational experience. I warned you that if you don't do this, you risk leaving them behind.

One of the consequences of training to be a therapist is that you will change fairly dramatically. In this theory course alone, you will be exposed to many new ideas that will reshape the way you look at the world and yourself. In addition, therapist preparation places great emphasis on developing greater intimacy in relationships, being more honest and direct, and using a variety of interpersonal skills to communicate more powerfully and persuasively. If you don't think this will change all your relationships, you aren't paying attention.

If you are not already doing so, it would be an excellent idea to invite your closest friends and family members to become involved in your education. Talk to them about what you are learning. Recruit their help with assignments in which you need to practice new skills. Introduce them to some of your classmates and instructors. If they show an interest, invite them to read some of your texts and especially your own papers and projects. Most of all, talk to them about what you are experiencing and the changes you are making.

A significant number of students find that their primary relationships and friendships become strained, or even end, as a result of the changes they go through during training. If you begin experiencing troubles in this regard that you can't work through on your own, consult with a counselor or therapist for help. This is perhaps the single best thing you can do to truly experience the power of therapy in action.

WHAT IS AN EXPERIENTIAL APPROACH?

This text takes a very personal approach to the subject of theory. I favor this method not only because it makes learning fun but also because active involvement is required in order to help the ideas stick with you over time. After all, you won't do your clients much good if sometime in the future you have only the vaguest possible notion about how to make sound clinical decisions. You might not remember all the names of things, but you must have instant recall of the principles that guide your professional behavior.

This sort of experiential approach is consistent with what is known about how human learning takes place. Real change occurs not only on an intellectual level but also involves a person's whole being (Bohart, 1993; Kottler, 2001). This is not only the case with how you do counseling and therapy but also how you learn to do it.

In order for you to become thoroughly familiar with the major theoretical structures that guide therapeutic action, you will need to study the material so that it becomes personally meaningful to you. First, as you are well aware, you tend to remember those ideas that seem most relevant as well as those that you can use daily. Second, you will need to understand the theories to the point that you can talk about them intelligently to colleagues, explain them to clients, and combine the best features of divergent approaches into a coherent framework to guide your actions.

An experiential approach to this subject means that you must have direct and intimate connections with the content, not as something that is "out there," but as something that is part of you. It is not enough to *know* the ideas; you must *use* them in your daily functioning. The theories become integrated into the routine and normal ways that you relate to the world.

How does this transformation occur that transcends mere superficial learning such as memorization or recall? Deep learning takes place through direct experience in which you become actively involved in the process. You can't learn this stuff merely by reading about it, or by sitting still in a seat while an instructor—no matter how entertaining and interesting—tells you about it. Seeing demonstrations of the theories in action and watching videos of master practitioners are also extremely useful in making the ideas come alive, but this still doesn't engage you actively to personalize what you are learning.

■ ■ ■ ■ ■

FOR A CLASS ACTIVITY

Talk to one another about the ways that have been most effective for learning new, complex ideas. Think about one specific instance in which you felt particularly successful in this regard and provide examples of what helped you the most to retain the learning.

As a counterpoint, talk about times that you learned things to pass an exam or get through a series of obstacles, but the results were not enduring. Compare the two experiences and come to your own conclusions about what matters most.

In order for you to hold onto this content for the rest of your life you must integrate the new material with what you already know. Then you have to figure out ways to combine the material with reality-based practice. The theories that will be most enduring in your work will be those that fit with your experience. They explain things that make sense to you. They predict behavior accurately. They are congruent with the ways you view the world. Finally, such theories are useful to you in making good decisions about how to do your job most effectively.

To aid you with this challenging mission, each chapter contains a number of experientially based activities, assignments, and reflective exercises that are designed to help you not only remember the theories but also to apply them where they can help the most. I can't stress how important it is that you complete these assignments so that the active process of learning continues even when you aren't studying the text.

To help you begin the difficult job of organizing the material you read and linking related concepts from different approaches, this text treats various theories in broad categories. Throughout your exposure to each individual approach, you will also begin looking at how it is similar to and different from others.

I will do my best to maintain your interest by including lots of stories, case examples, practical applications, and humor. It will be your job to relate what you learn to what you already know, what you are doing in your life, and what you hope to do in the future.

■ ■ ■ ■ ■

REMINDERS OF HOW TO STUDY THEORY

1. Read consistently and steadily throughout the semester.
2. Think critically about what you read.
3. Talk about the concepts with family members and friends.
4. Form a study group with classmates to talk about the ideas.
5. Complete the exercises and activities.
6. Manage your frustration and stress levels so that you remain patient and realistic about what can be done.
7. Get the basics down and then focus on a few theories that appeal most to you.
8. Take responsibility for applying what you read and do in class to your daily life.

SUGGESTED READINGS

Kopp, S. (1985). *Even a stone can be a teacher: Learning and growing from the experiences of everyday life*. New York: Jeremy Tarcher.

Kottler, J. A. (1995). *Growing a therapist*. San Francisco: Jossey-Bass.

Kottler, J. A. (Ed.). (1996). *Finding your way as a counselor.* Alexandria, VA: American Counseling Association.

McClintock, E. (1999). *Room for change: Empowering possibilities for therapists and clients.* Boston: Allyn and Bacon.

Pipes, R. B., & Davenport, D. S. (1999). *Introduction to psychotherapy: Common clinical wisdom.* Boston: Allyn and Bacon.

Ram Das, & Gorman, P. (1985). *How can I help? Stories and reflections on service.* New York: Knopf.

Weinberg, G. (1993). *Nearer to the heart's desire: Tales of psychotherapy.* New York: Plume.

Welch, I. D. (1998). *The path of psychotherapy: Matters of the heart.* Pacific Grove, CA: Brooks/Cole.

Yalom, I. (1990). *Love's executioner and other tales of psychotherapy.* New York: HarperCollins.

■ ■ ■ ■ ■

CHAPTER 2

THEORY IN CONTEXT

You are sitting in session with a client who does not seem to be cooperating with your best efforts to get him to talk about his childhood abuse. In previous sessions he has been quite willing to explore his traumatic past; in fact, he brought up the issue as something he wanted to work on. In the last meeting, you experienced a bit of a breakthrough as the man was able to recover lots of memories that had previously been buried. But now he seems reluctant to continue further. He appears listless and depressed, not at all like his usual demeanor. Finally, after sitting quietly for some minutes, he suddenly looks up at you and starts screaming that you've betrayed him. Quick! What do you do?

This five-minute scenario is not unlike any critical incident that will arise in a session. Something happens that seems puzzling, or at least unanticipated. As a counselor or therapist, you know you have to do something to intervene, but you can't act until you first figure out what is going on. In other words, you rely on some theory to account for the phenomenon and then to guide your efforts to intervene most effectively.

■ ■ ■ ■ ■

FOR PERSONAL REFLECTION

What do you think transpired in this brief episode to explain why this client returned so uncooperative and volatile? Although you have limited information and don't know the context for the behavior, that does not stop you from forming hypotheses to explain confusing situations.

Someone may cut you off on the freeway, and although you don't know the first thing about this person, you still have a theory to explain the erratic behavior—he didn't see you, or he was drunk, or he's the sort of person who doesn't care about others. Someone else does you a favor and you also have a theory to explain the gesture, even with limited data.

Based on the sparse information at your disposal in this therapeutic scenario, what is your best guess about what may be going on?

How do you trace the origins of this belief—from what reasoning did it evolve?

There are actually many legitimate hypotheses that might explain this client's behavior. Perhaps things got a little too threatening last time and defenses are kicking in to protect him from further perceived assaults. Or maybe he is mad at you about something else that is completely unrelated to the prior incidents. Another possibility is that something came up during the week that led him to mistrust you. Maybe he went home, talked about the session, and his spouse told him it was all bunk and he'd need to stop his therapy. There are probably a hundred other possibilities, each of which might logically follow the reasoning of a practitioner who identifies those factors that seem most significant and relevant.

All actions taken by a counselor or therapist depend on the particular theory that is adopted as an organizing framework. In this example, the clinician happens to hold some strong beliefs about what is good for people, how they best change, and what interferes with that progress. Furthermore, there are very well-developed conceptions about what causes resistance and how it must be overcome. Even the belief that resistance is something that exists in reality stems from a theory that is being followed.

A NARRATIVE OF THEORY-IN-ACTION

This chapter continues with a description and review of what counseling and psychotherapy are all about and what practitioners actually do. Based on interviews with therapists in a variety of settings, the concepts in this chapter are highlighted with first-person narratives about the ways that theory is used.

In the opening example that began the chapter, the therapist shares what she was thinking at the time:

> If you want to know the truth, I don't know what was going on inside my head when this happened. I felt scared. I was so disappointed and hurt that the progress I thought we'd made was now washed out. I also felt misunderstood and attacked.
>
> After I calmed down—and I knew I had to do this because he was getting progressively more agitated—I tried to reason through what he might be saying, or really, what he wanted from me. I had to stall first to buy some time.
>
> It's hard, really, to sort out what I was thinking at the time versus what I thought afterward. I've had lots of time to think about this case and talked to lots of colleagues about it to get their perspective on things. You can't believe how many different opinions I've gotten. . . . Okay, maybe you can imagine it.
>
> In the session itself, I went back to basics, which is what I always do when I'm stuck or feel panicky. I reflected back what I was feeling

and sensing from him, hoping not only to gather my wits about me, but also to clarify further what he might be experiencing. He had obviously been having trouble putting it into words.

Let's interrupt the narrative at this point to highlight how different this session would look on the outside from how it feels to the practitioner on the inside. If you were watching this interaction on video, all you'd see in the space of a few minutes is the client yelling at his therapist and the therapist responding calmly and deliberately. Inside, however, the therapist is experiencing a storm of feelings, searching desperately for the "right" handle on what she is facing. Until she can sort out what is really happening, she won't have a remote possibility of choosing the best intervention.

I just knew I'd pushed him too far last time. When the previous session was over, I felt so exhilarated about the progress we'd made but I also felt apprehensive because we'd opened up so many doors. All this stuff from the past just flooded out of him. And I had no idea what he'd do with it all after he left.

Now here are some clearer inklings of this clinician's theoretical orientation. First, she seems to believe that dealing with material from the past is important in order to resolve current issues. Not every practitioner subscribes to this theory, but it is not an uncommon way to proceed. Second, she has some relatively clear notions about what might be contributing to his unusual behavior, labeling it "defensive" and "resistant." She is, thus, not taking what is happening at face value but believes that there is some underlying process going on.

The therapist considered other theoretical frameworks as well to explain the situation, those that look at the systemic context of the behavior (its meaning in light of his other relationships) and its secondary gains (the hidden benefits). In other words, in the span of just a few minutes, she reviewed almost everything she could think of that might be useful.

■ ■ ■ ■ ■ ▬▬▬▬▬▬▬▬▬▬▬▬▬▬▬▬▬▬▬▬▬▬▬▬▬▬

FOR PERSONAL REFLECTION

It is helpful to get into the habit of processing puzzling interactions after they occur. This involves not only playing back what was said and what things looked like but also how they felt to you inside.

Think of a time recently in which you were involved in some struggle or conflict with someone that ended unsatisfactorily. Review that interaction by focusing on some probable hypotheses to explain why things turned out the way they did. Avoid placing blame on yourself or the other person(s) and instead try to make sense of what happened. Pay particular attention to what you were feeling and thinking at the time.

If time and circumstances permit, share this incident and your analysis with a partner. Recruit his or her assistance in formulating a theory to account for the incident. If you were going to revisit the struggle with the intention of improving the outcome, what might you do that is consistent with your theory?

This sort of internal processing is exactly the kind of thing that you will experience firsthand when you are in the helper's chair. Just about every minute, something will happen that you don't understand. About every two or three minutes, you will have to make some response or therapeutic intervention. In each case, you will need some organizing framework that will guide your thinking and actions.

WHAT THEORY WILL DO FOR YOU

A theory is an organized series of propositions that help you explain phenomena, predict behavior, and inform your decisions (Patterson, 1986). Rather than a stable conception, it constantly undergoes revisions in light of new experiences (Peterson & Nisenholz, 1999). What all this means is that you have a hundred theories that you operate from every day of your life. You have a theory about why you do not always get what you want. You have a theory about why there are lousy drivers on the road. You have theories about the way the world works, the way business gets done, and how people should behave. You even have a theory about the best way to get people to do what you want. The main difference between your theories and those you will read about in this book is that you have not spent the time to research systematically your ideas, to organize and field-test them, and then to record them for others to use. If you are serious about becoming a skilled practitioner, that is going to change.

Theory serves a number of different functions for practitioners of most professions, whether that involves architectural plans, legal cases, or therapeutic relationships (Boy & Pine, 1999; Kottler & Brown, 2000). Theory is helpful in that it:

1. Organizes and synthesizes information in such a way to make it more readily accessible.
2. Provides a blueprint for action, plotting choices available based on what is believed to be good for people.
3. Helps us to stay on track, assessing outcomes in light of stated goals.
4. Directs attention to selective data that are deemed most useful.

5. Guides the development of new ideas and interventions that are consistent with standard practices.
6. Encourages continued research to test hypotheses and formulate new questions for investigation.

There are limits to theory, naturally. That's why it is called a theory instead of a reality or a truth. English statesman Lord Chesterfield (1774/1901) once wrote a letter to his son in which he advised him: "The world can doubtless never be well known by theory: practice is absolutely necessary; but surely it is of great use to a young man, before he sets out for that country, full of mazes, windings, and turnings, to have at least a general map of it, made by some experienced traveler." That is *exactly* what the theories in this book are all about: they were constructed by experienced travelers who have already been where you are going, intended to provide you with a general idea of what to expect along the path of your journey. The confusing part, of course, is that there are so many different maps to get to roughly the same destination. Furthermore, these experienced travelers may not have actually visited the same places that you are going, nor will they have encountered the same exact situations along the way.

IS A THEORIES COURSE OBSOLETE?

Some would wonder if it is now obsolete to present theories of intervention as discrete entities. For one, most practitioners are eclectic and tend to borrow strategies from several approaches in their work, depending on what the situation calls for. Second, treatment manuals have been developed to describe specific interventions for particular problems, say, exposure techniques for anxiety or behavioral techniques for sexual dysfunctions. Third, theories are rarely practiced in pure form anymore. The most orthodox psychoanalyst now abbreviates treatment in some cases, as well as employing a variety of methods borrowed from other approaches. Finally, the managed care movement has forced practitioners to be far more flexible, pragmatic, and brief in what they do.

An example of this is the move toward a generic approach to training, driven not only by research but also accrediting bodies that recommend standardized curricula. Any particular course you now take includes facets from many different theoretical families. In a techniques class, for instance, you will most likely learn reflecting feelings (client centered), interpreting (psychoanalytic), goal setting (behavioral), reframing (strategic), role-playing (Gestalt), disputing beliefs (cognitive), and others.

Although there is a movement toward finding generic skills and standardized treatments for a host of clinical situations, most practitioners still favor a particular school of thought as a conceptual base. You don't need to be a card-carrying member of a specific school in order to use the ideas as an organizing framework to assess and treat client complaints. Moreover, the study of the various theories provides a historical context for present standards of practice and future developments.

POINTS OF AGREEMENT

You could very well get the idea that practitioners don't agree on anything in this field, that there are a dozen or more different theories to explain most phenomena and apply to most situations. Although that is indeed true to a certain extent, there is also a consensus among practitioners about consistent standards of practice.

Ethical Practice

If you look at the ethical codes of all the different helping professions (American Association for Marriage and Family Therapy, 1998; American Counseling Association, 1995; American Psychological Association, 1995; National Association of Social Workers, 1996), you will see virtually unanimous agreement about what constitutes appropriate behavior. The basic rule of thumb is that you don't do anything that might harm someone else, either as a result of neglect, incompetence, negligence, or meeting your own needs. Furthermore, therapists are expected to act with the highest standard of moral conviction, fighting against injustice, prejudice, and oppression (Cohen & Cohen, 1999).

Regardless of the setting in which you practice, the clients with whom you work, and the methods you might employ, your behavior is expected to be consistent with the following ethical principles (Corey, Corey, & Callanan, 1998; Cottone & Tarvydas, 1998; Weifel, 1998):

1. *Informed consent.* Clients have a right to make their own choices regarding their treatment, based on accurate information.
2. *Confidentiality.* Conversations are held in the strictest confidence and the client's right to privacy is protected, except under those circumstances in which the client might be a danger to himself or herself or others.
3. *Dual relationships.* Because therapists are in positions of power over clients, such circumstances may lead to exploitation. Therapists are prohibited from taking advantage of their clients in any way.

4. *Competence.* Therapists are not permitted to practice outside the scope of their training and preparation. This means therapists may engage only in those methods for which they are qualified.
5. *Respect for differences.* Each client comes to the relationship with a unique personal and cultural background. Therapists make every effort to respect the client's worldview and to refrain from imposing their personal values on others.

■ ■ ■ ■

FOR PERSONAL REFLECTION

Among the major ethical challenges you will face are those that involve practicing within the scope of your competence (item 4). This means that before you attempt any intervention or therapeutic strategy, you must first receive sufficient training and supervision in its use.

Imagine that an issue comes up in session that leads into an area that you know little about, for instance, impulse disorders or side effects from antidepressants. It is important that you appear to know what you are doing to instill confidence in your ability to be helpful. Yet you also want to be completely honest regarding your relative ignorance about these issues.

The easy part is what you *say* you would do. The correct response, of course, is to admit that this is outside your area of expertise and then to seek additional supervision before the next session. At the very least, you would stall until you could do your homework. Much more challenging, however, is what you would actually do in the session because there is sometimes a large discrepancy between what people say (their espoused theory and beliefs) and what they practice.

Assessment and Diagnosis

Although developed primarily by psychiatrists, the *Diagnostic and Statistical Manual (DSM-IV)* of the American Psychiatric Association is the closest thing to an operating manual that therapists have. It is based primarily on the medical model, which means that it uses an approach that classifies disorders with accompanying symptoms as would be found for any disease. Nevertheless, social workers, nurses, family therapists, and counselors are also inclined to use the *DSM-IV* in their work, making it possible for practitioners to have a common source for assessing client problems. Basically, this classification is supposed to be atheoretical, making it possible for practitioners from a wide range of orientations to employ its system.

It is reassuring that in spite of the theoretical differences among practitioners, there is agreement on the major diagnostic entities that therapists should look for during initial interviews. Basically, the categories are divided as follows:

1. *Personality disorders.* This means consistent personality styles that are usually maladaptive. These are often severe kinds of problems to treat because the patterns have become entrenched and are part of the person's usual way of relating to the world and others. Often the interpersonal style can be manipulative, deceitful, or controlling. Varieties you will encounter include narcissistic, borderline, hysterical, antisocial, schizoid, and so on.
2. *Adjustment reactions.* These are logical reactions to stressful situations, accompanied by anxious or depressed feelings, or a combination of both. The best way to make this diagnosis is to find out if the person can identify exactly when and where the problems started.
3. *Schizophrenic processes.* In this case, you will observe severe distortions of reality. The person may have thought disturbances, hallucinations, inappropriate reactions, and gross behavior dysfunctions.
4. *Mood disorders.* These are all severe problems that involve major incapacitation, including major depression and bipolar disorders mentioned earlier.
5. *Addictive disorders.* People become addicted to drugs, alcohol, gambling, sexual acting out, and other compulsive behaviors that interfere with healthy functioning.
6. *Organic and somatic complaints.* These involve some interaction between mind and body. It is likely that some underlying disease process (a tumor, degenerative neurological disease) may be influencing the psychological symptoms.

The diagnostic system currently in use by mental health professionals is only one example of a consistent standard of practice that transcends theoretical allegiances. There is also a variety of complaints that most practitioners would attempt to treat in basically the same way. I say "basically" because it would still be necessary to customize the sort of relationship you develop, as well as the way you implement the interventions, depending on the unique personality, needs, and cultural background of the client.

CONTEMPORARY TRENDS

One final area to examine the context of theories in the field is the cultural landscape in which therapists must practice. There are a number of trends that have emerged in recent years that shape not only which theories are rising to greatest prominence but also the ways in which they are applied.

■ ■ ■ ■ ■ ▬▬▬▬▬▬▬▬▬▬▬▬▬▬▬▬▬▬▬▬▬▬▬▬

FOR A CLASS ACTIVITY

Working in teams, come up with a list of the major cultural movements, trends, and forces that you believe will most impact the practice of counseling and therapy in the future. Consider such factors as technology, social evolution, political climate, economics, and moral development, as well as cultural fads in music, recreation, entertainment, and lifestyle. Make some predictions about the kinds of theories that will evolve to meet these changing circumstances.

It would appear as if the decision about which theory you adopt in your work is made by individual choice, according to your own individual values, preferences, philosophy, and inclinations. Although you certainly have some say in the matter, especially after you become a veteran, particular theories are often thrust upon you because others in power feel they are most suitable.

Managed Care

The managed care movement has had a huge impact on the cultural context for the practice of therapy, strongly shaping which theories may be used (see Brothers, 1999; Frager, 2000; Weisgerber, 1999). This has spawned much greater emphasis on briefer forms of therapy, especially those that are well suited to measuring outcomes (Holt, 2000). What this means is that when a new client walks in the door, the choice you make about treatment decisions and plans of action are not only influenced by the supervisors in your organization but also by case managers (often nurses or administrators) whose main priority is keeping costs under control.

It is likely that in the future you will see even more determined efforts on the part of third parties to hold therapists accountable for their treatment plans. Although many practitioners resent these intrusions and restrictions on clinical options, this pressure has forced them to develop theories that can be tested by assessing their outcomes.

Working Quickly

Managed care is not the only reason that therapists feel increasing pressure to employ brief methods. Prospective consumers have become more impatient, wanting instant results.

"How long will this take?" you will be asked by new clients repeatedly. "I mean, if we can't take care of this today, I am willing to come back for a second session." This may strike you as humorous, but many people really do expect that you have a magic wand that is capable of fixing lifelong problems by just saying a few incantations or casting a spell.

To put even more pressure on you to work quickly, clients often see therapy as a second choice to taking pills. During the last decade, new pharmacological advances have made it appear as if medications such as Prozac will cure every problem, often within a matter of days. In fact, these drugs have been found to be no more effective than those of previous generations and not any better than therapy for many problems. But there is nothing like aggressive marketing and advertising to convince consumers that there really is a magic cure. "The message is seductive and it works," write Duncan, Miller, and Sparks (2000, p. 26) in their review of research on the subject. "If these drugs were books, they would be runaway bestsellers. More than 130 million prescriptions were written for them last year alone, and more than $8 billion spent on them."

This is going to be your competition.

Cultural Diversity

As our society becomes more culturally diverse, therapists will be forced to become far more flexible in the ways they help people. Theories must be elastic enough to accommodate individuals and families who hold very different values and present issues that must be understood within different contexts. In the case example that began this chapter of the angry man who felt betrayed, the way you interpret this behavior may very well be influenced by the cultural background of both participants. What if the client was African American, Native American, or Latino, and the therapist was of European descent? How would that put a different slant on the perception of betrayal? Or what if the differences between client and therapist were reflected in their sexual orientation, gender, or religious beliefs? Such differences can be a strength, as well as a weakness, but they absolutely must be considered while making sense of the behavior and choosing how to respond.

Imagine, in another example, the ways that two different clients might present symptoms of depression as well as attempt to cope with the difficulties. The first individual, a white male electrician in his forties, has been referred because of two convictions of driving while under the influence of alcohol. He does not see himself as depressed even though he hates his job, his youngest child is dying of leukemia, and he drinks himself to sleep each night. The second case involves a 16-year-old Vietnamese American girl who attempted suicide after receiving a

B+ on an assignment in school. "I just can't accept this," she tells you with tears in her eyes, "and neither will my parents."

■ ■ ■ ■ ■

FOR A CLASS ACTIVITY

In the same teams as in the previous assignment, talk about the ways you might treat these cases of depression differently. Based on the clients' ages, genders, ethnicity, life situations, and their perceptions, how would you adapt your therapeutic approach to fit their needs?

Just as with this case, or any person who might seek your help, theories must be adapted to the client's unique cultural view of the world. Most contemporary books on the subject of theory make some effort to address this challenging issue, but according to Sue, Ivey, and Pedersen (1996), most fall short because of (1) continued ethnocentricity that emphasizes the European-dominant culture, (2) a failure to clearly articulate the cultural biases and assumptions of each theory, and (3) lack of attention to cultural factors that are at the core of most helping relationships.

As you study the various theories presented in this text and elsewhere in your career, you will want to remember that each of these conceptions represents its own cultural worldview about the nature of reality, what gives life greatest meaning, and what is good for people. Because these philosophies were developed by theorists who have their own personal notions about the world, they may be at odds with others who come from different backgrounds. This text will discuss this challenge further in almost every chapter that follows.

■ ■ ■ ■ ■

FOR PERSONAL REFLECTION

Consider the factors that are most influential in shaping your own cultural worldview. If you were going to see a counselor or therapist for help about a personal issue in your life, what would this professional need to know and understand about your own background in order to be helpful to you?

Fill in the basics about yourself as follows:

1. *Gender.* How was the conception of yourself as a man or woman formulated in your life? Who have been your primary role models?

2. *Sexual identity.* What is your sexual identity? This includes your sexual preferences as they have been part of your ongoing development.

3. *Ethnicity and racial heritage.* Going back in your family history, what have been the strongest influences in how you identify yourself culturally? What does this mean to you?

4. *Religious and spiritual beliefs.* This includes your affiliation with those who share your values and also the way you practice these beliefs.

5. *Geographic background.* How has a sense of place been a strong influence on who you are and what you value? This includes whether you have an urban or rural background and the particular region of the country from which you come.

For a Class Activity: Get together in small groups and share with others which cultural factors have most strongly shaped your worldview. How would counseling theories need to be adapted in order to respond best to your unique background?

Postmodern Movement

There have been some radical shifts in the intellectual climate of the field of counseling and therapy. Once there was a primary emphasis on the study of individual cases in therapy. When Freud, Jung, Adler, and others were first starting out, it was considered standard practice to look at the effects of treatment on one individual at a time. This was consistent with medical practice as well.

During the early part of the twentieth century, empiricism and the scientific method came into their own. Large-scale research studies have since been undertaken with huge samples, making it possible for practitioners to apply this knowledge to individual cases. Of course, there are limits to both approaches. When you try to generalize from a huge group to one person, you may be failing to account for this individual's unique situation. Likewise, if you try to generalize from a small number of cases to the population at large, you may also be missing a lot. Thus, debate has raged for some time whether we ought to be using case samples or empirical data, qualitative or quantitative methods, for the primary source of our theories.

In the last few years, a compromise seems to be developing in which both approaches to data collection and analysis are valued. Empiricism is still alive and well, but so-called postmodern theories are also exerting tremendous influence. In this paradigm (see Chapter 8 for further description) several features are prominent (Burr, 1995; Winslade & Monk, 2000):

1. You can't look at an individual and his or her problems without considering the social, cultural, and political context of the situation.
2. Reality is shaped by a person's individual perceptions, which are, in turn, strongly influenced by social forces.
3. Language is the primary means by which thoughts, feelings, and experience are formulated.
4. Rather than looking at behavior in general (like empiricists), or thoughts and attitudes (like cognitive theorists), or free will (like humanists), postmodern theorists examine everyday interactions and discourse for clues as to what is going on.

■ ■ ■ ■ ■

FOR PERSONAL REFLECTION

A person you are helping is not improving as you would expect. As far as you can figure out, you have followed procedures exactly as prescribed. Furthermore, what you have done with this case is the same as you have tried before, always with good results.

You are obviously missing something in this scenario but you can't figure out what that might be. When you are stuck like this, a good place to begin is with the right questions. Many of them are suggested by the various theoretical paradigms.

■ What does the literature and research inform you about this situation?
■ How have other similar cases that you have worked with proceeded along a different course?
■ What are you expecting of this person that he or she is unwilling or unable to do?
■ What is it about this person's unique perceptions of the world that are at odds with your favored theoretical approach?
■ What is it about this person's cultural background that would be important for you to take into consideration?

- What would the client say is going on and what does he or she think you should be doing differently in order to be helpful?
- What might you be doing (or not doing) that is creating these difficulties?
- What are you doing that is not working? What could you do instead?

What all this means for your study of theory is that you are going to be required to master the intricacies of traditional, scientific paradigms (courses such as statistics and research), case study paradigms (developmental courses and qualitative research), and postmodern approaches. The good news is that this will give you lots of options about how you can approach your work.

Technology

Your guess is as good as mine about what the future will bring in the ways that technology will affect your life and practice. Certainly, the increasing use of the Internet, wireless communication devices, computers, and such will make the world a very different place than it is now. Furthermore, the sheer magnitude and pace of these changes are staggering.

Therapists and counselors are now helping people in ways other than face-to-face contact through self-help programs on the Web, real-time interactions on the Internet, and brief consultations on videophones. These methods require the development of change theories and strategies that can work in a variety of media and delivery systems. It will also mean that many of the theories that were essentially designed for face-to-face interactions must be reworked and adapted for delivering services in other media.

Technology is also changing the kinds of problems that people present for help. Young children are spending hours each day playing video and computer games, isolating them from peers. Teenagers and adults become "addicted" to the Web, spending as much as five to ten leisure hours each day in front of a screen. Cable television, with hundreds of channels, keeps families immobile, sitting on their couches every night. Technological innovations in both prescribed and elicit drugs present additional ways for people to medicate themselves for the slightest discomfort. Even the tools people use—wireless phones, computers, vehicles—are rendered obsolete every few years, requiring more and more energy to be invested in mastering these new devices. Jobs are becoming obsolete as often as software versions are updated.

■ ■ ■ ■ ■

FOR A CLASS ACTIVITY

How will technology impact our field and the ways we think about and do therapy? In small groups, or as a class, talk about your predictions about how therapy and counseling will evolve to meet the needs of a changing world.

Consider how technological advances will alter not only the problems that clients present but also the ways that therapy will be delivered. How will diagnostic and assessment procedures take place? How will innovations in technology related to simulations, cyberspace, virtual reality, communication devices, neurobiology, and behavioral science change the field?

Integration and Synthesis

There has been a trend developing over the past few decades in which more and more practitioners are describing themselves as eclectic or integrative in their approach, using a variety of approaches depending on what is needed. This means a lot more work for you because you will probably not be able to pick only one of the theories in this text and expect to stick with it throughout your career.

It requires a high level of conceptual mastery to understand one or more theories and then to combine several of their features into an individualized model. Yet that is exactly the task that we have before us during this journey.

SUGGESTED READINGS

American Psychiatric Association. (1994). *Diagnostic and statistical manual of mental disorders* (4th ed.). Washington, DC: Author.

Cohen, E. D., & Cohen, G. S. (1999). *The virtuous therapist*. Pacific Grove, CA: Brooks/Cole.

Corey, G., Corey, M. S., & Callanan, P. (1998). *Issues and ethics in the helping professions* (5th ed.). Pacific Grove, CA: Brooks/Cole.

Frager, S. (2000). *Managing managed care: Secrets from a former case manager*. New York: Wiley.

Kottler, J. A., & Hazler, R. (1997). *What you never learned in graduate school*. New York: W. W. Norton.

Peterson, J. V., & Nisenholz, B. (1999). *Orientation to counseling* (4th ed.). Boston: Allyn and Bacon.

Seligman, L. (1998). *Selecting effective treatments: A comprehensive, systematic guide to treating mental disorders* (2nd ed.). San Francisco: Jossey-Bass.

Weifel, E. R. (1998). *Ethics in counseling and psychotherapy: Standards, research, and emerging issues*. Pacific Grove, CA: Brooks/Cole.

Weisgerber, K. (Ed.). (1999). *The traumatic bond between psychotherapists and managed care*. New York: Jason Aronson.

■ ■ ■ ■ ■

CHAPTER 3

THEORY IN A CLINICIAN'S LIFE

It is one of the myths of our profession that theories are developed purely out of scientific, objective inquiry in which a scholar slaves over data, analyzes empirical literature, systematically reviews case notes, and then constructs a logical paradigm that sequentially follows the blueprint. In truth, theory construction and development so often follow the intensely personal events in a clinician's life.

Certainly, theory emerges and evolves as a result of clinical experience and a synthesis of the literature, advancing previous work. But I would not wish to give you the impression that such conceptual frameworks necessarily represent some objective reality that was identified purely from scientific scrutiny. Actually, many of our field's theoretical innovators were driven by very personal motives. It is very important that you appreciate this point before you begin delving into conceptual ideas that will become so much a part of your professional life.

THREE THEORIES, THREE LIVES

In what is certainly the first comprehensive therapeutic system, Sigmund Freud clearly went in the directions he did because of many unresolved issues related to intimacy, sexuality, and his own past (Gay, 1998; Masson, 1998; Rand & Torok, 1997). It was hardly a coincidence, for instance, that his theory followed a path that excavates buried material when his lifelong obsession was with archaeology. Not only did Freud spend his day digging into people's past to uncover the meaning of their experiences, but he also spent most of his vacations on archaeological digs, as well as collecting ancient artifacts that adorned his office. This was a man who believed in his soul that the past shapes who we are, and his theory reflected this intensely personal conviction.

Likewise, Victor Frankl, the inventor of one school of existential theory called logotherapy, developed his notions as a result of traumas he suffered in the concentration camps of Nazi Germany (Frankl, 1997). Day after day, as he watched friends, neighbors, and family members give up and die, or actually kill themselves by running into the guarded fence, he searched for some larger purpose to his tortuous existence. This investigation into the meaning of his own suffering gave way to a whole system of helping others that was rooted in the construction of personal meaning.

"He who has a *why* to live for," writes Frankl (1962, p. 121) paraphrasing Nietzsche, one of his favorite philosophers, "can bear with almost any *how*." Frankl believes this should be the motto for any therapeutic effort: "Woe to him who saw no more sense in his life, no aim, no purpose, and therefore no point in carrying on. He was soon lost." Remember now, Frankl is not talking about people he has observed in some scientific study or even in his consultation chambers; these are the observations of a man who is a prisoner, who faces death every day, who has already lost everything else in his life except the choice as to how he wants to view his own predicament.

In a third example of how theories are influenced profoundly by the personal experiences of their inventors, Carl Rogers, the founder of person-centered therapy, developed an approach that followed perfectly his most deeply held convictions. In his autobiography, Rogers (1980) reflects on one of his earliest memories from childhood—the pure pleasure he felt when he could really *hear* someone.

FOR A FIELD STUDY

Watch videos of prominent theoreticians doing therapy. You will find several representative examples in your school or department library that include many of the greatest thinkers in the field demonstrating their ideas in action.

Observe the ways the theorists appear so effortless and natural in the ways they work with clients. Compare the ways their distinct personalities and personal values reflect the professional styles they have developed.

If you ever watch a video of Rogers, you will see the embodiment of the perfect listening being. All his love, his caring and compassion, and his focused attention are directed toward his client. When you watch him work, you may feel this longing to crawl into his lap as the perfect grandparent, to have him hold you and tell you everything will be all right. And you would believe him.

It is hardly surprising that Rogers would have developed a theory of helping that emphasizes authentic relationships when he felt such an emptiness in his own life growing up. He moved around a lot as a kid, never felt any roots, and admits he never had close friends. "I was socially incompetent," Rogers discloses, "in any but superficial contacts" (1980, p. 30). Yet, lo and behold, later in life he develops a theory of helping that holds as its most sacred principle the significance of an accepting, caring, nurturing relationship.

So, what is the point of including these three examples? This is a reminder that each theory you will study was most likely conceived by someone who was frustrated with the choices already available and sought to develop a framework that would fit better with his or her own values, interests, personality, and life experience. Each theory reflects the personal biases and preferences of its inventor.

It is hardly a coincidence that someone such as Fritz Perls, once an immigrant with a poor command of the English language, developed Gestalt therapy that emphasized nonverbal forms of communication. Likewise, Albert Ellis grew frustrated with the conventional psychoanalysis he was practicing because he likes to talk a lot, and his theory wasn't allowing him that indulgence. So he developed rational-emotive therapy to express perfectly his love of logical analysis and rational thinking. In so many other cases, as well, if you take the time to search through their backgrounds, you will find that the architects of various theories were influenced as much by their personal histories as by their professional experiences.

What this means is that if you ever hope to practice effectively and naturally yourself, you will someday have to become your own theoretician. You will evolve a personal style of practice that adapts what you have learned from your supervisors, mentors, teachers, and theoretical allegiances. Just like your predecessors, you will develop a theory that more closely fits your personal and professional style.

■ ■ ■ ■ ■ ▓▓

FOR A FIELD STUDY

Read the biographies or autobiographies of prominent theoreticians in several fields. You might start with those of Sigmund Freud (Gay, 1998; Jones, 1961; Rieff, 1979) and Carl Rogers (1980), or even thinkers outside our profession such as Charles Darwin (Darwin, 1888/1969; Wright, 1994), Margaret Mead (Bateson, 1984), Albert Einstein (Folsing, 1998), Mahatma Gandhi (Chadla, 1999; Erikson, 1969; Gardner, 1993), or Franklin and Eleanor Roosevelt (Goodwin, 1995).

As you read the stories of their lives, observe the ways their theories evolved from their personal experiences. Trace the roots of their thinking as they emerged in various significant events and critical incidents. Note in particular the ways their theories reflected the context of their times, culture, gender, and home life.

PERSONAL AND PROFESSIONAL INTERACTIONS

It isn't only in the lives of famous therapists that you can witness the interaction between personal and professional lives. In a book edited by Gerson (1996), a number of practicing therapists discuss how various life transitions, crises, and experiences impact their work and influence their theories. They talk about how traumas, transitions, and tragedies they survived helped to shape their views of helping. Not surprisingly, most of the seventeen contributors have chosen a psychoanalytic framework that works through past traumas as they are manifested in current problems. Warshaw (1996), for example, talks about how losing her father as a child influenced her development as a practitioner. She is big into control issues as a defense against the terror of helplessness. She is focused a lot on the experience of loss in her sessions. And she chose a psychoanalytic framework because of the way it provided the sort of "soothing containing relationship" she missed in her own life. "Undoubtedly," she writes, "my fascination with theory that supported that work was an outgrowth of my deeply felt need for missed parenting" (pp. 219–220).

■ ■ ■ ■ ■

FOR PERSONAL REFLECTION OR A CLASS ACTIVITY

Spend a few minutes making a list of the three most significant events that have occurred in your life. These could be traumatic experiences (i.e., loss, physical illness, failure), normal developmental transitions (i.e., riding a two-wheel bike, thirtieth birthday), or joyful incidents (i.e., marriage, birth of a child, job promotion).

Make a second list of the three most deeply held convictions that guide your life. These should involve those personal values and beliefs that most strongly influence your behavior. They could be related to things such as justice, fate, spirituality, lifestyle, relationships, work, and related issues.

Find connections between the two lists, noting the ways that your most significant experiences helped you to formulate your guiding philosophy.

In small groups, talk to each other about what you discovered. As with any cooperative learning group, (1) allocate your time equitably so that everyone has a chance to speak, (2) show respect and caring for each person's contribution, and (3) stay on task so you complete the assignment.

After all group members have had a chance to share their experiences, look for common themes that emerged.

Rarely do therapists and counselors admit so honestly the way their professional choices have been influenced by their personal experiences. Other contributors in the volume mention how divorce, pregnancy, parenthood, sexual abuse, death of a child, aging, and obesity have all had a huge impact on the ways they currently operate. You can expect a similar course throughout your own career: Your selection of which theories to employ and the ways you adapt them to your work will be strongly influenced by *everything* you encounter—not only in your work but also in your life.

THEORIES IN A THERAPIST'S LIFE

Although this book is focused primarily on theories of intervention, there are many other conceptual frameworks that are part of a therapist's work. For instance, before you can ever hope to select the best treatment strategy for a given client, you will first need to have a thorough understanding of the person's development in a host of areas.

Before we review these specific domains of human experience, it would be useful for you to realize that theories are not something created only by experts or professionals; everyone creates and invents theories to make sense of the world and explain phenomena. What separates the theories in this book from those that you have made up on your own is basically that the ones here have been published and well researched so we are reasonably sure that they have maximum generalizabilty.

Social scientists have spent the past century creating and testing theories to describe and predict human behavior in every possible area. Although our efforts will be concentrated primarily on theories related to helping strategies, you will also need to be familiar with those that deal with other facets of human conduct.

■ ■ ■ ■ ■ ▬▬▬▬▬▬▬▬▬▬▬▬▬▬▬▬▬▬▬▬▬▬▬▬▬▬▬▬▬▬

FOR PERSONAL REFLECTION

Think of one theory that you find especially useful in your life. This could be related to your job or any other facet of your life.

For instance, I am attracted to a theory called evolutionary psychology because of its value in explaining why people do the things they do when surface motives are not apparent. According to this theory, people act in accordance with their drive to increase the likelihood their genes will continue until the next generation (Breuer, 1982; Buss, 1999; Wilson, 1978). This helps explain, for instance, the value of gossip as a source of intelligence, or the reasons why dominance plays such an important part in relationships (holding on to the best resources for one's kin), or even why maternal grandparents often have closer relationships with their grandchildren than do paternal grandparents (because the mother's parents can be certain the offspring has their genetic material but the father's parents can never be sure) (Dugatkin, 1999; Wright, 1994). There is even some application to therapy in explaining why people so hunger for closeness and affiliation with others, and how therapeutic relationships fill the void left by the disbanding of our tribal heritage (Glantz & Pearce, 1989).

What are some of your favorite theories that you use every day? Think about what makes them so valuable to you.

■ ■ ■ ■ ■

FOR A CLASS ACTIVITY

Get together in small groups and create a theory among you to explain why you are taking this class. Don't rely on anything I've said in this text, or anything your instructor has volunteered: Formulate your own explanation.

After you have reached a consensus among you as to the best theory to account for this class requirement, go back and review the process you followed together to arrive at a conclusion. What steps did you follow?

After sharing your conclusions with the class, talk about the collaborative nature of theory building and what advantages you see are possible in team efforts over individual achievements.

Physical Development

It was Robert Havighurst (1972) who popularized the concept of developmental tasks for humans, meaning those challenges that arise at a predictable age that must be overcome if healthy development is to proceed. For each of several stages in life, people must tackle certain physical, social, and emotional tasks in order to develop further.

During infancy, for instance, a baby must learn to take solid foods, to sit up, and eventually to crawl and walk if he or she expects to advance much further in life. In middle childhood, or the elementary school years, a child must learn to get along with others, to read and write, to develop a moral system, and so on. Developmental tasks are specified for each stage of life, listing what is absolutely required of the individual in order to be reasonably competent in our culture.

■ ■ ■ ■ ■

FOR A CLASS ACTIVITY

Divide the class into eight groups. Each group must tackle one of the following six stages of life by listing all its developmental tasks:

- ■ Preschool (3–5)
- ■ Childhood (6–12)
- ■ Adolescence (12–18)
- ■ College or apprentice years (18–22)
- ■ Young adulthood (23–35)
- ■ Adulthood (36–48)
- ■ Middle age (49–65)
- ■ Later maturity (66–and older)

It will help you generate a more complete list of tasks if you think of categories including (1) physical activities, (2) social activities, (3) career-related activities, (4) civic/community activities, (5) family activities, and others that come to mind.

After you are done, talk about how therapists could and should help people to achieve the developmental tasks expected of their age group.

Other Developmental Theories

Surely you remember something about Jean Piaget and his early work plotting the ways that children develop their capacities for making sense of the world. As another strong developmental theorist, Piaget and subsequent followers described the sequential stages that people progress through as they age and gain experience. Basing his initial observations on the behavior of his own daughters, and later watching children play, Piaget noted several distinct stages from early infancy (sensorimotor), preschool (preoperational), elementary school age (concrete operations), and middle school age (formal operations) in which children finally learn to think abstractly, reason logically, and develop concern for social issues.

Other developmental theories soon followed after this initial work, creating a blueprint for how humans evolve in a host of different areas, including moral development (Lawrence Kohlberg), ego development (Jane Loevinger), gender development (Carol Gilligan), personality development (Erik Erikson), and career development (Donald Super). Before you start to panic, remember that there are several other courses that cover these theories. It is important, however, that you develop some degree of background knowledge about the ways that people typically develop.

■ ■ ■ ■ ■ ▬▬▬▬▬▬▬▬▬▬▬▬▬▬▬▬▬▬▬▬▬▬▬▬▬▬

FOR PERSONAL REFLECTION OR A CLASS ACTIVITY

A new client is referred to you because of difficulties sleeping and chronic stomachaches. A physical exam has ruled out any physical causes. This young woman is 22 years old, just graduating from a university with a business degree.

    Based on this person's age, what are some of the developmental issues that you would expect that she would be struggling with right now? How might these be related to her presenting complaints?

It should now be clear that before you can hope to understand and use theories of therapeutic intervention, it is crucial that you also have a grasp of developmental theories that help you to understand the age-related context of a person's struggles. Once you know the client's approximate life stages, you can make some reasonable predictions about where he or she ought to be operating. This allows you to compare actual functioning to what would be expected. It also makes it possible for you to plan what sorts of interventions would be most likely to stimulate growth to the next successive stage.

    Let's say, for instance, that a 29-year-old client has been having difficulty making commitments to a primary relationship. Although he expresses a deep interest in this love relationship, he senses that things will soon end unless he is prepared to take things to the next step. In conducting an assessment, you discover that his parents were divorced when he was 13, and that he experienced a traumatic breakup with a girlfriend in high school, swearing to himself never to get hurt again. As you dig further, you find other significant events in his life that may be related to his present problems: chronic asthma that he developed as a child, as well as a learning disability that interfered with his ability to read. Finally, you note that he is approaching the "age 30 transition" that marks one of the most significant life passages. He must now come to terms with the reality that he will never reach, some of his dreams, yet he is still young enough to reassess new priorities.

    When you apply developmental theories in this way, you are thinking in terms of how a person is doing in all the areas of human competence that matter most. You will find this model especially useful when conducting diagnostic and intake interviews.

Learning Theories

Since counseling and therapy are all about change processes, you must be familiar with the typical ways that people learn, as well as which structures are most likely to foster such growth. At one time, you were probably exposed to many of these ideas, such as reinforcement theory (B. F. Skinner), discovery theory (Jerome Bruner), humanistic theory (Carl Rogers), and so on. Even if these theories are a bit hazy (if you remember them at all), you have some idea about how you believe that people best learn.

Complementing the more biologically, instinctually based theories previously mentioned, learning theories are about the ways that people change as a result of personal experience. This is where you come in as a therapist because your essential job is to teach people how to get their needs met more effectively. In order to do this, naturally, you had better have a very good idea about how learning works and what you can do in order to further this process.

■ ■ ■ ■ ■

FOR PERSONAL REFLECTION

Consider the most significant learning experiences you have had in your life. Either write down in your journal, or talk to a partner, about life's lessons that have been most important to you. For instance, I might mention the time I learned to ride a two-wheel bike without training wheels, or when I first understood that rejection is more a state of mind than circumstances, or when I realized for the first time that I might be smart.

Now identify what forces and factors most contributed to these significant learnings. What is it that made the most difference?

As a therapist, what can you do to capitalize most on those elements that you believe are most conducive to promoting significant learning?

WHAT YOU NEED TO UNDERSTAND NEXT

You may already be feeling a little overwhelmed by all the terms, names, and ideas that have been introduced as part of this contextual presentation. Let me remind you that in this course we are after the big picture. Certainly it is important to learn the important figures and concepts in the field, but unless you can put all the stuff together into a fairly coherent view of what therapy is all about, why and how it works, you are not going to do your clients much good.

Before beginning an investigation of specific theoretical frameworks covered in the text, there are a few things that you will need to understand first.

Confusion and Ambiguity

If you are looking for truth or even consistent answers to your questions, you won't find them here. If you need clarity or concrete answers, you might try law, engineering, or physics, but you won't encounter much of that in counseling and therapy. For every explanation you hear that makes sense, there will be a dozen other ones that directly contradict this point of view. For every possible course of action you could take with a particular client, afterward there will occur to you several others that seemed more advantageous. Once you get input from colleagues and supervisors, you will feel the burden of even more alternatives.

One perspective states that the most important factor in therapy is the client's own self-healing (Bohart & Tallman, 1999). It is the client who determines how far progress will go, based on his or her own readiness levels and motivation. The therapist's role is merely to facilitate this process by providing an atmosphere that is rich in both creativity and resources.

Of course, as you have no doubt already realized, for every point of view in this field, there is another one that takes the opposite argument. In this case, there are some other approaches that believe the therapist is the expert who determines whether the experience is worthwhile or not. Even with so-called resistant or unmotivated clients, strategic maneuverings on the part of the clinician can be implemented to overcome a lack of commitment.

Fervor and Zeal

Practitioners become rather attached to their theories. It like a club, a fraternity or sorority, or even a religious affiliation to which you belong. There are secret handshakes, special code words, designated books, even a particular wardrobe associated with the followers of one theory or another. Furthermore, professionals get mad when you subscribe to another theory that directly contradicts their own preferred ideas.

Typical of the zeal that theory developers attach to their own ideas, Ellis (1996) asks the question whether his theory of Rational Emotive Behavior Therapy (REBT) is superior to all others. Perhaps unsurprisingly, he answers that assuredly it is, although he admits there is little empirical evidence to support his belief. Certainly REBT works quite well, but so does almost every other theory you will study.

Again and again, attempts to demonstrate that one approach is more effective than all others have resulted in a tie. Even when isolated studies do indicate that one approach such as REBT might be better for certain kinds of clients or presenting complaints, it is difficult to sort out whether the positive results occurred because the theory was better or because the clinicians selected for one group were more skilled than the others.

Points of Departure

All of the approaches to helping that are covered in this text have points in common, as well as areas in which they diverge significantly from one another. You will notice that each theory differs primarily in the following dimensions (Fishman & Franks, 1997):

1. *Historical context.* From which traditions did this theory emerge? Some are heavily steeped in classical philosophy, others in neurological science, education, anthropology, physics, or humanities. The theory is also influenced by the era in which it was spawned (compare nineteenth-century Vienna to the sixties in California or the urban setting of contemporary Hong Kong, London, or Sydney).

2. *Underlying philosophy.* Each therapeutic approach follows an organized set of assumptions, as well as a basic philosophy of change. Theories differ in their views of human nature, most legitimate focus of attention, scope of treatment, who has primary responsibility for outcomes, treatment goals, counselor roles, and criteria for success (Kottler & Brown, 2000).

FOR PERSONAL REFLECTION

Consider where you stand on each of the following dimensions of personal philosophy:

People are born good.	People are born neutral.	People are born evil.
Clients control outcomes.	Therapists decide outcomes.	Responsibility is shared.
Feelings are most important.	Thinking is most important.	Behavior is most important.
Focus on the past.	Focus on the present.	Focus on the future.
Goals should be specific.	Broad themes are best.	Concentrate on the process.
Use structuring most often.	Use interpreting most often.	Reflect feelings most often.
Be active.	Be nondirective.	Let client decide which is best.
Function as a friend.	Function as a consultant.	Function as a teacher.
Use one primary theory.	Use several theories.	Combine theories into one.
Theory is most important.	Skills are most important.	Therapist personality is key.

3. *Values held most sacred.* Separate from a guiding philosophy are the values implicit in a particular approach. Therapists who flock together tend to adopt similar attitudes about the work and the best way to do it. Psychoanalytic therapists will be inclined to be more patient whereas their strategic or brief-oriented colleagues prefer incisive, directive operations. Humanistic practitioners value relationships and process above specific goals and content, whereas behavioral and cognitive therapists emphasize the opposite. You do not have to apologize for identifying with a theory that reflects most closely what you believe—that is among the most important factors to consider.

4. *Data that are used to support premises.* Theories cannot evolve and remain influential without compelling evidence to support their claims. They must not only be field-tested and found to produce desired results but also subjected to systemic scrutiny by research efforts. The interesting part, however, is that the practitioners tend to collect their data in different ways and even interpret the results according to their own preferred outcomes.

■ ■ ■ ■ ■

FOR PERSONAL REFLECTION

Think of something you do well. This could be cooking a favorite dish, engaging in some athletic activity, playing a particular video game, talking convincingly about a subject, or doing anything that stands out as being (in your judgment) exceptional. Now ask yourself how you know you are good at this. What evidence do you have to support this claim?

Perhaps you would say that other people (those whom you trust) tell you that you are good at this (but they may be lying to make you feel good). You may be confident in your competence because you know you are good (but perhaps you are in denial or not seeing things clearly). You could use some more objective measure, such as amount of money won gambling, grade point average, or place you finished in a race (but perhaps the competition was not all that good, you were lucky, or your data are not representative of your total performance). Well, you get the point: It is really hard to determine personal effectiveness and there are so many different ways to do it.

5. *Techniques employed.* Each of the theoretical approaches not only differs in its underlying beliefs but also in the ways it is applied. Sometimes it is difficult to tell what sort of therapy someone is doing just by watching because we can't really get inside the participants' heads. The skills therapists use are somewhat generic and universal—everyone uses reflection, interpretation, summarization, and so on. Nevertheless, each approach has certain trademark interventions that are immediately identified with that theory. Mention the "hot seat" or "empty chair" and most experienced practitioners will know that they come from Gestalt theory. Disputing beliefs is associated with cognitive theory, dream analysis with psychodynamic approaches, "spitting in the client's soup" as Adlerian, systematic desensitization with behavioral therapy, script analysis with transactional analysis, circular questioning with narrative therapy, and reframing with strategic therapy.

Basically what this means is that it is worth becoming familiar with all the theories in the text (and many others that were left out because of space limitations) so that you can collect a variety of techniques for your arsenal. This gives you the option of having a huge bag of tricks at your disposal when faced with inevitable resistance and challenges.

Expanding Your Options

I have heard more than a few instructors who teach this course claim that the whole idea of teaching theories as discrete entities is counterproductive. Why introduce students to a bunch of models that are rarely, if ever, practiced any longer in pure form? It has been widely cited that there are over 400 distinctly different theories of counseling and therapy (Karasu, 1986) and that none of them are clearly better than the others (Smith, Glass, & Miller, 1980; Stiles, Shapiro, & Eliott, 1986). The vast majority of practitioners don't identify with any single theory, calling themselves integrative, pragmatic, or eclectic (Norcross & Prochaska, 1988). This means that they have either combined several approaches into a more personalized approach, use a variety of different theories depending on what is needed, or find common factors that appear universal in all approaches.

To complicate matters further, what professionals say they do in their sessions isn't always what they are really doing. In therapy, just as in life, there is a marked discrepancy between espoused beliefs versus theory-in-action (Schon, 1983).

Not all the theories are treated equally, nor are they used with equal frequency. Interestingly, the choice one makes often is influenced more by a professional identity than anything else. In a study of the theoretical preferences of various professional groups, the following results were found (Prochaska & Norcross, 1999):

PROFESSIONAL GROUP	FIRST CHOICE	SECOND CHOICE	THIRD CHOICE
Clinical Psychologists	Integrative (27%)	Cognitive (24%)	Psychoanalytic (18%)
Counseling Psychologists	Integrative (40%)	Psychoanalytic (12%)	Cognitive (11%)

PROFESSIONAL GROUP	FIRST CHOICE	SECOND CHOICE	THIRD CHOICE
Psychiatrists	Integrative (53%)	Psychoanalytic (35%)	Interpersonal (3%)
Social Workers	Integrative (34%)	Psychoanalytic (33%)	Systemic (13%)
Counselors	Integrative (37%)	Humanistic (13%)	Psychoanalytic (11%)

You can see from this chart that, hands down, the consistent winner is an integrative approach. This means that regardless of training and professional identity, the majority of practitioners combine several different theories in their work or use a variety of methods depending on what is called for. Among those who describe themselves as eclectic or integrative as their dominant approach to therapy, clinicians draw on many different approaches. In one study of over 400 family therapists, psychologists, social workers, and psychiatrists, 68% of participants mentioned that they chose four or five different theories as their base (Jensen, Bergin, & Greaves, 1990). The theories were listed in the following order of popularity:

1. Psychoanalytic   72%
2. Cognitive   54%
3. Behavioral   49%
4. Systemic   48%
5. Humanistic   42%

The preceding results are presented not so much to show the winners of a popularity contest but rather to demonstrate how flexible most practitioners are in the ways they employ theory in their work. Because you will certainly have your work cut out for you just to master the basics of a single theory that you can apply with clients, augmenting that base with other ideas will come later in your career.

A REVIEW OF BASIC HISTORY

It would appear as if theories in the field of counseling and therapy began with Sigmund Freud's pioneering efforts to invent the first talking cure. In fact, the next chapter begins the story by introducing psychoanalysis as the first "official" model of intervention. But this is a gross simplification. The modern era of psychological helping may have started when Freud and his collaborator, Josef Breuer, first began experimenting with hypnosis to relieve people of their annoying problems, but the story actually begins a long time before that.

It is important that you understand the historical context for the theories you are about to study. As mentioned before, they are presented to you with an authority and confidence that would lead you to believe they are actually the truth about the way change takes place. You are entitled to your suspicions, especially when you discover just how contradictory many of the ideas are in light of others that directly refute them. Keep in mind that throughout the ages there have always been individuals who have believed with all their hearts that they have finally found the true path to enlightenment. If they couldn't get people to listen, they might even raise armies to impose their will on others, or perhaps even subject nonbelievers to a very persuasive type of discourse (imprisonment, exile, or execution).

When you study the theories that currently exert the most influence on contemporary practice, remember that a hundred years from now our colleagues in the future will most likely laugh uproariously at the methods we were using as being primitive and archaic. Remember that this discipline is only a century old; a single generation ago our professional forebearers attempted to cure people solely through talking about their dreams on a couch. This was a time before antidepressant medications, before generic helping skills, and before supervision was possible by reviewing videotapes. It was a time when progress was measured in years rather than weeks.

■ ■ ■ ■ ■ ▬▬▬▬▬▬▬▬▬▬▬▬▬▬▬▬▬▬▬▬▬▬▬▬▬▬▬

FOR PERSONAL REFLECTION OR A CLASS ACTIVITY

Either on your own or with several partners make a list of everyday practices that you believe will be laughably obsolete in twenty years. Make some predictions about what you think the future holds for some aspects of our current existence. For instance, do you think we will still be transported from one place to another by automobiles? What will be the state of communication devices? More relevant to our present subject, how would you expect that the practice of therapy will change in the next twenty years?

In order to keep a historical perspective on the role of our present theories, let's go back a few centuries to a time when there was a major outbreak of disturbing psychological maladies. If you were so unfortunate to have been experiencing these symptoms during the fifteenth century, it is highly likely that both your diagnosis and your treatment would have consisted of "trial by water." I know this certainly sounds like a better option than being burned at the stake but only as a matter of personal preference. When someone was suspected of manifesting identifiable signs of weirdness, she would be trussed up and tossed in the nearest lake. If this patient sank to the bottom and drowned, then it was obvious (after the fact) that she had not actually been afflicted with any sort of malady. If, however, the unfortunate subject should float—a most difficult undertaking with one's feet tied to one's hands—then the diagnosis was clear that she was a witch and she was then burned at the stake.

This was not the most compassionate of therapies but I suppose it was effective in discouraging further outbreaks of the symptoms, or in drawing too much attention to yourself. If you think this treatment was somewhat archaic, consider that in the centuries preceding it, bloodletting was the most reliable cure employed. And before that, going back to ancient times, a whole host of nasty brews were created to cure emotional suffering. Even this would have been a significant improvement over the techniques employed by our cave-dwelling ancestors. Skulls have been found with holes drilled in them, presumably intended to let the demons escape.

It was actually the generation before Freud when the most dramatic improvement in mental health services was recorded. Philosophers such as John Locke and Jean-Jacques Rousseau were preaching the merits of enlightenment. The scientific method was just coming into its own as a preferred avenue of investigation. Anton Mesmer (recall the term *mesmerized*) and Jean-Martin Charcot (one of Freud's first teachers in medical school) began experimenting with hypnosis as a means for treating mental disorders.

They might have been getting impressive results from their clinical methods, but the theories they advocated to explain the outcomes were somewhat amusing. Mesmer, for example, believed that people were possessed in varying degrees with something called animal magnetism, a kind of fluid that fills the universe and acts as a conduit between people, the Earth, and heavenly bodies. Using a collection of magnets, flowing water, and a stage that would rival stage magicians, Mesmer managed to restore the sight of (supposedly) blind people, cure depression, and do anything within the power of a contemporary faith healer. He may not have understood how he worked his healing powers, but he did produce results.

One can only imagine what historians will say about our own theories used to explain how and why people change. I do suggest that you retain a degree of caution, humility, and skepticism as you examine the ideas now believed to form the backbone of helping. It all seems to make sense to us now, but so did bloodletting, witch burning, and animal magnetism to our ancestral therapists.

Cultural Worldviews

A worldview is the way a client makes sense of the world and it is usually strongly influenced by a person's cultural identity (Sue & Sue, 1990). It involves a person's basic values and perceptions, the window through which the world is seen and experienced (Ibrahim, 1985). It is through interactions with others, especially with those of one's identified cultural groups, that views about relationships, family, productivity, control, time, intimacy, love, and similar values are developed (Okun, Fried, & Okun, 1999). It also includes the attitudes one has about seeking help from a stranger.

In Kingsolver's (1999) novel about cultural adaptation, a missionary family goes into the Congo during the 1960s to preach the Word and convert the native people to Christianity. Each family member is allowed to bring only a limited number of items (by weight) on the long flight. The father elects to bring with him a hammer because he finds great satisfaction in repairing things, just as he does saving souls of the nonbelievers. As a metaphor for the conflicts likely to ensue, the father soon discovers that there is absolutely nothing in the village to hammer. There are no wood structures, nor even any nails. This heavy hunk of metal and wood is absolutely useless even though it is his favorite instrument.

As you would predict, this missionary was not very successful trying to help the people he was sent to assist. Rather than learning their worldview and trying to approach helping relationships in terms his clients would understand, the missionary insisted that they adopt *his* worldview. Of course, the guy was so rigid and dogmatic that nobody bothered to tell him the reason he could not get any volunteers to be baptized in the crocodile-infested river. There is a lesson to remember here because quite often you will be trying to convert your clients to a particular worldview, and they will tell you in no uncertain terms that they prefer their own perspective.

Therapists have their own definite worldviews. Each theory you will study represents its own cultural group. Each has a language, special rituals and customs, and a shared identity that shape values and behavior. Humanistic practitioners are inclined, for example, to hug a lot and talk in the language of feelings. Their worldview is based on faith and trust in the human capacity for growth and self-healing. On the other hand, attend a gathering of cognitive therapists and you will see interactions that are far more formal. They speak a different language and value other aspects of human experience. They embrace a worldview that is logical, rational, and ordered, based on thinking rather than feeling. They would be less inclined to hug one another and more inclined to talk about what they think about things.

In a comparison of theoretical worldviews, Ivey, Ivey, and Simek-Morgan (1997) summarize differences between four popular approaches:

1. *Existential-Humanistic.* Human beings are naturally inclined to grow and develop in positive ways, especially when they experience trusting, caring relationships. It is important to find personal meaning in one's life and to come to terms with one's personal choices. People have problems when something blocks their natural tendency toward self-actualization. The therapist's job is to facilitate this process through a close relationship, exploration of feelings, and search for personal meaning.

2. *Psychoanalytic.* People are ruled by their instincts, especially the drive to need satisfaction. Problems in the present result from unresolved issues in the past, especially those related to early childhood interactions with parents. Analyzing dreams, labeling defenses, and looking for unconscious, repressed material are the best ways to help people resolve their difficulties. The relationship with clients is important mostly as it relates to clients' fantasies and projections.

3. *Cognitive-Behavioral.* People get in trouble when they fail to think clearly and logically about their situations. They distort reality and subscribe to beliefs that are self-defeating. Because negative feelings are actually caused by irrational beliefs, people can alter their moods by choosing alternative interpretations of the situation. In order to help people, it is necessary to challenge their beliefs and teach them alternative ways of thinking.

4. *Systemic.* Individual problems really represent larger family conflicts. Rather than looking at how the action of one person causes problems for another, therapists should be examining instead the reciprocal, circular exchanges that take place between individuals. This is most effective when therapists work with the whole family and seek to restructure family interactions in a way that is more healthy.

I could have picked any of a dozen other theoretical worldviews, but my point is that you must understand that both the client and therapist enter the encounter with well-developed ideas about the way the world works and the way change should most easily take place. If your clients were totally honest with you, and you asked them what they wanted to happen in sessions, they would probably tell you something like the following:

"I will tell you my troubles. You will listen to me . . . and agree with me. Then you will tell me what I should do and how to do it."

This, of course, is a very different view of change than the one that you intend to apply in your work. You can appreciate, therefore, the intrinsic conflict that is so often a part of your client relationships. You will each be trying to "sell" one another a particular ideology that you think is optimal. One of three things usually happens: (1) You will be convincing enough that the client buys what you are selling and agrees to adopt your worldview, (2) the client insists that you agree with his or her worldview (a not unreasonable request considering who is the "customer"), or (3) the client leaves to find satisfaction elsewhere. Needless to say, this clash of worldviews presents some interesting challenges and is at the heart of the therapeutic process.

The Main Attraction

So, enough with the opening acts. Enough with all this preparation for the main attraction. It is time now to begin the study of the principal therapeutic worldviews that are currently most dominant. Study them with an open mind. Embrace each theory as if it has something valuable to teach you and something important that you can use to become more effective in your work.

SUGGESTED READINGS

Bankart, C. P. (1997). *Talking cures: A history of Western and Eastern psychotherapies.* Pacific Grove, CA: Brooks/Cole.

Beck, L. (2001). *Development through the lifespan.* Boston: Allyn and Bacon.

Buss, D. M. (1999). *Evolutionary psychology: The new science of the mind.* Boston: Allyn and Bacon.

Frankl, V. (1962). *Man's search for meaning.* New York: Washington Square.

Gay, P. (1998). *Freud: A life for our time.* New York: W. W. Norton.

Gerson, B. (Ed.). (1996). *The therapist as a person: Life crises, life choices, life experiences, and their effects on treatment.* New York: Analytic Press.

Kingsolver, B. (1999). *The poisonwood bible.* New York: Harper.

Okun, B. F., Fried, J., & Okun, M. L. (1999). *Understanding diversity: A learning-as-practice primer.* Pacific Grove, CA: Brooks/Cole.

Rogers, C. (1980). *A way of being.* Boston: Houghton Mifflin.

Schon, D. A. (1983). *The reflective practitioner.* New York: Basic Books.

Smart, N. (1999). *Worldviews: Crosscultural explorations of human beliefs.* Englewood Cliffs, NJ: Prentice-Hall.

Slavin, R. E. (2000). *Educational psychology: Theory and practice.* Boston: Allyn and Bacon.

Wachtel, P. L., & S. B. Messer (Eds.). (1997). *Theories of psychotherapy: Origins and evolution.* Washington, DC: American Psychological Association.

■ ■ ■ ■ ■

CHAPTER 4

LOOK TO THE PAST TO SET YOU FREE

Psychodynamic Approaches

Theories differ according to a number of dimensions. Some require a very active therapist role whereas others put more responsibility on the client. Some focus particularly on changing cognitive activity whereas others stress observable behavior or inner feelings. And theories vary in where they think most of the action takes place: the present, the past, or the future.

In our first set of therapeutic approaches, the emphasis is clearly on the past. Each of the psychoanalytic conceptions shares a strong belief that until you help people to resolve issues in the past, they will never come to terms fully with what is bothering them in the present.

■ ■ ■ ■ ■

FOR PERSONAL REFLECTION

What are some of the ongoing personal struggles that *you* have faced throughout your life? These could involve difficulties with intimacy, authority figures, or poor self-esteem, among others.

What are some possible sources in your early life that could be responsible for these personal struggles? What have you suffered previously that continues to plague you today?

EARLY BACKGROUND

For all practical purposes, the fields of counseling and psychotherapy were launched when a young physician in the middle of the nineteenth century began using hypnosis to help his patients talk about their difficult problems. Sigmund Freud had been trained as a neurologist with the finest medical scholars of his day. In addition, he had a lifelong interest in reading novels, studying philosophy, and practicing amateur archaeology. In a sense, Freud fancied himself as much a historian and archaeologist as he did a medical practitioner.

In one of his first published papers, Freud collaborated with a mentor, Joseph Breuer, to describe cases of hysteria (physical symptoms of psychological origin) they had treated using hypnosis. It was their hypothesis that these patients suffered some sort of trauma at an early age and that they attempted to cope with this pain by blocking it out, repressing memories of the events (suspected to be sexual abuse). They theorized that strangling this emotional energy resulted in the development of symptoms that could only be treated by getting at the root of the problem. Although hints of the problem may slip out in dreams and unconscious acts, until the person can be helped to excavate and unearth the buried memories, the symptoms would endure.

During the next fifty years, Freud collaborated with a number of other medical colleagues, as well as students, to formulate a comprehensive theory of human development that includes the origins of problems as well as how they might best be resolved. Many of these individuals, whose names may be familiar to you, went on to establish their own unique brand of psychoanalytic theory that better fit their personalities, values, and therapeutic style.

PSYCHOANALYTIC DISCIPLES AND REVISIONISTS

"While it is not true that there are as many psychoanalytic theories of personality and treatment as there are psychoanalysts, it often seems that way" (Buirski, 1994, p. 1). You have probably heard of many different names in this movement—Carl Jung, Alfred Adler, Harry Stack Sullivan, Theodore Reik, Anna Freud, Melanie Klein, Karen Horney, Erich Fromm—all once disciples of Freud who went on to develop their own schools.

Sullivan (1953), for example, created an interpersonal theory that is based on the quality of infant–mother bonding. Jung (1926/1954) was even more influential, creating a theory that is still quite popular among contemporary practitioners. Whereas Freud was big on sexual and biological roots of behavior, Jungian analysts favor more spiritual and cultural factors, which access the collective rather than the individual unconscious. In Jung's theory, he remained true to Freud's original idea about the importance of the past and inaccessible memories, but he expressed these as archetypes, which are enduring cultural symbols.

Just as in traditional psychoanalysis, the Jungian therapist encourages clients to talk about their dreams and fantasies, but the interpretations of this material are constructed very differently. That is one of the curious aspects of this field: Jungian patients will dream in Jungian symbols of mythology, folklore, and religious icons whereas Freudian patients dream in phallic symbols, Oedipal complexes, and wish fulfillment. Does this phenomenon validate the theory or rather reflect that people were indoctrinated into a particular system?

Jungian therapy remains popular precisely because it can be so easily combined with religion, spirituality, and cross-cultural experiences. Because Jung wasn't nearly as sexist, pessimistic, or rigid as Freud, he is also often embraced as an alternative.

BASIC PRINCIPLES
OF PSYCHOANALYTIC THEORY

It would normally take you at least five to ten years of intensive study in order to get a handle on psychoanalytic theory and its nuances. This would include reading the two dozen or more volumes that Freud wrote, plus ten times that many of other related works. While you were completing this bookwork, you would also be expected to participate in psychoanalysis as a patient for five or more years because it is considered crucial that you work through your own issues before you attempt to help anyone else with their problems. Once your training began as a practitioner (traditionally open only to M.D.'s and Ph.D.'s), you would then be meeting with your training analyst several times per week to work on cases, as well as attend seminars at an approved psychoanalytic institute.

■ ■ ■ ■ ■ ▬▬▬▬▬▬▬▬▬▬▬▬▬▬▬▬▬▬▬▬▬▬▬▬▬▬▬▬▬▬▬

FOR PERSONAL REFLECTION

Bring to mind the image of someone you don't like very much, someone who really gets underneath your skin. This may be a person who once betrayed you, someone who rejected you, or someone who has been repeatedly abusive toward you.

Now imagine that a new client comes in to see you who bears a striking resemblance to your nemesis, either in appearance or mannerisms. How do you suppose you would feel working with this individual who reminds you of another person whom you despise? Do you think there is any way possible that your strong feelings would not affect your relationship with this client?

Situations such as this (called countertransference) are why psychoanalytic theory considers it so crucial for you to work through all your own unresolved issues before you attempt to help others. Otherwise, your unconscious desires, repressed memories, and unresolved issues can infect the work you try to do with others.

Fear not, however, if you have no inclination or intention of making this sort of commitment to the study of Freud. You would certainly be well advised to read a biography about him (see Breger, 2000, or Gay, 1998, as examples) because his life's work was so interesting and influential. You would also find it interesting to read a few of his classic works, notably *Interpretation of Dreams, The Psychopathology of Everyday Life,* or *An Outline of Psychoanalysis.* Because so many of Freud's original ideas are now part of our universal language and therapeutic principles, you would hardly be considerate literate as a therapist if you didn't at least familiarize yourself with the following basic concepts of the theory.

Intrapsychic Conflicts

Psychological symptoms and self-defeating patterns are the result of internal struggles in which a person attempts to reconcile battles between basic aggressive and sexual instincts (id) versus the conscience and moral beliefs (superego). It is the ego that mediates in the middle, attempting to reconcile raw desire with socially appropriate behavior. Even though this theory is rarely applied as it was originally conceived, it supplies a valuable metaphor for looking at the struggles that people have between their raw aggressive/sexual instincts and their conscience.

FOR A CLASS ACTIVITY

In groups of three, each person should take on the role of the id (raw impulses), superego (moral conscience), or the ego (reasoning, logical self). Situate yourselves with the id facing the superego, and the ego sitting in the middle like a referee. Now begin a conversation (more likely an argument) in which the id wants to do something wicked or socially inappropriate and the superego tries to cajole and scold the id into restraining himself or herself. Before things get totally out of hand, the ego's job is to mediate this struggle, trying to get the two sides to agree to a reasonable compromise.

According to psychoanalytic theory, this sort of debate among the three intrapsychic parts of the self occurs internally all the time. The therapist's job is to strengthen the ego as much as possible so it can do a more effective job of helping the client live productively and happily.

The Past

Current problems stem from unresolved issues that have occurred in early childhood. Freud focused on such things as the impact of breast-feeding, toilet training, and early sexual feelings, but it is far more useful to expand this idea to include the influence of any traumatic or significant events. This not only includes early traumas that have been *repressed* (buried) but also templates for all our relationships. It is an interesting concept, for example, to assume that the ways that people currently engage in intimacy is related in some way to what they witnessed in their parents as a child, or experienced themselves.

Unconscious Drives

People are motivated by forces beyond their awareness. This may sound rather obvious, but this idea was not given great meaning until Freud popularized ideas that, until that point, had only been portrayed in plays and novels. Freud believed that there were actually three levels of consciousness: (1) *conscious awareness* that includes everything that a person perceives, senses, and experiences, as well as remembers, (2) *preconscious memories* that lie just beneath the surface ready to be accessed with just a little prodding, and (3) *unconscious memories* that lie deeply buried because they were threatening, traumatic, or involved unacceptable impulses.

The important thing to remember about memories is that they are *very* selective, ordering things according to the way a person wished they were rather than the way things really were. This has been described as the difference between historical truth, the way things really happened, and narrative truth, which is the way the story is told (Spence, 1982).

■ ■ ■ ■ ■

FOR PERSONAL REFLECTION AND A FIELD STUDY

Without having to look very hard, you will find evidence for all three levels of consciousness in your own experience, especially if you spend the time interviewing family members to compare what you remember to their own recollections.

For the sake of this exercise, assume that you have buried, repressed, or forgotten some powerful experiences in your life because they were too painful for you to deal with. They might have involved traumatic events about which you have no memory. They could involve abuse you suffered as a child. There could also have been some "convenient" rearranging of facts in which you remember things very differently from others who were around.

Get together with family members and look through old photograph albums together. Before you begin this task, tell yourself that you are going to remember things that you have forgotten previously. Tell stories to one another that are elicited by the photos but resist telling the same old tales. Instead, try to drum up new ones. Compare your different versions of the same events.

Resistance

People are not crazy about the idea of delving deeply into buried secrets and painful memories. Psychoanalytic theory predicts that there will be a certain amount of resistance to probes, however subtle, that are intended to bring unconscious material to the surface. A certain amount of client reluctance is, therefore, expected and anticipated. Another useful concept from this theory states that when you encounter ambivalence on the part of clients who say they want to change but sabotage their own efforts, it is a sign that progress is being made.

When practicing this theory, you anticipate and expect that your clients will become resistant during those times when you are getting close to painful, repressed material. This is considered a normal part of the growth process and is expected to be part of the treatment. In fact, practitioners would get suspicious if clients were being a bit too enthusiastic and cooperative.

Whether you subscribe to this idea or not, it is of immeasurable help to remind yourself when you encounter client resistance and reluctance that clients are just doing the best job they can to protect themselves from perceived threats. In such circumstances, it may not only be that clients are being resistant but also that their therapists are unwilling to be more compassionate and flexible (Kottler, 1992). Here you are meddling in their lives, stirring up painful stuff, pressing and pushing them in areas they would rather not venture. It is like you are pulling on old scabs—and it hurts. A lot.

Defense Mechanisms

When threatened, people try to defend themselves with a variety of strategies including withdrawal and counterattacks. As a neurologist, Freud noticed this same sort of process operating within the body when a system would mobilize defenses to deal with a perceived threat. It seemed reasonable to imagine that the same thing happens psychologically during those times when individuals believe they are under attack, sometimes even beyond their awareness. It is, thus, one of the therapist's roles to help clients identify their favored defenses and understand their impact on present behavior (Clark, 1998).

Many of the ego defenses have become part of everyday language. You have heard before, for example, things such as "You are in denial," or "You're just projecting your stuff on to me," "Stop intellectualizing," "He became so freaked out he just regressed." In each of these instances, what is being described is a way that a person is combating a situation that is experienced as overwhelming and so attempts are made to hide.

■ ■ ■ ■ ■

FOR A CLASS ACTIVITY

Working in small groups, supply examples for each of the following common defense mechanisms:

Rationalization—justifying a situation by making up rational reasons to explain irrational behavior.

Repression—censoring painful experiences by excluding them from conscious awareness.

Projection—perceiving that others have those characteristics or behaviors that you find unacceptable in yourself.

Denial—pretending that something undesirable is not really happening.

Sublimation—converting unacceptable or forbidden impulses into socially acceptable behavior.

Regression—a retreat to an earlier stage of development because of fear.

Dreams

According to Freud, dreams were seen as the "royal road to the unconscious," the most useful means by which to decode what a person longs for most. In the traditional psychoanalytic format, complex symbols and metaphors were uncovered and interpreted as the means to discover hidden impulses and repressed material.

Along with many of Freud's original ideas, his notion of dreams as repressed wish fulfillment has not stood the test of time. Many other theories are now advanced to describe the purpose and meaning of dreams. That is not to say that dream interpretation cannot play an important role in therapy, just that the possible interpretations are now open to greater possibilities. Nowadays, practitioners of all orientations tend to be more flexible, asking the client to supply meaning in the images. A common intervention is, thus: "What is the dream saying to you?"

■ ■ ■ ■ ■

FOR HOMEWORK

Whenever a client brings a dream into session, it is often useful to explore possible meanings. Before you can hope to help others make sense of their dreams, it would be useful for you to have some practice examining your own inner experiences.

Keep a notebook and nightlight by your bed. Since you tend to forget your dreams unless you immediately write them down, make a promise to yourself that you will write down all your dreams for a week. Before you go to bed each night, tell yourself that you will remember your dreams. Each time you wake up in the middle of one (which is the only time you will actually remember them) scribble down some notes about the gist of what happened. In the morning, review your notes and draw some hypotheses about what the dream means to you.

Catharsis

This is the release of pent-up emotional energy that occurs through clients telling their stories. Almost all therapeutic approaches make some use of this process by allowing people to dump a lot of stored-up frustrations. It is generally not a good idea to let this go on and on without some intervention or rechanneling because clients can end up just feeling sorry for themselves or engaging in "poor me" victim roles.

You have experienced the power of catharsis many times in your own life. Perhaps you were talking to a friend or family member about something very upsetting and afterward you noticed how much better you felt. This confidante may have done nothing else but listen to you, allow you to leach out all your frustration, but that was quite enough.

It may strike you that it is not nearly enough to just sit there and listen to someone pour his or her heart out, but this is so often exactly what some people need to do (at least in the beginning). It is so rare that most people have anyone in their life who will really listen to them and make a sincere effort to understand without judgment.

Corrective Emotional Experience

Rather than merely talking about feelings, the contemporary analyst and other practitioners seek to help clients to alter their self-perceptions and behavior in light of their increased awareness. Once there is some degree of emotional arousal, sometimes directed toward the therapist in the form of transference, attempts will be made to help him or her work this through in constructive ways. This becomes a model for undertaking similar conflict resolutions in the outside world.

TREATMENT PROCEDURES

The psychoanalytic style of therapy is a relatively long-term relationship that is designed to help people explore their unconscious issues that are at the core of current problems. Through the use of interpretation, dream analysis, free association, transference, and other methods that access repressed material, the practitioner helps clients to understand the source of their troubles and apply what they learn to their daily lives. There are several strategies that are used to bring about this process, many of which are embedded in the special kind of relationship that is established.

Detachment

Freud was the first to advocate a type of helping alliance in which the therapist would appear cool, calm, and collected. Consistent with Freud's scientific training, practitioners were schooled in the importance of objectivity and neutrality in their chairside manner. It was hoped that the more bland and anonymously you present yourself, the more pure will be the client's *projections* (subjective perceptions) about who he or she believes you are. Thus, clients are actually encouraged to create fantasies toward their therapists, providing material for exploration and working through.

There is a very delicate balance to reach in which, on the one hand, you present yourself as neutrally as possible so as to not contaminate the transference that must naturally develop. On the other hand, you don't want to appear so withholding and aloof that it is perceived as punitive. Psychoanalytic practitioners, while appearing somewhat neutral and objective, present themselves as empathic, caring, nonjudgmental, with a kind of "evenly hovering attention" (Wolitzky & Eagle, 1997, p. 46). Remember that many people who attend counseling or therapy may have already experienced lots of rejection in their lives from parents who were neglectful.

■ ■ ■ ■ ■ ▬▬▬▬▬▬▬▬▬▬▬▬▬▬▬▬▬▬▬▬▬▬▬▬

FOR A CLASS ACTIVITY

Practice detachment in helping relationships with a partner. One of you takes on the role of a client, thinking of a very provocative, sensitive, perhaps shocking issue you could talk about (being an abuser, a drug dealer, or perhaps a person in a witness protection program). Imagine that you are feeling very reluctant about your life because of fears of being judged.

The other person will be the therapist. Your job is to listen with neutrality, detachment, and evenly hovering attention. Present yourself as interested, nonjudgmental, and noncritical, encouraging the person to speak about his or her experience. For now, it does not matter which skills you use because this is only an exercise in practicing a relatively detached therapeutic stance.

Afterward, talk to one another about what the experience was like. Give feedback to one another. If time permits, switch roles and try another round.

Transference

Freud (1915/1953) originally conceived of transference as a projection of unconscious desires onto the therapist. Through the analysis of this fantasy, it becomes possible to work on repressed memories and unresolved conflicts of childhood, especially those involving parental figures. Whereas Freud saw the distortion that occurs in therapeutic relationships as a manifestation of past struggles, Kohut (1977) reconceived of transference as something else altogether: a real alliance in which the client creates a new parental relationship rather than merely reliving an old one. In contrasting these two perspectives, Menaker (1991) feels that a far more useful view of transference in contemporary practice is one that helps clients to examine three facets:

1. Unconscious and unfulfilled needs that are played out in sessions.
2. Ways the therapist is idealized by the client as a need for more constructive parenting.
3. Use the transference as leverage without bringing the client's attention to this process. This third option avoids interrupting the developmental work taking place.

Whether you subscribe to psychoanalytic thinking or not, it's rather obvious that therapeutic relationships have elements that are based on reality and fantasy. You see people as they really are, as well as how you imagine them to be. You impose onto others the images of others who have resembled them, often responding to them based on these prior associations. Sometimes you even project attributes that are created by your own past experiences rather than people's actual behavior.

■ ■ ■ ■ ■

FOR PERSONAL REFLECTION

Think of a time recently in which you projected onto someone feelings that were transferred from another relationship. One especially fertile place to look for such a process is related to authority figures. Notice, for example, the ways you perceive your instructor that are based less on his or her behavior and more on your images of what he or she is like. Whom does your instructor remind you of? What are ways your interactions with your instructor are similar to other relationships you have experienced before?

Typically, transferences involve the repetition of some previous relationship pattern, one that is inappropriate and distorts reality (Greenson & Wexler, 1969). For instance, when you look at your instructor for this course, you react to him or her not only as she appears in reality (if you could watch a totally objective video) but also as you imagine him or her to be. This perception is based on all the prior experiences you've had with other authority figures who have served in a similar role. Sometimes you may feel judged or criticized by your instructor less because of his or her actions than by your prior associations with other teachers that have reminded you of this situation.

Whereas Freud and traditional psychoanalysts believed that almost all the feelings one has toward a therapist are projections, fantasies, and distortions, some of the reactions are genuine and reflect what is actually occurring between two people involved in a very intimate, intense relationship (Gill, 1984; Kottler, Sexton, & Whiston, 1994).

The relationship between client and therapist becomes a source of conflict and ambivalence, especially considering it is designed to be a blank slate upon which people may project their fantasies about unresolved authority figures. Once clients gain insight into their distortions, they are then able to work through the conflict first with the therapist and later by resolving issues related to other relationships in the past and present.

Countertransference

The client isn't the only one who projects and distorts the relationship. Therapists, as well, have strong feelings toward their clients—both positive and negative—that have little to do with that person. Our buttons sometimes get pushed by people who remind us of others we have encountered in our lives. We respond to them not as they really are but as we imagine them to be.

Some of the most easily identifiable signs that countertransference may be going on include:

- The arousal of guilt from unresolved personal struggles that parallel those impulses and emotions of the client.
- Impaired empathy in which you find it difficult to feel caring and respectful toward the client.
- Inaccurate interpretations of the client's feelings due to your identification and projection.
- Feelings of being generally blocked, helpless, and frustrated with a particular client.
- Evidence of boredom or impatience in your inner world during work with a client.
- Unusual memory lapses regarding the details of a case.
- Mutual acting out in which the client begins living out your values and you begin acting out the client's pathology.

- A tendency to speak about a client in derogatory terms.
- An awareness that you are working harder than the client.

I remember one instance in which I was seeing an elementary school principal as a client. Because I had been a rather precocious child who frequently found myself in trouble with the principal, I did not have the best of feelings toward this woman who reminded me of my former nemesis. Although ordinarily I am quite flexible about the ways I schedule sessions, doing my best to arrange appointments in a way that is most convenient for clients, with this woman I was more than a little unyielding. I might normally say something such as, "When would you like to reschedule?" but with the principal, I said instead, "I'll see you next Thursday at 3:00."

"But I can't make it then," she replied with astonishment. "You know I can't get away from school until 3:30 when the last children have left."

"Well then," I said with a scolding tone that gave me more pleasure than I'd like to admit, "if your therapy is really important to you, you'll find a way to be here, won't you?"

I am certainly not proud of the way I handled this case but it is a good example of how my own personal feelings got in the way of my compassion. The worst part is that I really wasn't seeing this woman the way she was because I had projected onto her the image of other authority figures from my own past.

■ ■ ■ ■ ■

FOR A FIELD STUDY

Talk to experienced therapists about instances in which they have had strong countertransference reactions toward particular clients. This is a difficult, risky area to discuss because it represents a loss of control and poor judgment on the part of the therapist, so be prepared from some resistance unless you have a trusting relationship with the professional.

CONTEMPORARY THEORISTS

In the past thirty years there has been a strong movement among psychoanalytic practitioners to move away from Freud's emphasis on instinctual drives and psychosexual stages of development and focus instead on the ways that primary relationships are internalized as templates for future intimate relations. Termed *object relations* or *ego psychology,* several different theorists have concentrated their treatment efforts on the basic bonds between infant and parent(s).

Donald Winnicott (1958) conceived of therapy as a kind of "holding environment" to provide a safe, secure, dependable relationship in which clients might work through early relationship conflicts. Typical of the way so many other revisionists took a central idea of Freud's and ran with it, Heinz Kohut (1971) was intrigued with one of Freud's papers on narcissism, which is the condition of excessive self-involvement. Although Freud and current diagnostic manuals treat narcissism as a pathological state marked by obsession with one's own needs, Kohut's theory stresses that the development can be healthy if it leads to productive activities and balanced self-esteem. Kohut (1984) emphasized the role of empathy in the therapeutic alliance, believing that one of the most important ingredients is helping people to feel understood.

Jacques Lacan was a maverick analyst who stirred up tremendous controversy because of his unconventional methods. He believed, for instance, that it was ridiculous to schedule sessions in fifty-minute intervals because not all people need that exact amount of time, and some people needed more. He was, thus, notorious for not taking appointments—clients would simply show up to his office and wait until he would call them in. If he felt that someone was playing games or not in the mood to do serious work, he would abruptly stand up after five minutes of conversation and dismiss the client. If, on the other hand, he felt that a few hours of treatment were indicated, then he would make himself available for that as well.

This text will look in greater detail at two of the contemporary theorists who have been most influential in today's therapeutic practice.

Object Relations Theory

Otto Kernberg (1975, 1984) applied concepts of self-psychology to the understanding of one severe type of personality disturbance known as borderline disorder. Unlike what it sounds, someone caught between the boundaries of being sane and insane, this type of personality disturbance is characterized by intense, contradictory interpersonal patterns. Such individuals tend to be manipulative and extremely difficult to deal with. It would be the consensus of most therapists that this is the most challenging case of all because such individuals are unpredictable and often do their best to get underneath others' skins as a means of self-protection. In fact, one of the major determinants as to whether a client is bestowed with this toxic label occurs when the client appears so annoying, manipulative, and irritating that the therapist can't get him or her out of mind.

More recently Kernberg (1997) has sought to integrate the contributions of other therapeutic systems into a more contemporary and responsive version of psychoanalytic treatment that brings in elements of empathy, the here and now, affective experience, and a more genuine relationship.

Just as in traditional psychoanalytic practice, object relations therapists see the past as a strong influence on behavior in the present. However, rather than remaining aloof and completely detached, they often create a more natural, empathic, and supportive relationship that fosters a degree of attachment without complete dependence. The goal is to provide a secure environment with clear boundaries. This type of relationship encourages clients to explore the nature of their relationships with others, as well as with the therapist in sessions.

Self-Psychology Theory

Rather than only interpreting events of the past as a road to understand current problems, Heinz Kohut (1984) recommends a treatment in which here-and-now behaviors are identified and explored. Defenses are identified as they play themselves out in sessions. Rather than sparking further resistance, if handled sensitively, such interpretations can lead to greater ego strength and resilience.

According to this theory, it is excessive self-centeredness and narcissism that lead to many personal problems. When you get stuck in the stage of egocentrism and grandiosity typical of a 4-year-old, you are likely to feel awfully disappointed with others not living up to your expectations. Like Masterson and Kernberg, Kohut specialized in working with severe personality disorders by structuring an empathic relationship with clear boundaries. Self-psychologists often call this type of relationship a "holding environment" because you are metaphorically holding someone with caring but consistent, stable force. Because you are likely to be tested a lot with these types of cases, it is crucial that you have in place clear rules and boundaries for handling inevitable acting out.

Whereas traditional psychoanalytic therapy as it was originally conceived by Freud is now virtually obsolete, self-psychology and object relations therapy are very much alive and flourishing. These psychodynamic approaches have evolved in such a way that they reflect more accurately the needs of contemporary practice. The applications of these theories will be described further in the next sections.

A Different Set of Rules for Therapy

The type of cases that interested these theorists—narcissistic and borderline personality disorders—involve a very different type of treatment than does "ordinary" therapy. As one example, you might usually present yourself as a very open, warm, and flexible professional. In my own work, I tend to smile a lot, use humor, and appear as supportive, empathic, caring, and flexible as I can. I might adapt this style if I am working with someone who is more strait-laced, older, or a member of some traditional culture in which formality is valued, but basically I am pretty easygoing.

The one major exception to this fluid approach is when I discover—often a little too late—that I am dealing with someone who might have one of these toxic interpersonal styles (I don't like to use the *DSM* terms of personality disorders because they sound so intractable and hopeless). Because people who are manipulative for a living are adept at making a good impression when they need to, it isn't until the third or fourth session that I might realize what is happening. I might begin to notice increasing intrusions on my time—phone calls at home, requests for special consideration, excuses to contact me. I also might sense that the person seems somewhat frightening to me—not that I feel in any physical danger—but rather that it seems as though this person is working awfully hard to figure me out to gain some leverage and control.

It is about this time that something dramatic happens—the client accuses me of abandoning him or her, or figures out some vulnerable spot to exploit, or engages in some self-destructive gesture—that I realize that my usual kind of relationship is not going to work. With clients who display these manipulative patterns, it is very important to structure the type of relationship that is consistent, predictable, and with very firm boundaries. Because this type of person probably never had parenting in such a way, this holding environment becomes therapeutic beyond anything else that you do.

■ ■ ■ ■ ■

FOR PERSONAL REFLECTION AND A CLASS ACTIVITY

The management of boundaries plays an important part in ego psychology and self-psychology. Because these theories have been applied often to cases of severe personality disorder, it is especially important to provide a predictable, solid relationship to set appropriate limits that clients might not be able to maintain on their own.

Think of times you have been involved in teaching or helping relationships in which someone set firm boundaries about what you could and could not do. You understood that these rules existed for your own safety and welfare rather than as part of some arbitrary bureaucracy or the helper's convenience. How did this structure help you?

In small groups, identify the boundaries that have been established in your class. These include all rules, both explicit and implicit, that are designed to further goals, maintain safety, and keep things running smoothly. Talk about the ways these boundaries are enforced.

The hard part, of course, is recognizing as early as possible that you might be dealing with a "disordered self" type of client, requiring a kind of relationship that might be different from others you create. I say "might" because in most psychoanalytic relationships there are always clear boundaries that are strictly enforced.

CONTEMPORARY DEVELOPMENTS

Obviously, the world today is very different from nineteenth-century Victorian Vienna that spawned Freud's original ideas. Furthermore, advances in neurology, psychology, and related social sciences have demonstrated that although many of Freud's theories have withstood the scrutiny of empirical investigation (i.e., unconscious conflict), others have not (i.e., dreams as repressed wishes, Oedipal complex).

Some of Freud's original disciples such as Alfred Adler, Franz Alexander, and Otto Rank began making revisions in the basic psychoanalytic model almost from their first involvement in the movement. They realized that if this novel psychological approach was going to help those who needed it the most, then somehow it would need to be abbreviated in such a way that symptoms could be relieved in a matter of months rather than years.

Most contemporary psychodynamic practitioners have abandoned many of Freud's original tenets, such as use of the couch or reliance on instincts as the primary source of motivation. It makes sense, of course, that any theory devised over a hundred years ago in another world would need considerable revision and adaptation to fit our current needs. Most dramatically, the changing therapeutic landscape of managed care and an increasingly diverse client population have forced practitioners to shorten their treatment methods.

Although there are as many different theories of brief treatment as there are traditional approaches to psychoanalysis (Book, 1998; Davanloo, 1980; Frank, 1992; Gill, 1984; Horowitz, 1988; Kernberg, 1997; Kohut, 1984; Levenson, 1995; Luborsky & Crits-Christoph, 1990; Malan & Osimo, 1992; Mander, 2000; Mann & Goldman, 1982; Messer & Warren, 1995; Sifneos, 1987; Strupp & Binder, 1984; Wachtel, 1997), most of them follow similar clinical principles in their work.

1. Treatment has been abbreviated from the mandatory four times a week for five years to structures that are more realistic and cost-effective (weekly sessions for several months).

2. As with any form of brief therapy, clients are carefully screened and selected to make certain they are good candidates for abbreviated treatment (Levenson, 1995; Strupp & Binder, 1984). This includes those with:
   a. adjustment reactions (depression and anxiety that are the result of life events)

    b. problems in everyday living (relationships, work, and family problems)

    c. milder forms of personality disorder

3. The best clients for this approach (or probably any other therapy) are those in acute pain, willing to attend regular appointments, and those who can relate to the therapist in a meaningful way. Level of motivation is also a key consideration, assessed by determining the client's degree of honesty, openness, psychological-mindedness, realistic expectations, and willingness to make reasonable sacrifices (Sifneos, 1987).

4. Sessions are devoted not only to coming to terms with the past but also to looking at present behavior and concerns. This might sound like a rather obvious approach but actually represents a recent innovation.

5. Treatment goals are defined in more specific, limited ways. Rather than seeking to reshape a person's whole personality, the brief dynamic therapist focuses on identified, negotiated goals related to presenting complaints. You would usually stick with one theme or set of issues—maladaptive relationships, ineffective coping styles, unresolved parental issues, unsatisfying work—rather than trying to cover the whole spectrum of a person's life.

6. Attention is directed more toward ego functioning rather than instinctual drives. This means that clients are helped to look at their characteristic ego defense mechanisms (i.e., denial, rationalization, sublimination).

7. Severe forms of personality disorder (borderline and narcissistic disorders) have been especially fertile ground for psychoanalytic theorists (e.g., Masterson, Kroll) who have combined traditional thinking with a more strategic type of therapeutic relationship.

8. Within a psychodynamic framework, practitioners are inclined to use a variety of interventions from many other approaches. In the treatment of sexual dysfunctions, such as erectile problems in men and orgasmic problems in women, one of the pioneers in the field was a practicing psychoanalyst who combined the theory with behavioral methods. Thus, Kaplan (1974) believed that it was virtually unethical to treat these disorders with insight-oriented therapy alone, when it has been found that couples therapy in conjunction with behavioral exercises is far more effective.

■ ■ ■ ■ ■

FOR A FIELD STUDY

Interview several people who have participated in psychoanalytic therapy to find out about their experiences. Ask them to comment on what they found most useful about the sessions. As they look back on the therapy, what stands out as having been the most enduring result?

9. Most psychodynamic clinicians make similar adaptations when borrowing behavioral, cognitive, systemic, or other strategies for specific presenting problems. Experience and empirical research have shown that insight alone often isn't enough, especially for those with impulse disorders, addictions, and other behavioral disorders. Thus, practitioners are far more inclined to be confrontive and direct instead of waiting patiently for clients to figure out things on their own.

10. It is no longer enough to rely purely on case studies, personal experience, and the collected works of Freud in order to plan interventions and seek guidance for treatment plans. For example, a number of empirical outcome studies (Barber, 1994; Svartberg & Stiles, 1994) have been undertaken to demonstrate the effectiveness of short-term psychodynamic therapy when compared to other approaches.

Psychoanalytic practitioners are also licensed psychologists, counselors, psychiatrists, and social workers; as such, they are mandated by their professions to practice in a way consistent with established standards of care that are based on empirical research.

In other words, psychoanalysts have been influenced strongly by developments outside their own discipline and have sought to integrate these innovations with their own training. Several writers, for example, have combined psychoanalytic thought with humanistic approaches (Appelbaum, 1995), behavior therapy (Wachtel, 1997; Wheelis, 1973), family systems models (Ackerman, 1958; Framo, 1992; Gustafson, 1986), and even crisis intervention (Bellak, 1992) to name just a few of the permutations.

GENERAL PRINCIPLES OF BRIEF PSYCHODYNAMIC PRACTICE

As you will see in a later chapter on brief therapies in general, long- and short-term practitioners embrace different values in their work (Budman & Gurman, 1988; Levenson, 1995). In traditional psychoanalytic treatment, the therapist attempts to deal with underlying characterological changes and expects to be around throughout the whole process of transformation. Therapy is viewed as the most important part of a person's life and the participant is expected to make a major investment of time, money, and commitment. In any short-term treatment, including brief psychodynamic models, the emphasis is not on a cure but rather on relief of presenting symptoms. In addition, there is considerable reality-based attention to time constraints and limited financial resources.

Among the various abbreviated psychoanalytic methods is the work of Davanloo (1980), Wolberg (1980), McCullough (1991), Levenson (1995), and Book (1998), who developed methods that could be followed within prearranged sessions as agreed, yet they still didn't abandon many of Freud's original premises. Basically, the process follows several distinct stages:

1. Help the person to tell his or her story.
2. Establish a solid relationship.
3. Deal with initial resistance to the therapy.
4. Gather relevant background information and limited history.
5. Select the problem(s) most amenable to short-term intervention.
6. Explore the precipitating events in a limited way.
7. Collaborate with the client to formulate a diagnosis and treatment plan.
8. Increase the client's awareness of defensiveness and self-defeating thinking.
9. Revisit resistance to interventions.
10. Explore the client's personal reactions to the relationship (limited transference).
11. Monitor personal reactions to the relationship (limited counter-transference reactions).
12. Examine ways that the past is influencing the present.
13. Help the client to behave more effectively in the relationship and in the outside world.
14. Provide feedback and confront discrepancies.
15. Negotiate homework assignments.
16. Continuously remind the client of the prearranged termination date.
17. End therapy as agreed.
18. Schedule follow-ups as needed.

Just as in regular versions of psychoanalysis, the relationship is critical but in an altered form that emphasizes a more present-oriented, authentic alliance in which the therapist becomes more of a teacher/consultant rather than a parent figure. This approach does not much resemble the method first developed by Freud over a hundred years ago, but then not much in the way any profession currently operates is the same as it was in the last century.

Thinking Psychodynamically

Whereas there once was a time when almost all practicing therapists expressed allegiance to psychoanalytic theory, this approach is now restricted to mostly those in private practice, those doing relatively long-term personality reconstruction work, and those in urban areas with a fairly affluent client population. Obviously, because psychoanalytic therapy has been traditionally very time-consuming and expensive, it has been most well suited to those who have the time, inclination, and capacity for insight-oriented work. Recent manuals (see Fredericks, 1999; Hollender & Ford, 2000; Mander, 2000), however, have been designed to help clinicians adapt to the demands of contemporary practice.

There has been over a century of criticisms leveled at Freud and his disciples—that the theory is too complex, that its concepts have not been empirically validated, that it is sexist and culturally biased, that it ignores the pragmatic realities of the disadvantaged and poor, that it overemphasizes the influence of the past to the exclusion of the present, and so on. There are literally hundreds, perhaps thousands, of books written that attack the model with passionate vehemence.

■ ■ ■ ■ ■

FOR PERSONAL APPLICATION

Thinking psychodynamically means that when someone is encountering difficulties, you might ask yourself and the client several relevant questions such as the following:

1. What is the relation of what you are experiencing now to what you have encountered in the past?
2. Which experiences in your early life have most shaped who you are today?
3. What motives and forces beyond your awareness might be affecting your judgment?
4. What fantasies and dreams have you had that might be related to your presenting problem?
5. How have your feelings for me, as your therapist, reflected the kind of relationships you have experienced with others?

In spite of the many limitations of psychoanalytic theory it has become the foundation for all forms of therapy. It was the first systematic model and the one most widely practiced. Furthermore, many of its essential ideas have been so integrated into the public consciousness and therapeutic lore that it is very difficult *not* to think psychodynamically when looking at personal problems.

SUGGESTED READINGS

Ackerman, N. W. (1958). *The psychodynamics of family life.* New York: Basic Books.

Book, H. E. (1998). *How to practice brief psychodynamic psychotherapy.* Washington, DC: American Psychological Association.

Breger, L. (2000). *Freud: Darkness in the midst of vision.* New York: Wiley.

Erikson, E. (1982). *The life cycle completed.* New York: W. W. Norton.

Fredericks, J. (1999). *Psychodynamic psychotherapy: Learning to listen from multiple perspectives.* New York: Brunner/Mazel.

Freud, S. (1900) *Interpretation of dreams.* In Collected papers. London: Hogarth Press.

Hollender, M. H., & Ford, C. V. (2000). *Dynamic psychotherapy: An introductory approach.* New York: Jason Aronson.

Jones, E. E. (2001). *Therapeutic action: A guide to psychoanalytic therapy.* Northvale, NJ: Jason Aronson.

Jung, C. (1963). *Memories, dreams, reflections.* New York: Pantheon Books.

Kohut, H. (1984). *How does analysis cure?* Chicago: University of Chicago Press.

Levenson, H. (1995). *Time-limited dynamic psychotherapy: A guide to clinical practice.* New York: Basic Books.

Luborsky, L., & Crits-Christoph, P. (1998). *Understanding transference: The core conflictual relationship theme method* (2nd ed.). Washington, DC: American Psychological Association.

Mander, G. (2000). *Psychodynamic approach to brief therapy.* Thousand Oaks, CA: Sage.

Spense, D. P. (1982). *Narrative truth and historical truth.* New York: W. W. Norton.

■ ■ ■ ■ ■

CHAPTER 5

THE PRIMACY OF PERSONAL EXPERIENCE

Humanistic Approaches

The family of humanistic therapies is just as diverse as the psychoanalytic approaches in the previous chapter. Although the theories may share a set of basic assumptions about human nature, they go about their work in very different ways. Some humanistic theories (existential) are rather intellectually dense and philosophical in nature, whereas others tend to focus on unexpressed feelings (client-centered) or primary experience (Gestalt). What makes them all humanistic in orientation is a strong belief in the power of people to heal themselves, especially in the context of a genuine, authentic type of relationship. Rather than adopting a stance of aloofness and detachment common to psychoanalytic theory, the humanistic practitioner seeks to create a relationship with clients that is warm, caring, genuine, and engaging. The therapist is not only allowed to be authentic and real in the relationship but also is encouraged to be so.

SOME SHARED BELIEFS

At the time that humanism was spawned in the sixties, there were two major forces in the field: behaviorism and psychoanalysis. Each was fighting for dominance, arguing that the best way to do therapy was either to concentrate on presenting symptoms or underlying causes. Although psychoanalytic practitioners did advocate that the therapeutic relationship was the core of healing, they stressed a kind of alliance that was fairly antiseptic. Furthermore, consistent with Freud's thinking, they believed that humans were essentially driven by their most base, instinctual drives: sexuality and aggression. The object of therapy was to help people to control their basic nature.

By contrast, humanism views people as essentially good and growth oriented. If they experience problems or engage in destructive acts, it is because they have wandered away from their basic nature. Given the proper sort of fertile environment that is characterized by an accepting, respectful, and caring relationship, people can be helped to regain their emotional and spiritual footing.

Basic Assumptions

There are several characteristics of a humanistic approach, regardless of which brand is practiced:

> *The primacy of experience.* Rather than quantifying or measuring be-havior, the humanist seeks to understand personal experience in its essence. Every individual is unique. Human experience is irre-ducible. Subjective, inner states should be honored and respected.
>
> *Growth orientation.* People have the tendency to grow and actual-ize their potential. Increased self-awareness and self-acceptance will help people in their journey toward greater fulfillment and productivity.
>
> *Free choice.* Rather than being deterministic, humanists believe that people can become almost whatever they choose.

You can see that these assumptions are quite different from those presented in the previous chapter. If psychodynamic theory has been de-scribed as deterministic and instinct driven, then the humanistic ap-proaches focus much more on the choices that people make and the freedom they have to determine their own futures. Of course, with that freedom comes awesome personal responsibility.

The Healing Relationship

It is through the relationship with a helper (therapist, counselor, teacher, coach, parent) that people are able to sort out their troubles and regain their composure. This special type of relationship includes a kind of nonpossessive loving, caring, and respect. It is characterized by three facets (Moustakas, 1986):

1. *Being in.* Empathy means crawling inside someone else's skin so that you can feel what he or she is experiencing. All of your ability to read what another is feeling, to respond sensitively, and to mirror what you hear and see is based on the accuracy of your "felt sense." In order to experience pure empathy, you must leave your own self-centeredness and enter into the being of another. Needless to say, this is a very challenging journey.

2. *Being for.* Helping relationships are hardly neutral ones in the sense that you act as an advocate for your clients. You may not support the destructive things they do and the irritating behaviors that get in the way, but you never waver in your acceptance and respect for them as people. When times are tough, you are the one person they can count on for support and encouragement.

3. *Being with.* As an individual, distinct person, you have your own perceptions, beliefs, and feelings that are separate from those of your clients. Even when you are involved in the empathic activity of "being in," you are still apart, aware of your own internal reactions and perceptions. The authentic sharing of selves in therapy is a reciprocal process in which both participants are profoundly influenced by the interaction. Just as the client is affected by the encounter, so too is the therapist impacted dramatically. The humanistic relationship is, thus, an authentic engagement. "Being With," writes Moustakas (1986, p. 102), "certainly means listening and hearing the other's feelings, thoughts, objectives, but it also means offering my own perceptions and views."

FOR A CLASS ACTIVITY

Form small groups of about six participants. Each of you talks to one another about a time in your life in which you were having a difficult time and a strong relationship with a helper (teacher, coach, counselor, neighbor, etc.) made all the difference. Rather than focusing on what this helper did that was most valuable, focus instead on the kind of relationship that developed between you.

After each of you has had a chance to share something personal, then discuss what it feels like to be in a group together talking about your experiences.

FOR PERSONAL APPLICATION

One of the most useful concepts that you can use to improve the quality, intimacy, and satisfaction of *all* your relationships is to practice empathic listening. This means focusing your full and complete attention on the other person, resisting all distractions, both internal and external. It involves putting yourself in a place of perfect openness so that you can enter the other person's world without judgment or criticism. You simply make yourself present for the other person, doing your absolute best to listen carefully and respond compassionately.

I warn you: This is *very* hard to do. It is so natural to divide your attention, let your thoughts wander, and become critical and judgmental of what another person is saying or doing. Empathic listening, however, requires you to suspend your own needs in the process of entering another person's world.

Report back to class how this practice went, what problems you encountered, and what you noticed was different about your conversations.

BACKGROUND AND HISTORY

Humanism emerged as much as a cultural artifact as a scientific revolution. It was a product of the 1950s, a time of eternal optimism, faith in the human spirit, material affluence, and a search for personal meaning. It was a time of Eisenhower, the Mickey Mouse Club, Ozzie and Harriet, and Elvis (Moss, 1999).

It was Abraham Maslow, perhaps more than any other thinker, who converted the widespread cheerfulness and optimism of postwar America into a psychology of positive mental health. Remember that at this time the only alternatives available were largely mechanistic (behaviorism) or deterministic (psychoanalysis). Then Maslow's (1954) voice was heard advocating that psychology should not just focus on the emotionally dysfunctional and mentally ill but also on those who are most fully functioning. He decided to identify the individuals who were exceptionally "self-actualized," contemporaries such as Eleanor Roosevelt and Albert Schweitzer, and use them as models for human potential. He also believed it was possible to study scientifically not only observable behavior but also internal experience.

■ ■ ■ ■ ■

FOR PERSONAL REFLECTION OR A CLASS ACTIVITY

Among his findings, Abraham Maslow discovered that self-actualized people have a high frequency of peak experiences—magical moments of insight, creativity, spiritual transcendence, intimacy, or harmony. Think about the peak experiences of your life, those moments of sublime ecstasy in which you transcended ordinary reality. These could have been religious, creative, intellectual, emotional, or physical experiences.

Try to recall the texture of what took place—how you felt, saw, heard, and experienced reality in a distinctly different way. Recapture the power of those moments and how they changed forever your perceptions and lived experience.

Select one such event from the past year. Talk to classmates about what happened and what it meant to you.

Although Maslow started the ball rolling (with a little help from some friends), others worked independently of his efforts, making their own discoveries about the best in human nature. These included names you might have heard before, such as Carl Rogers (the developer of client-centered therapy), Rollo May (the first American existential therapist), Erich Fromm (popular writer of books on love and personal meaning), Clark Moustakas (author of books on the meaning of loneliness), James Bugental and Alvin Mahrer (both psychologists who developed humanistic approaches to therapy), and many others. I am not throwing all these names at you because I think you should commit them to memory but merely to highlight that dozens of people were involved in promoting the humanistic movement, each of them with a unique viewpoint.

EXISTENTIAL THEORY

Rather than a coherent theory, this is really a philosophical approach to helping people that examines issues of personal meaning. This model is much less about therapeutic techniques and more about offering a perspective on the human condition to guide helping efforts.

Some Background and History

Existential theory has its heritage in the philosophical writings of European theologians and philosophers, who make for some very difficult bedtime reading. Unless you have a strong background in this discipline, it's likely that tackling the original sources of Søren Kierkegaard (1813–1855), Frederick Nietzsche (1844–1900), Martin Heidegger (1889–1976), Jean-Paul Sartre (1905–1980), Martin Buber (1878–1965), and Karl Jaspers (1883–1969) will be quite a challenge. To give you the "one-minute existentialist" version of their ideas, they were basically concerned with the meaning of human existence. Some took the approach that God (Jaspers, Buber) provided the foundation for finding meaning in life, whereas others (Sartre) believed that in the absence of God it is up to each individual to find his or her own reason for living. This overwhelming sense of freedom is also a kind of prison in that we must accept responsibility for the choices we make.

The existential themes are the stuff of movies and novels. Indeed, some of the most thought-provoking stories you have ever heard or read probably deal with the search for meaning in life. Many of the world's greatest writers (Franz Kafka, Fyodor Dostoyevsky, Albert Camus) have presented provocative themes in which human characters struggle with existential issues and their consequent moral choices. In fact, the term *existentialism* was first coined by writer and philosopher Jean-Paul Sartre to describe the state of despair expressed by characters in his novels.

■ ■ ■ ■ ■ ▬▬▬▬▬▬▬▬▬▬▬▬▬▬▬▬▬▬▬▬▬▬▬▬▬▬▬

FOR PERSONAL REFLECTION

Existentialists are fond of being provocative by encouraging people to wrestle with life's ultimate questions. One of the most disturbing of all subjects is our own mortality. According to this approach, it is the prospect of our own impending death that forces us to confront the urgency of living each moment to its fullest.

When philosopher Bertrand Russell, well into his nineties, was once asked about what he'd like for a gift, he said with great passion that he'd like to get on his knees on the busiest street corner in London and beg passersby to give him the precious moments of their lives that they waste. This was clearly a person who was in the throes of facing his own existential mortality.

Consider your own path. Regardless of what you think happens after you die, whether you go to heaven, purgatory, nirvana, whether you believe yourself destined for reincarnation, or whether you will simply be food for worms, your time on this planet is certainly limited. With each tick of your heart, the precious moments of your life are forever being used up. How many such heartbeats to you think you have left before this ordinary muscle stops forever? A million? A billion? Not so many really, especially when you consider how long you're going to be dead.

When you ponder your own impending demise, what does that bring to the surface? Knowing that your time is limited, realizing that the precious seconds of your life are ticking away (already several hundred more just since you started reading this reflective exercise), how do you wish to spend your life? Do you really want to waste time feeling depressed or bored or lonely?

How might you engage more completely with your life? If you knew you only had a few weeks left to live and every day you are granted is a precious gift, what choices would you make as to how you'd spend your time differently?

Victor Frankl and Logotherapy

A far more personal approach to the subject of human existence was also undertaken in Europe, but rather than in academic settings or philosophical societies new ideas were spawned in the concentration camps of Auschwitz. Within the span of just a few years, psychiatrist Victor Frankl ended up being "transferred" from head of the most prestigious department in Austria to being interned in the death camps of Germany. As he watched his family and friends perish, Frankl mused about why some of the inmates managed to survive while others seemed to give up. He postulated that those who found some underlying meaning to their suffering, even if it was simply to last long enough to tell the world about what was happening, were able to cope in ways that others could not. The will to live seemed to emanate from a strong conviction that there was some reason or purpose for the challenges put in their path.

In his book, *Man's Search for Meaning,* now regarded by many as one of the most important works of the twentieth century, Frankl (1962) set forth his ideas about existential theory that were to form the foundation for a system of helping that he called logotherapy. Foreshadowing quite a number of schools that would emphasize the value of one's attitude even in the most horrible conditions, Frankl (1962) presented his credo of survival:

> We who lived in concentration camps can remember the men who walked through the huts comforting others, giving away their last piece of bread. They may have been few in number, but they offer sufficient proof that everything can be taken from a man but one thing: the last of the human freedoms—to choose one's attitude in any given set of circumstances, to choose one's own way. (p. 104)

The implications of this message are profound: that regardless of the circumstances in which we find ourselves, in spite of the trials and tribulations we must face, it is the choices we make about our attitudes and actions that determine our ultimate reactions. This means that as therapists, one of our main jobs is to help people to examine their personal choices in life to find their own personal meaning.

FOR PERSONAL APPLICATION

Some of the best films you have ever seen are steeped in existential themes related to freedom, responsibility, lack of meaning, and especially to death. There is no subject more terrifying nor one that forces us more directly to confront the choices we make in life.

A number of fine movies, many of them Academy Award winners, chose death as the main backdrop from which to explore how people struggle with their own existence. Consider the following list as just a few of the existential films in this genre: *Dead Man Walking, Sophie's Choice, Philadelphia, Leaving Las Vegas, Schindler's List, Life Is Beautiful, American Beauty, The Big Chill, Midnight Cowboy,* and *Born on the Fourth of July.*

Watch one or more of these films with classmates or family members. Afterward talk to one another about what the film(s) stirred up in you, especially as related to your own mortality.

Existential Principles

Existential philosophy forms the foundation for all the other humanistic approaches and many others as well. To be an existentialist means that you make an effort to include in your sessions discussions of the following issues (May & Yalom, 1995; Yalom, 1980):

1. *Self-awareness.* There is only the present. Nothing else exists except the now. To the extent that you are living in the past or future, you are dead, not fully alive.
2. *Isolation.* Each of us is born alone and will die alone. Everything else is illusion. We will spend our lives seeking intimacy and trying to connect to others, but ultimately we must confront our own essential aloneness.
3. *Personal meaning.* It is up to each individual to find his or her own purpose for living. This is not a one-time proposition but an ongoing struggle to continuously redefine our lives in light of new experiences.
4. *Freedom.* Each of us is confronted with choices every day. Freedom may be the foundation of democracy, but it also presents some awful choices. Freedom is terrifying; most people want a whole lot less of it. They fear making bad decisions. They want others to make decisions for them.
5. *Angst.* This is another word for anxiety, but in German it means a more general, free-floating kind of dread. The consequences of dealing with existential issues or of trying to hide from them is that we must all live with angst. It is always there, just below the surface. You can try to ignore it, medicate it, or distract yourself as much as possible, but angst will remain your lifelong companion.
6. *Responsibility.* We are responsible for our lives—for the choices we make or don't make. We are also responsible for our own freedom. Many people live in a type of prison of their own creation, trapped by their own refusal to be responsible for their lives.
7. *Death.* This is the biggie. This is the one you'd like to run from the most. Death is what kills us, but ultimately it is also what makes us most alive.

To be an existentialist means that you think a lot about life's ultimate issues. Regardless of the issues your clients present and the problems they face, you see at their core the fundamental themes of what it means to be alive. You incorporate discussions about these themes as part of any intervention you attempt. No extra charge.

■ ■ ■ ■ ■

FOR A FIELD STUDY

Interview or talk to several other people about what gives their lives greatest meaning. What is it that most drives them to get out of bed in the morning, to make sacrifices, to work hard? What are they searching for most in life?

Get in the habit of talking to as many people as possible about existential themes. Spend considerable time yourself writing in your journal and reflecting privately about the meaning attached to your own existence.

Existential Therapy

It wasn't until Rollo May (1958, 1967, 1983) adapted existential ideas for contemporary therapeutic practice in North America that this approach really began to exert a significant influence. Other practitioners such as Jim Bugental (1965, 1992), Clark Moustakas (1961, 1994), Alvin Mahrer (1986, 1996), and Irvin Yalom (1980, 1989) also played an influential role in developing systems of therapy that used existential ideas as their core.

Should you decide that you want to be an existentialist or practice existential therapy, I warn you that you have your work cut out for you. There is no easy path if you walk this way. Existential philosophy is dense, complex, and difficult to master. Furthermore, there is precious little guidance for the practitioner because the emphasis is not on technique but on therapist stance. You can *be* an existentialist, but you can't *do* it. This, of course, gives you even more freedom to use whatever methods you want as long as they are embedded in an underlying existential way of life and practice.

Contemporary developments in existential theory and practice have made the approach far more pragmatic and flexible than other models. Although this brand of therapy still recognizes the value of long-term work as the best means to improve people's quality of life and promote profound change, it has also been adapted to briefer systems of intervention.

Potash (1994) makes the point as well that because eclecticism can be rather unsystematic in that practitioners use whichever techniques they desire, existentialism provides a theoretical framework to organize helping efforts. This kind of pragmatic-existential approach permits a therapist and client to co-invent unique ways of working together that can change from moment to moment, depending on what is needed.

If you are the type who needs concreteness, who thrives only on action plans, and who likes specificity, then you will likely feel very frustrated with this approach. Then again, maybe that is *exactly* what you need most. There is an idea that the most direct path to growth is not to follow the way that is most convenient, comfortable, and familiar but rather to pursue a journey that presents reasonable obstacles to be overcome.

A Different Sort of Relationship

A huge component of existential work is the relationship you develop with your clients. Although this approach was really just an offshoot of psychoanalysis (in Europe it was even called existential analysis), a fundamental change was implemented in which the connection with clients became a more authentic engagement. Rather than using detachment and transference as the leverage by which to promote exploration and insight, existential therapy uses as its core the genuine, human connection that clients and therapists feel toward one another.

Keeping in mind the importance of boundaries, the dangers of dual relationships, and the exploitation of clients through inappropriate boundary violations, an existential relationship is highly professional but also quite personal. The therapist presents himself or herself as a real person. The goal is make an authentic connection to clients in such a way that they feel they are treated as persons rather than as objects.

This type of relationship is not just unidirectional because the therapist must not only help the client to increase self-awareness but also must do this as well. The psychoanalytic practitioner seeks to monitor personal reactions to deal with transference issues. The existentialist also does so but for quite a different reason: Rather than to guard against personal reactions that might pollute the relationship, the goal is instead to use these feelings.

In practice, this means that when you are *with* clients (note the emphasis on *with*), there are two parallel processes going on in the relationship. On the one hand, you are closely following the client's experience, using your heart, head, and soul to really get a sense of his or her world. At the same time, you are following what is going on inside of you as well, noting your very personal reactions to what is taking place. You might not always share your own process because therapist self-disclosure is probably the single most abused skill, but you would monitor closely and carefully how each of you in this relationship is responding and reacting to what is happening.

Whereas other systems of therapy emphasize objectivity in the relationship, the existential practitioner seeks to be "a participant 'in' the relationship rather than the detached observer who stands 'outside' the client's psychic world and comments upon or interprets it" (Spinelli, 1997, p. 7). As you no doubt can imagine, this sort of commitment requires a high degree of personal involvement.

The Therapeutic Process

The techniques of existential therapy may be inconsequential and the method extremely flexible; nevertheless, some practitioners have taken the time to set forth a general sort of overview of the process involved in helping people. In describing what occurs in every session he conducts, Mahrer (1986, 1996) describes four sequential steps:

1. *Being in the moment.* This means focusing totally and completely on the here and now, as well as teaching the client to do the same. Both participants in the process note internal feelings, identify those affective states, give them names, and then access the feelings at the deepest levels.

2. *Integrating the felt experience into primary relationships.* This means making connections between what is felt to more fulfilling relationships with others. The relationship comes into play again because it is through the therapeutic encounter that clients are able to apply what they have learned to other relationships. The trust and intimacy become generalized to other contexts.

3. *Making connections to the past.* Although things start out in the present with self-awareness and presenting complaints, these are linked to experiences that have occurred previously. The client is invited to relive early life scenes and reexperience what was felt. This is one major difference from psychoanalysis in that clients are not merely encouraged to talk about past events but to experience them emotionally all over again, working them through in ways that were not possible previously.

4. *Integrating what was learned.* This means being a new person in the present.

■ ■ ■ ■ ■ ▬▬▬▬▬▬▬▬▬▬▬▬▬▬▬▬▬▬▬▬▬▬▬▬▬▬▬▬▬

FOR PERSONAL APPLICATION

Try being in the moment. First, prepare yourself to embrace whatever comes into your mind and heart as you read these instructions. Start with the very first thing that comes to mind. Anything! It doesn't matter.

Be aware of how you are censoring and limiting yourself. Just let yourself go. Don't be concerned with what is important.

What are you feeling that is rather prominent in your life right now? This can be a good feeling or a bad one. Let yourself feel this emotion right now. Don't block yourself but let it flow.

As you experience this feeling, what are you aware of in your body? What sensations are present? Which images come to mind? Just attend to whatever is happening.

Whatever has come to you—use it in some way. Make some connections between what you just experienced and what you have lived before. Make yourself receptive to whatever emerged. Ask yourself what you just learned.

If possible, talk to a friend, classmate, or family member about what you experienced. Let the experience deepen the intimacy between you and another.

Consistent with the demands of contemporary practice, some existentialists such as Strasser and Strasser (1997) have made an effort to abbreviate the treatment approach to include a more systematic, focused, and confrontive method. After a working relationship is established and an exploration is undertaken of the client's world, the therapist might very well challenge underlying beliefs that are seen as self-defeating, point out discrepancies and paradoxes, dispute misconceptions that aren't based in reality, and identify new choices useful in developing personal meaning. As you will read in the next chapter, this may sound suspiciously like cognitive therapy, but as I've mentioned, one of the strengths of this approach is its willingness to adapt methods to an existential perspective.

Some Limitations

I have mentioned previously that the existential approach can be very intellectual, complex, and cerebral, although offshoots of it such as Gestalt and client-centered theories applied the concepts to far more practical circumstances, emphasizing felt experience over the intellect. This is quite a good thing because people in crisis, those who are experiencing acute trauma, or those with limited interest in insight, would not be good candidates for an existential approach, at least initially.

Although much of the foundation theory comes from Western philosophers, there is actually quite a lot in the approach that is compatible with Taoist, Buddhist, and other Eastern philosophies that look at ways of being (see Chapter 10). Nevertheless, one would have to be especially vigilant in adapting this approach to members of different cultural groups. Issues of responsibility and freedom are interpreted very differently by women than men and also quite differently by members of oppressed minorities and marginalized groups.

CLIENT-CENTERED THEORY

In the 1920s, at the time that Carl Rogers was training as a psychologist, he was offered essentially two approaches to his craft—one as a behaviorist, the other as a psychoanalyst. Yet neither theory provided the sort of warmth and human contact that he believed people crave in their lives. Rogers envisioned a kind of helping relationship quite unlike the rather sterile, objective, detached encounters preferred by his contemporary practitioners.

In his autobiography, Rogers (1980) writes about several individuals who influenced the development of his ideas: John Dewey and his philosophy of educating the whole person, Otto Rank's (a disciple of Freud) relationship-oriented therapy, theologian Martin Buber's notions about intimate relationships, Søren Kierkegaard's philosophy on the meaning of life, and the Chinese Buddhist thinking of Lao-tse. Then there was the practical streak in Rogers, which drove him to learn from his students and clients.

Like so many other theoreticians who would come before and after him, Rogers was a voracious reader and synthesizer who was able to pull together many diverse ideas into a coherent stream of thought. (Freud did much the same thing in his own early development, reading philosophy, literature, and archaeology as the main sources of his work.) Prior to developing his client-centered style of treatment, he had written a manual on personality assessment (Rogers, 1931) and another on working with difficult children (Rogers, 1939). In both cases, he showed an early proclivity for describing practical things that could be done during the diagnostic and treatment process.

Basic Assumptions

It was during his tenure at Ohio State University during World War II, and later at the University of Chicago, that Rogers formulated his model of therapy that had several distinct features that were considered radical for the time (Barrett-Lennard, 1999):

1. Building on the work of Theodore Reik and Otto Rank, both students of Freud, Rogers sought to incorporate the concept of listening with the "third ear," and responding with empathy, into his helping system. The therapist gives full and complete attention to the client, concentrating on the internal experience of self, and then reflects back what was heard.

2. Applying his training as social scientist and empiricist, Rogers (1957) attempted to research systematically the core conditions of helping, which he labeled *congruence, unconditional positive regard,* and *empathic understanding.* These variables, which he believed were the necessary and sufficient conditions for change to take place, were later tested empirically by several of his followers (Carkhuff & Berenson, 1967; Truax & Carkhuff, 1967).

■ ■ ■ ■ ■

FOR A HOMEWORK ASSIGNMENT

Watch a video of Carl Rogers doing therapy with a client. (There are many such recordings available by a number of publishers.) Rather than concentrating on the limited skills and interventions he uses (mostly active listening), observe the way he builds a relationship with his client, valuing trust and authenticity above all else.

Compare the style Rogers uses to that of his daughter, Natalie Rogers, James Bugental, and yours truly (all three videos are published by Allyn and Bacon in the "Psychotherapy with the Experts" series), or other humanistic practitioners. Notice the ways that each therapist adapts the basic principles into a style that matches his or her personality.

3. Rogers developed a structure for conducting interviews and facilitating counseling sessions that relied on the therapeutic relationship as the means to encourage greater self-acceptance. You have certainly heard of "active listening" or "reflecting feelings," techniques that emerged from the client-centered style.

4. Rogers was never content to restrict his interventions to the traditional individual session format. From the very beginning, he was interested in facilitating growth in groups and classrooms. The whole encounter group movement of the sixties was encouraged in part by Rogers's contributions to the concept of a safe, trusting, supportive community that made it possible for participants to express their most authentic selves.

Core Conditions

Throughout his career, Rogers (1957) talked a lot about the role of therapists and teachers in creating conditions that are optimal for producing change. He didn't really believe that you could teach anyone anything worth learning; the job of a helper is to facilitate change by structuring a climate that makes it possible. This atmosphere emphasizes the core ingredients of trust, caring, and empathy in the relationship (Mearns & Thorne, 1999).

■ ■ ■ ■ ■

FOR A GROUP ACTIVITY

In small groups, talk to each other about what you would consider the optimal conditions for promoting positive growth and change. This discussion should include features that would be universally present in good therapy relationships, the classroom, parenting, coaching, and even in your group right now.

Look to your own experiences in which you have made the most significant and lasting changes. What variables were present in the setting or circumstances that made your growth possible?

Rogers identified several factors that he considered necessary and sufficient for change to take place. It would be safe to say that although these core conditions are often useful and sometimes necessary, they are hardly enough for some people to get off dead center and maintain their momentum over time.

Contact. The relationship between a helper and client, whether that involves a teaching, coaching, parenting, or therapeutic service, must involve some sort of psychological contact in which the participants are open to one another and subject to mutual influence.

Genuiness. Rogers believed that it was critical for a helper to be real with a client, that is, to be authentic, congruent, human, and transparent. This sort of modeling makes it possible for the client to follow the therapist or teacher's lead and risk revealing himself or herself as well.

Unconditional positive regard. There are times, of course, when it is very difficult to accept what certain people do, especially when their behavior involves abusing others or acting in disrespectful ways. There is a difference, however, between not accepting people's actions and not accepting their core being. Rogers felt it was critical to communicate consistently that clients are accepted unconditionally even if certain behaviors are not.

Empathy. Rogers defined empathy as the ability to crawl inside someone else's skin and feel what he or she is feeling. It is a process of knowing another deeply, resonating with his or her experience, without judgment or evaluation. Needless to say, this is *very* difficult to do.

Okay. It's test time.

A new client walks in to see you. You take a deep breath, clear your mind of all distractions, and put away the work you were doing so you can give this person your full attention. You remind yourself about the importance of staying focused and clear. You put away all judgmental thoughts so you can be fully present with this other person. Once your mental checklist is completed, you nod your head for the client to begin.

With minimal preliminaries, the man tells you that he has a habit of becoming sexually involved with several farm animals. He feels a little guilty about this because he doesn't wish to cause harm to the calves or sheep that he prefers, but he would rather not stop this behavior because he finds relationships with human women far too threatening.

You remember not to scream, laugh, or otherwise show shock and disgust on your face, directing him in the most casual voice to tell you what he wants you to do to help him.

"I don't know," he tells you. "Maybe just tell me that I'm not screwed up or anything because of what I do."

Let's put aside what you might actually *say* to this client, whether you would offer him reassurance or tell him you think he is very disturbed. My question for you is what you would *feel* inside toward him. Granted, you have only just met him and hardly had the chance to develop any sort of alliance. Nevertheless, Rogers's core conditions demand that no matter what a person does, or how he behaves, everyone deserves to be respected and valued as a human being. You might very well consider this behavior to be maladaptive and self-destructive (not to mention abusive toward animals), but the true test is whether you can engage this person—and others like him who present behavior that you may personally find quite distasteful—with genuine caring and respect.

This man was actually my very first client, during my very first session during an internship. I had been concentrating so hard on being empathic and nonjudgmental during the interview that I really didn't even notice that his behavior seemed the least bizarre until after he left. It was only upon reading my notes, and picturing myself presenting the case to my colleagues, that I started laughing to myself about how unusual I found this sexual conduct.

I think what I did to help him most (and I did help him within a relatively short period of time) was to listen to him and be with him without judging him as a person. I did eventually confront him about his cow and sheep courting rituals and gently suggested that he might want to consider members of his own species, but he was open to hearing me because he felt that I respected him and genuinely cared for him. It would be difficult to underestimate the power of such unconditional regard.

Features of a Client-Centered Session

As is so often the case, when one innovator comes up with a good idea, others adapt it for their own purposes. While at the time, it seemed downright radical to construct an interview based on humanistic principles, today almost every practitioner makes use of the core message behind healing relationships based on respect and caring.

It is actually rare these days that professionals practice a pure form of client-centered therapy. There have been too many changes in the cultural landscape, research base, and professional demands since the sixties and seventies when humanistic approaches were most popular. Nevertheless, many of the features described here still have value in our times of managed care and brief therapy, even if they must be adapted accordingly.

Full and Complete Presence.   Regardless of the way you practice, it is important to give clients the best part of yourself. Often they are used to being neglected, ignored, or devalued, so you owe them the commitment to be as fully present and attentive as possible.

Openness and Unconditional Regard.   There has been considerable debate about whether unconditional regard toward clients is possible, much less desirable. I prefer to think about the concept with respect to people's essence rather than their behavior. Quite often clients do annoying, obnoxious, self-destructive things that I find difficult to accept unconditionally. But you can unconditionally accept a client, as a person, and still *conditionally* accept his or her behavior.

Authenticity, Genuineness, Transparency, and Warmth.   These are all different ways of saying that you present yourself as a real, authentic person in the relationship. You provide the sort of support, trust, and caring that make it possible for clients to take risks and face themselves in new ways.

Immediacy.   This is one of my absolutely favorite interventions that involves being as present as possible with a client. Instead of talking about something, it is far more dramatic to bring it into focus by pointing out ways that the very behavior is unfolding before your eyes.

> **Therapist:**   You've been talking for some time about the difficulties you have getting close to people. I was wondering how that applies to our relationship.
>
> **Client:**   Excuse me?

Therapist: I think you know what I'm saying.

Client: I'm not sure.

Therapist: Okay, right this moment I'm trying to get closer to you, to talk about our relationship, and you act like you don't know what I'm talking about as a way to push me away.

Client: I still don't know what you mean.

Therapist: Look at how you are sitting right now. You've pulled your chair back and you are leaning as far away as you can. Your arms are crossed and I can feel you visibly pull away, as if what we are talking about is so frightening that you need to put some distance between yourself and me. This is exactly what you were talking about that occurs in many of your other relationships.

Client: [Shrugs and looks down]

Therapist: What you are you aware of right now?

The immediacy brings the discussion into the ultimate present moment. Instead of merely talking about an issue, it is being played out in the session.

Empathy and Active Listening.   This concept is now so universal that it is hardly worth mentioning. Yet the importance of empathy and the application of active listening skills (reflection of feeling) are one of the major contributions of this theory to mainstream practice.

You will have numerous opportunities in other courses to practice the core helping skills of active listening that are now considered so generic they are no longer exclusively identified with client-centered therapy. The skills of listening, reflecting content (restating), and reflecting feelings are among the simplest of interventions but also the most difficult to master. In the following example notice how the helper tries to take the student to a deeper level:

Student: I just don't see the point of learning all this stuff. And the idea of giving us a test on the material sounds ludicrous.

Instructor: You're pretty frustrated and overwhelmed with the sheer volume of ideas that you have to learn. [Notice the way the helper did not give into the temptation to explain or defend. The focus is kept on the student's feelings.]

Student: Well, you gotta admit, you give us all these new theories at once. You say you're trying to teach us to work cooperatively and to develop compassion and empathy, but you're really teaching us to memorize a bunch of facts that have little meaning. I mean, how are we supposed to apply all this stuff?

Instructor: You're really having some doubts about how you're going to do on the first exam. You're scared that you might not do very well. [Among all the many messages conveyed in the student's communication, the instructor chose to focus on the fear of failure. There are many other things that could have been said instead.]

Student: No. That's not it at all! The point I'm trying to make is that you're just asking too much of us.

Instructor: You're feeling annoyed, even angry with me, because I've misunderstood you. Your main concern isn't so much how you will do on the test but rather that you're not learning as much as you would like to.

The beauty of this approach is that this last intervention, which is not a particularly accurate reflection of what the student is thinking and feeling, nevertheless encourages further exploration together. The instructor is still resisting the urge to be defensive and is trying hard to really understand what the student is experiencing and trying to reflect back what has been heard.

When you first learn these skills, you will practice initially repeating verbatim what the other person says (parroting). Once you can do that consistently, you'll move on to restatements in which you reflect the content of what was communicated ("You find the workload and structure of this course to be unreasonable"). After you can do this fairly well, you will then add to your repertoire reflections of feeling that take considerably greater sensitivity and deftness because you must go as deeply as you can to find the true essence of what the person is experiencing. In the preceding example, for instance, it may very well be that the problem has little to do with the class itself and may be more related to other pressures the student is feeling in life. Or the feelings of anger and frustration may be legitimate responses to the instructor's behavior. In any case, the client-centered approach uses empathy to get to the heart of the matter.

■ ■ ■ ■ ■ ▬▬▬▬▬▬▬▬▬▬▬▬▬▬▬▬▬▬▬▬▬▬▬▬▬▬

FOR PERSONAL APPLICATION

You can never get enough experience practicing active listening skills. The method involves (1) listening as closely and carefully as you can to what another person is communicating, (2) using both verbal and nonverbal means to communicate interest, respect, and caring, (3) decoding the underlying meaning of what is being said by asking yourself what the person is feeling deep down inside, and (4) reflecting back to the person what you hear, see, sense, and feel.

Active listening skills work equally well to deepen relationships with family and friends as they do with clients. Keep in mind, however, that until you make these skills part of your natural repertoire, they will not only feel awkward to you but also your loved ones may ask you to stop trying that "counseling stuff" on them. Over time, you will notice how much more intimate and open your conversations become as you become more fluent and proficient in reflecting others' felt experiences.

Focus on Affect and Feelings.   In contrast to the other theories that were most prominent at the time (behavioral, psychoanalytic, existential), Rogers concentrated on the importance of accessing and expressing feelings. Whereas almost all therapists use active listening skills, client-centered practitioners focus as much as they can on the unexpressed feelings in the communication. This approach is evident in the following interaction led by a school counselor:

> **Client:** It could be that my parents won't be home later when I get done with school.
>
> **Counselor:** You don't sound sure about that and you're a little anxious because you don't know what to expect.
>
> **Client:** It's no big deal. I'm used to being on my own a lot of the time.
>
> **Counselor:** You do strike me as very capable of taking care of yourself, especially for someone so young, but I also hear some hesitation in your voice. Being alone isn't something that you greatly look forward to.
>
> **Client:** Well, sometimes I get a little scared. There was this one time . . .
>
> **Counselor:** You don't want to be a burden on your parents because you know they've already got a lot to take care of. But still, you wish you could spend some more time with them. You miss them.
>
> **Client:** Yeah.

In this brief dialogue, you can appreciate how quickly you can move a client from superficial conversation to a deeper-level exploration of underlying feelings. When this skill of reflecting feelings is combined with other skills you will learn, many of which are borrowed from other theories, you have a powerful repertoire of interventions to deal with anything that might arise.

■ ■ ■ ■ ■

FOR PERSONAL APPLICATION

Sit down with someone who is important to you in your life—a partner, family member, friend, coworker, or classmate. Spend some time talking to one another about your feelings toward one another. Avoid the temptation to say what you think, or what you imagine, or what you know, and instead say what you *feel.* This is a difficult task, one that you may feel some resistance to complete. I can only assure you that if you expect your clients to talk about their innermost feelings, you have to be prepared and skilled to do this yourself. Any of your relationships can profit from becoming more intimate and fulfilling if you regularly spend time not only talking about business matters, routine subjects, and predictable topics (politics, sports, kids, health) but also talking to each other about what you really feel.

I have tried on more than a few occasions to get this sort of discussion going at a party or social gathering when everyone is talking about superficial, predictable things. As you probably imagine, about half the time I am ignored and the other half indulgently humored. It is fun, though, and stimulating to get together with friends or loved ones and break through the usual conversational routines by talking on a much deeper level.

Contemporary Revisions

Even after sixty years, theoreticians and practitioners are still advancing Rogers's basic ideas. In particular, several writers (Barrett-Lennard, 1999; Bugental, 1992; Mearns & Thorne, 1999; Rennie, 1998) have made solid strides in their attempts to adapt the theory to the demands of contemporary practice (see Schneider, Bugental, & Pierson, 2001). Boy and Pine (1999) have sought to integrate client-centered premises with a more practical approach to therapy that responds to the contemporary demands of practice. Using the caring relationship as a base, they stress the importance of the therapist as a person. Indeed, much of what all therapists do in their work is related far more to who they are than what they do (Kottler & Hazler, 2000).

Working collaboratively, the client and therapist next use a variety of avenues by which to deepen the intimacy and address specific complaints. Whereas Rogers once described his approach as "nondirective," Boy and Pine see value in being directive in certain circumstances. Nevertheless, in spite of increased flexibility and eclecticism on the part of the practitioner, they still believe that therapy should be *person*-centered rather than *problem*-centered, meaning that the focus should always remain on the distinctly human experience.

Eugene Gendlin, one of Rogers's students and colleagues, had a special interest in applying client-centered theory to more severely disturbed populations. Like his mentor, Gendlin wrote about his schizophrenic patients with a special sensitivity, avoiding the use of medical terms and instead trying to describe the human experience. Like so many creative thinkers in the field, Gendlin (1962, 1981) later went his own way, developing a theory that has its focus on accessing primary experience.

Although the client-centered approach continues to enjoy widespread popularity, it has limitations like all the rest. For one thing, in this era of symptom-oriented, quick treatments, Rogers seems almost quaint by comparison. Also, he was flat-out wrong in thinking that the therapeutic relationship is a necessary and sufficient condition for change to occur. It may be a highly fertile environment from which to promote changes, but with some clients it is hardly enough to make a difference. In fact, several other successful therapeutic approaches since Rogers's time have been developed that downplay the relationship altogether.

Finally, the theory may value feelings over other domains of experience, but some individuals and some cultural groups would find it extremely intrusive and inappropriate to talk about deep feelings with a nonfamily member. Furthermore, some people don't really need to get a handle on their feelings as much as they would profit from controlling their behavior or managing their thoughts.

GESTALT THEORY

No other theory was carved more closely from the personality of its inventor than Gestalt therapy. In fact, in its early days, the approach was known as the "Fritz style," referring to Fritz Perls. Like several other theories (i.e., Rational Emotive Behavior Therapy), this close association between the approach and its charismatic leader is a mixed blessing. Gestalt therapy became known as an aggressive, combative, anti-intellectual approach largely because Perls thrived on controversy and provocation. Yet many of the subsequent innovators (Latner, 1992; Polster & Polster, 1973; Wheeler, 1991) demonstrated a sensitivity that would make the practice of this theory almost unrecognizable to Perls.

Early Background

Perls escaped Nazi Germany to set up a psychoanalytic practice in New York. Following the lead of Wilhelm Reich, another disciple of Freud, Perls was as concerned with the body as the mind. This proved especially convenient for Perls because language barriers made it difficult for him to communicate effectively in his new, adopted language. Clearly, he needed a working method that relied less on talk and more on action.

You may recall from a psychology class that in the early years of studying how learning occurs, some theorists borrowed ideas that were percolating among German physicists. At the time, scientists were attempting to study the minute particles of nature by breaking everything down to its most basic elements. Another approach was taken by scientists who believed that true understanding of the physical world can only occur by looking at the whole rather than reducing something down into parts.

This same Gestalt approach was applied to humans as well. Several German scientists, such as Kurt Lewin and Wolfgang Kohler, concentrated their attention on learning processes that were described as a form of insight in which the person (or animal) solves problems by looking at the whole. It is a kind of "eureka" phenomenon that contrasts with the other theories (such as behaviorism), which believed that learning occurs incrementally through successive reinforcement.

■ ■ ■ ■ ■

FOR PERSONAL REFLECTION OR A CLASS ACTIVITY

Think about a time recently in which you experienced insight as a gestalt, meaning that you had a single moment of revelation or inspiration rather than (apparently) a slow, gradual process of learning. Although, in fact, there may well have been a series of accumulative events that led you to this transformative moment, the integration of everything occurred swiftly, decisively, and without warning.

Tell your own stories to one another about a transformative experience that occurred as a sudden moment of insight. As you look back on the event, what do you think most contributed to this learning?

In one classic Gestalt experiment that you might remember, monkeys were presented with bananas that were just out of reach. In order to get the food, they had to figure out a way to use a stick as a tool or a box as stepladder, thus solving the problem. Rather than resolving this dilemma through trial and error, it appeared that the monkeys learned through insight—an "aha" moment in which they realized what needed to be done.

Likewise, Perls used the concept of Gestalt to describe the irreducible nature of human growth. He believed that people became disconnected from their essential selves—fragmented—and that the process of therapy was one of helping them to reintegrate themselves into a whole.

Collaborating with his wife, Laura Perls, and Paul Goodman, an American who was conversant in both existential and Taoist philosophy, Fritz Perls began writing about his ideas that appeared extremely novel at the time. Like so many other ex-psychoanalysts, he was fervent in his desire to break with the ideas of Freud, from whom he became estranged after a brief encounter that he felt was disrespectful. He never forgave what he considered Freud's humiliation of him and did everything he could to refashion a theory that was as far from the master as possible. If psychoanalysis was formal, fate driven, and biologically based, then Perls would develop an approach that was whimsical, playful, and based completely in the present rather than the past.

A Theory of Doing

Just as important as Perls's publications were the workshops he began running at the Esalen Institute in California, an influential center devoted to personal growth. The rules in these seminars were few but rigidly enforced: (1) participants must stay in the here and now, (2) no talking about people who were not in the room, (3) focus must remain on personal awareness—the nervous tapping of one's finger or the tremor in one's voice, and (4) emphasis was placed on personal responsibility.

In the Gestalt approach, there is an emphasis on both awareness and action. The goal is to heighten one's awareness and then act on what is experienced. It seeks to integrate all aspects of the body, mind, and spirit (Wolfert & Cook, 1999). People are helped to stay in the moment and focus only in the present to become more fully alive.

■ ■ ■ ■ ■ ▬▬▬▬▬▬▬▬▬▬▬▬▬▬▬▬▬▬▬▬▬▬▬▬▬▬▬▬▬▬▬▬▬▬

FOR PERSONAL REFLECTION

One name for activities that remain completely in the present is *flow*. Based on his research with surgeons, athletes, musicians, rock climbers, and others, Csikszentmihalyi (1975, 1999) discovered that people are able to operate at peak performance and with maximum engagement when they are able to lose themselves in an experience with effortless action. It is as if the person and the activity flow together as one.

Locate a cracker, the most humble of all foods. (If none is available, any food item will work.) Put the cracker in front of you and spend a few minutes studying it intensely. Notice the different color gradations, the speckles of salt, the tiny holes, the geometric shapes and perfect symmetry. Notice as well the imperfections and unique qualities of this single item that appears at first to be like all others of its kind.

Pay attention to what is happening inside of you as you study the cracker. Notice increased salivation in your mouth, any body sensations, as well as where your thoughts drift. Just gently bring your mind back to a complete focus on the cracker.

Now, slowly, *very* slowly, reach for the cracker and hold it between your fingers. Note how it feels, its lightness and texture. In exaggerated slow motion, bring the cracker to your lips (take at least 30 seconds just to bring it to your mouth). Notice the way it feels in your hand, your arm, and any other part of body.

Bring the cracker to your nose first. Smell it. Take a deep breath.

Touch it to your lips. Gently. In slow motion.

Now, take a tiny, little bite of the cracker and slowly taste it.

Take several minutes and savor the cracker, eating it as slowly as you can. Through each stage of the process take your time feeling, smelling, and tasting the cracker with your whole being.

When you are done, consider what you learned.

According to this theory, you can't *do* Gestalt therapy; you must *be* a Gestalt therapist (Perls, 1969). This means that you must demonstrate a high degree of authenticity, creativity, sensitivity, and realness—not just in your work but in your being.

Gestalt Techniques

Although in theory the therapist's stance is more important than actions, this approach is known mostly for its techniques.

The Here and Now.   According to Gestalt theory, everything important happens in the present and all efforts are made to keep the client there. People are constantly asked what they are aware of and what they are experiencing.

Unfinished Business.   Fritz Perls's approach to therapy clearly had roots in psychoanalysis. Just as he talked about the polarities that people experience (reminiscent of id and superego), he also believed that things from the past continue to haunt us in the present. However, rather than focusing on the unconscious or repressed memories, Perls honed in on unexpressed feelings such as resentments.

Channels of Resistance.   Like Freud, Gestalt therapists subscribe to the notion that certain behaviors get in the way of growth. Rather than calling them defense mechanisms, Perls described several means by which people try to block themselves from having complete contact with themselves and others.

Choice of Language.   There are certain words and phrases that are verboten in Gestalt therapy. Clients aren't permitted to overgeneralize by using the term *you* to refer to others, or *it* to refer to some statement. If a client were to say, "*It* was a difficult situation," he or she would be redirected to say, "*I* had a difficult time with the situation." Ownership is critical.

■ ■ ■ ■ ■ ▄▄

FOR A CLASS ACTIVITY

Work with a partner to increase your skill using Gestalt present-moment oriented-interventions. This is a particularly difficult assignment because of the way it requires you to do some things that are not usually part of ordinary interactions (unfortunately).

Sit opposite your partner, facing him or her fully. Spend one minute (time it with a watch or you will quit early) staring into one another's eyes. As you do so, become aware of what you feel inside you and notice in your partner.

Talk to each other about what that was like for you.

Resume eye contact. Take turns completing the stem sentence: "One thing that I am aware of . . ." Complete at least five successive rounds. Afterward process the experience.

CONTEMPORARY REVISIONS OF HUMANISTIC THEORY

Just as psychoanalytic theory entered the twenty-first century with a pragmatic flavor that is more responsive to the demands of contemporary life and the managed care movement, so too has humanism continued to evolve. Although humanistic practitioners remain loyal to the basic tenets of the philosophy that stress free choice, personal responsibility, and authentic engagement, new theoretical innovations also emphasize briefer methods that combine features from other approaches, greater gender and cultural sensitivity, employing both qualitative and quantitative research methods, and far greater flexibility in methods (Greenberg & Rice, 1997; Kottler & Hazler, 2001). In addition, humanism has embraced some of the postmodern theories currently in vogue—or rather these constructivist approaches have really updated humanism. As you learn in a later chapter, constructivist thinking shares some of the beliefs of humanism in terms of looking at a person's inner perceptions but stresses the cultural rather than individual context for this experience.

The Skills of Humanism

Humanistic theory was empirically tested for a period of time in the sixties and seventies when Robert Carkhuff and several colleagues (Carkhuff

& Berenson, 1967; Truax & Carkhuff, 1967) attempted to examine the core conditions that Rogers first identified. Among other things, they discovered support for the importance of empathy in the helping process in which therapists who were accepting, open, and reflecting accurately the client's experience were seen as most effective.

Carkhuff attempted to measure these core conditions, with limited success, but also was instrumental in specifying the specific therapeutic skills that are involved in the empathic process. When Thomas Gordon (1975, 1986, 1987) devised a structured training program for teaching core helping skills to parents, teachers, and leaders, humanistic theory became translated into behavioral skills. Ironically, the core values of the philosophy became somewhat lost.

One example of the useful helping behaviors derived from Rogers's theory by Thomas Gordon was the idea that problems come in two basic varieties: those that belong to the client, and those that may appear to be of that nature but really belong to the teacher, counselor, or leader. For instance, consider the following examples that apply to classroom situations:

- A child is carving his initials in the desk.
- A child is talking to several friends while the teacher is talking.
- A child is upset because she got a poor grade on an assignment.
- A child doesn't understand a lesson.

In the first two examples, it is really the teacher who has the problem rather than the student. The big mistake that teachers make is trying to solve their own problems by missing this important point. "Excuse me, mister," the teacher says to the kid who is having a wonderful time carving up the desk. "Do you have a problem?" The child, of course, is thinking to himself that the only problem he really has is the teacher who won't let him finish the job.

■ ■ ■ ■ ■ ▬▬▬▬▬▬▬▬▬▬▬▬▬▬▬▬▬▬▬▬▬

FOR REFLECTION

In the following example who "owns" the problem—you or the client?

You: How can I help you this morning?

Client: Help me? You haven't done crap for me since we started these sessions!

Based on this assessment, would you use an "I" message or active listening?

Frame the way you would respond.

Whether applied to the classroom or to counseling or business situations, the helper is first taught to distinguish between who "owns" the problem. When it is the teacher, then the best intervention is called an "I" message, as in "*I* have a problem with what you are doing." When the child owns the problem, then the most suitable intervention is active listening, which you would recognize as reflecting content and feelings, skills that are easily recognizable in Rogers's style.

In the following example, a parent uses both skills during an interaction with her child:

> **Parent:** I wanted to talk to you because I have a problem with the way you have been acting lately.
>
> **Child:** [Defiantly] So?
>
> **Parent:** I realize that this is not so much your problem as it is mine. I am the one who doesn't like what you have been doing and you are perfectly fine with the way things are.
>
> **Child:** [Nods her head cautiously and suspiciously]
>
> **Parent:** So, I wonder if you could help me with my problem.
>
> **Child:** [Shrugs]
>
> **Parent:** It's just that I have been having a hard time lately, and I noticed that hasn't been easy for you.
>
> **Child:** Well, you gotta admit, it's not fair that I have so many rules.
>
> **Parent:** This has been so frustrating for you, feeling like I don't trust you.

Notice the subtle shift that just took place in which the parent started off owning the problem, using "I" messages to state clearly that she was the one who needed help. Once the child was engaged in the conversation and agreed tacitly to participate in the process of problem-solving, the parent used active listening skills to reflect her feelings. Now they are both involved in a mutual problem-solving process that will not only take care of the parent's problem but also explore the child's feelings at a deeper level.

Carl Rogers and other humanists never intended that their theories would become translated into such specific action skills, but many generations of counselors, teachers, and parents have been trained in these methods to enhance their professional and personal relationships.

TESTING HUMANISTIC IDEAS EMPIRICALLY

Leslie Greenberg and colleagues (Greenberg & Johnson, 1987; Greenberg & Rice, 1997; Greenberg, Rice, & Elliott, 1993; Greenberg & Safran,

1987) are among several researchers who have been continuing the work begun by Carkhuff and others who want to test this theory in several ways. It turns out, for example, that emotional arousal by itself is not particularly helpful unless clients are helped to resolve the internal struggle. This is in marked contrast to the philosophy of the encounter group movement that advocated getting feelings out on the table and expressing them as honestly as possible. Many, many people ended up as casualties in such groups because of the unbridled and irresponsible actions of group members who would lash out at others under the guise of being therapeutic (Yalom, 1995).

In other words, whereas it was once believed that expressing feelings, emoting, and otherwise giving vent to pent-up emotions were intrinsically therapeutic, this is not always the case unless people are helped to complete the cycle. As you have no doubt noticed in yourself and others, giving release to strong feelings such as anger can also lead to more potent emotional explosions.

Continuing the work of Greenberg in attempting to test empirically the assumptions of humanism, Bohart and several colleagues (Bohart, 1993; Bohart & Tallman, 1999) have looked at the primary role that clients play in their own self-healing. Rather than focusing on what the therapist does to promote growth, they have explored the elements that are most conducive to clients' change efforts. Similar to Gendlin, they also feel that helping people to become aware of their inner experience, including body awareness, leads to significant shifts in thinking, feeling, and behavior (Tallman & Bohart, 1999). It is the therapist's job not to change the client but rather to capitalize on those variables that are most conducive to self-change. The therapist, thus, collaborates with the client as a consultant to plan and implement changes. "Therapists," Tallman & Bohart (1999) write, "use their process expertise to support clients' natural healing tendencies" (p. 119). This should sound very familiar to you as it is quite consistent with the original tenets of Rogers and his colleagues.

Back to the Person

Another thread of contemporary humanism has not abandoned its original conception, even with the current emphasis on empirical validation of concepts and translating theory into specific skills. Eugene Gendlin (1962, 1995), Alvin Mahrer (1986), James Bugental (1967, 1991), and myself (Kottler, 1991, 1993, 1995, 1999, 2001), have been writing about the person of the therapist as much as his or her behavior. This means that in addition to the interventions you select, the techniques you employ, and the theory you follow, who you are as a person also has a significant impact on the client.

One of the most intriguing challenges of humanistic psychology is for its advocates to practice what they preach. Nothing is more frustrating than to hear stories about "crazy shrinks" or supposedly humanistic educators and therapists, who cannot apply in their own lives the same principles they espouse and teach to their clients and students.

■ ■ ■ ■ ■

FOR PERSONAL REFLECTION

One of the contemporary innovations in the humanistic movement has been to combine ideas from several different approaches. Prouty (1994), for example, combined Carl Rogers's original theory with the experiential approach of Eugene Gendlin (1998) to use with more severely disturbed clients with profound retardation and schizophrenia. The emphasis throughout this method is on direct experience and awareness.

Focus on your earliest awareness of waking up this morning. What was the first sensation and feeling that captured your attention? What did it feel like in your bed?

What are you aware of right now? Look and listen around you. Notice where you are. Now go inside and concentrate on what you are experiencing in your body. What thoughts are reverberating inside your head? What are the feelings and sensations that are most present for you?

An exercise such as this takes practice because it's difficult to recollect what you have experienced directly throughout the day, much less in the present moment.

The facets of humanistic psychology that have always appealed to me most are the attention given not only to the relationship between people but also the emphasis on the humane values of caring, compassion, authenticity, unconditional regard, respect, and honesty. Many humanistic practitioners have been encouraged to apply in their personal lives the knowledge and skills they learned for the benefit of their clients (Kottler & Hazler, 2000). It is certainly a major benefit of our profession that everything learned about therapy can make us more effective human beings, more loving and caring toward others, more skilled at communicating our needs and responding to others, more expert at reaching personal goals, and more highly evolved in our moral, spiritual, emotional, and intellectual development (Kottler, 1993).

The benefits of being a humanistic therapist, as positive as they might be, do not come without personal costs that are often burdensome. These personal costs are reflected in many ways including signs and symptoms of therapist impairment. Which part of the human is therapist and which part is humanist? How can the roles be integrated? What is the effect of their interaction on quality of life? These are questions that are yet largely unanswered with the exception of legal and ethical guidelines that tend to present the therapist as a "thing" rather than a living, breathing, changing being. Exploring these struggles will help therapists of all theoretical orientations to understand themselves better, as well as to become more effective models of humane values and humanistic behavior.

Some Concerns and Criticisms

Humanism has been attacked, quite legitimately, as being excessively self-oriented. There is all this talk about *self*-actualization, *self*-expression, *self*-awareness, *self*-fulfillment, leading to *self*-centeredness and narcissism (Solomon, 1989). Autonomy and independence are valued over cooperation and interdependence that are so much a part of other cultures (Latino, African, Asian, indigenous). Of course, Maslow, Perls, Rogers, and others died before the multicultural movement was launched, before humanistic psychology's focus on a person's lived experience morphed into contemporary constructivism.

Perhaps today self-actualization would be redefined in terms of social responsibility, relationship competencies, and cultural sensitivity rather than its original emphasis on personal freedom and self-expression.

SUGGESTED READINGS

Bohart, A., & Tallman, K. (1999). *How clients make therapy work: The process of active self-healing.* Washington, DC: American Psychological Association.

Boy, A. V., & Pine, G. J. (1999). *A person-centered foundation for counseling and psychotherapy* (2nd ed.). Springfield, IL: C. C. Thomas.

Bugental, J. F. T. (1990). *Intimate journeys: Stories from life-changing therapy.* San Francisco: Jossey-Bass.

Csikszentmihalyi, M. (1998). *Finding flow: The psychology of engagement in everyday life.* New York: Basic Books.

Frankl, V. E. (1992). *Man's search for meaning* (4th ed.). Boston: Beacon Press.

Kottler, J. A. (1993). *On being a therapist* (rev. ed.). San Francisco: Jossey-Bass.

Mahrer, A. (1996). *The complete guide to experiential psychotherapy.* New York: Wiley.

Moss, D. (Ed.). (1999). *Humanistic and transpersonal psychology.* Westport, CT: Greenwood Press.

Moustakas, C. (1994). *Existential psychotherapy and interpretation of dreams.* Northvale, NJ: Jason Aronson.

Perls, F. (1969). *In and out of the garbage pail.* Lafayette, CA: Real People Press.

Polster, E. (1995). *A population of selves: A therapeutic exploration of personality diversity.* San Francisco: Jossey-Bass.

Rogers, C. (1980). *A way of being.* Boston: Houghton Mifflin.

Schneider, K., Bugental, J. T., & Pierson, J. F. (Eds.). (2001). *Handbook of humanistic psychology.* Thousand Oaks, CA.: Sage.

Strasser, F., & Strasser, A. (1997). *Existential time-limited therapy: The wheel of existence.* New York: Wiley.

Yalom, I. (1998). *The Yalom reader: Selections from the work of a master therapist and storyteller.* New York: Basic Books.

■ ■ ■ ■ ■ ▰▰▰▰▰▰▰▰▰▰▰▰▰▰▰▰▰▰▰▰▰▰▰▰▰▰▰▰▰▰▰▰▰▰

CHAPTER 6

THOUGHTS BEFORE FEELINGS

Cognitive Approaches

This chapter represents a marriage of convenience. The various approaches to cognitive, cognitive-behavioral, rational emotive, Adlerian, and reality therapy don't really fit together as closely as it might appear to include them in the same chapter. Alfred Adler, as an original disciple of Freud, could technically be considered to have a neopsychoanalytic approach. Since it was also the first systemic model because of Adler's interest in underlying family structure, it could have been placed there as well. As for Reality Therapy, it is a kind of brief therapy, as well as a particular type of behavioral approach. Both therapies are also somewhat cognitive in nature, so they do belong here in one sense.

In recent years, several authors (Carlson, 1991; Nystul, 1999) have sought to combine Adlerian and Reality approaches into a single, integrated problem-solving model that capitalizes on the strengths of each. While I don't intend to confuse matters any further for you by merging these two distinctly different theories, they definitely share some common principles that make them compatible cognitive "chaptermates."

All of these approaches are enjoying a resurgence in popularity because of their emphasis on brief interventions and flexible strategies. They lend themselves, in particular, to application in educational settings, making them especially useful for school counselors. Each has a fairly structured, step-by-step process, which makes them easier to learn than other models that are more ambiguous. Each one also stresses the importance of accepting responsibility for one's choices and behavior. Apart from these similarities, the models also have some distinctly different features.

AARON BECK AND COGNITIVE THERAPY

Aaron Beck (1967) developed cognitive therapy as a way to treat depression by asking his patients (he is a psychiatrist) to examine their dysfunctional thinking that is leading to their problems. More recently (Beck, 1997) he has examined the self-defeating thought patterns that operate inside people's heads to keep them from improving. "If the patient is inclined to stay in bed and to neglect her family and work," Beck (1997) mentions as an example, "her observations of these behaviors and somatic symptoms are then 'translated' by her information processing into: 'I am lazy; I am an irresponsible person; I deserve to be punished' and a vicious cycle is established" (pp. 57–58).

Thus, Beck believes that in order to promote deeper, lasting changes, the therapist must go beyond the client's irrational thinking to reach the underlying belief structure. Unless this secondary change takes place, then the symptomatic relief may become only temporary and relapse will become inevitable.

■ ■ ■ ■ ■

FOR PERSONAL APPLICATION

During a twenty-four-hour period of time, carry around a notebook to jot down all the self-defeating, dysfunctional, and irrational thoughts that you tell yourself. Every time you are aware that you are feeling the least upset, disturbed, anxious, or worried about something, identify and write down what you were thinking to produce this emotional state.

At the end of the day, analyze the consistent themes that emerged.

Consider other things you might tell yourself instead of these thoughts.

Dysfunctional Styles of Thinking

In his early work, Beck was interested in the ways that his psychiatric patients developed thinking patterns that predisposed them to depression. He had found that their early childhood experiences and interactions shaped schemas, the underlying beliefs and assumptions that people carry around inside them. These cognitive schemas can be either positive ("I am good at overcoming adversity") or maladaptive ("I'll never get anywhere in life"). They may also be influenced by how much emotion is tied up in them, how long they have been operating inside someone's head, who was involved during their first inception (how significant that person was), how detailed and well developed they are, and how they dictate behavior (Freeman, 1993).

FOR A CLASS ACTIVITY

Working with a partner or in small groups, help one another to list the prominent schemas in your thinking. This includes the most common cognitive scripts that guide your life, the things you tell yourself about who you are, what you can and cannot do, and what the world is like. Examples might include schemas such as: "I'm not good at math"; "I have bad luck"; "I am the sort of person who does well in groups"; "A moral person is someone who always tells the truth no matter what."

After you have created a list of those schemas that are most influential in your head, talk about ways they are helpful as well as counterproductive.

There are a number of consistent patterns of dysfunctional thinking that are evident in people's schemas, as well as in their everyday behavior. Examples of this include:

1. *Overgeneralization* in which someone makes an erroneous assumption that a single case necessarily means that something is always true. "Because this guy won't go out with me, I'll never find anyone to love me."
2. *Personalization* involves exaggerating the extent that events in the world apply to oneself. "Every time I plan a party, it always rains."
3. *Dichotomous thinking* means dividing things into extreme categories. "Either I get the job and become destined for greatness, or lose the opportunity and become destined for mediocrity."
4. *Mind reading* represents a kind of arbitrary inference in which a person assumes that he or she knows what others are thinking. These conclusions are generally not supported by objective facts. "I can tell the instructor doesn't like me because he ignored the question I asked in class."

You can see a pattern emerging here, one in which there is cognitive distortion, denial, exaggeration, or some other form of illogical process. In any of the cognitive approaches, it is crucial to recognize and label these patterns.

■ ■ ■ ■ ■

FOR HOMEWORK

Begin to sensitize yourself to the ways that people express themselves with language that indicates dysfunctional thinking. One of the keys to the cognitive approach is being able to recognize instantly when someone is distorting reality, exaggerating his or her predicament, or otherwise engaging in self-defeating thought patterns. The main clues you will have to identify overgeneralizations, personalizations, dichotomous thinking, and mind reading are the ways that people talk to themselves, as well as speak out loud.

I wouldn't recommend that you continuously point out to people when they speak in the language of external control or helplessness (they will quickly become annoyed rather than grateful), but train yourself to notice evidence of this behavior.

Beck was also most helpful in developing the specific belief patterns for each of several major personality disorders (Beck et al., 1990). These are entrenched dysfunctional styles that transcend any specific presenting complaint. You have likely heard these terms before such as:

Narcissistic. "I am special and deserve more than anyone else."

Borderline. "Everyone will eventually abandon me so I should ruin things on my own terms."

Dependent. "I am helpless and need others to take care of me."

Avoidant. "It's senseless for me to try anything new because I will get hurt."

Paranoid. "Everyone is out to get me and ruin my life."

Antisocial. "It's everyone out for themselves, so if I don't take advantage of others they will get the best of me."

■ ■ ■ ■ ■

FOR A CLASS ACTIVITY

With partners get together and examine each of these dysfunctional beliefs that represent exaggerations or denial of reality. Write down a list of reasons why each of these should be considered irrational beliefs. Provide supportive evidence.

Principles of Cognitive Therapy

There are a number of similarities between this theory and others that follow, but it also stands out as being the one cognitive approach that is clearly empirically based and stresses collaboration in the relationship. You will see in the next theory, for example, how the therapist takes on a much more active, directive role, but this reflects more the style differences between Aaron Beck and Albert Ellis.

Beck and several colleagues (Beck & Emery, 1985; Beck & Young, 1985; Clark, Beck, & Alford, 1999) described the major concepts of this approach:

1. Emotions result from cognitive processes. In other words, thinking precedes feeling.
2. Therapy is brief, focused, and time limited. It deals with presenting problems.
3. It employs a solid therapeutic relationship as a means to a more important end. Practitioners value the importance of this alliance but don't dwell on it. The therapist and client work together as a team.
4. It uses the Socratic method of inquiry and dialogue. Clients are challenged to explore their underlying beliefs.
5. Homework is valued as an especially important part of treatment. Clients are expected to translate talk into specific action they will take in between sessions.

■ ■ ■ ■ ■

FOR PERSONAL REFLECTION

All the cognitive therapies are especially sensitive to language because the way people talk is the best clue as to how they think internally. The idea is that if you can change the way people express themselves out loud, you can also alter their cognitive processes. Compare, for example, the difference between someone who says "I *must* leave now because I *have* to take care of another *obligation*" and someone who says "I *choose* to leave now because I *want* to take care of another *commitment*." This is more than being a little nit-picky about a few words. In the first case, the person feels trapped because that's the way he is thinking about his situation. In the second instance, the action is identical but the internal perception of it is quite different.

In the statements that follow, catalogued by Gerber (1999), there are examples that reveal illogical or irrational thinking. For each one, change it to an alternative that is more empowering. I've started you off with a few. You finish the rest.

IRRATIONAL STATEMENT	ALTERNATIVE STATEMENT
"I should . . ."	"I want to . . ."
"You make me upset . . ."	"I make myself upset . . ."
"I must . . ."	
"I can't . . ."	
"It's awful . . ."	
"It's unfair . . ."	
"I can't . . ."	
"Everybody feels . . ."	
"This always happens . . ."	
"I never get . . ."	

If you can get in the habit of speaking out loud with carefully chosen words that imply self-control and rational expression, you can change the way you think inside your head. According to cognitive theories, it is this internal dialogue that determines how you feel based on personal interpretation of events.

Applications to Specific Problems

One of the real strengths of Beck's cognitive therapy is its application to common psychological complaints such as depression, anxiety, and obsessive disorder. In each case, he and several colleagues have been successful in plotting out the specific dysfunctional thinking patterns (schemas) that are most prevalent for each diagnosis. Followers of this theory have also been quite diligent in researching empirically the effectiveness of this approach with specific presenting problems such as anger and hostility (Beck, 1999) or depression (Clark, Beck, & Alford, 1999). Other sources (McMullin, 1999) have been helpful in providing practitioners with hundreds of cognitive techniques for use with a variety of problems.

As you would expect with any theory that emphasizes one domain of human experience (thinking) over all others (feeling, being, sensing), there is sometimes a problem applying it to individuals of particular cultural backgrounds and life experiences. The whole notion of logic and rationality as important values is, for instance, typical of the male-dominant culture. As such, traditional female ways of being that include intuition and feeling are often labeled as hysterical and illogical. Among certain members of cultural groups, such as those of indigenous peoples, a cognitive approach may also not fit their cherished beliefs, at least without considerable adaptation.

■ ■ ■ ■ ■ ▬▬▬▬▬▬▬▬▬▬▬▬▬▬▬▬▬▬▬▬▬▬▬▬▬▬

FOR A CLASS ACTIVITY

Get together with several classmates and imagine that you are depressed. Really get into this state of mind by recalling a time in your life (which hopefully isn't going on right now) in which you felt perfectly miserable and hopeless. Picture that you have low energy and difficulty with your sleep habits. You are feeling discouraged and incredibly helpless. You feel utterly worthless.

Adopting this mode of being, make a list together of all the thoughts you are experiencing inside your head that are part of your depression. Identify as many dysfunctional thoughts as you can.

Once you are done, talk to one another about the ways these ideas are based on distortions, exaggerations, overgeneralizations, and mislabeled beliefs. What might you tell yourself instead?

ALBERT ELLIS AND RATIONAL EMOTIVE BEHAVIOR THERAPY (REBT)

The title of this theory is a bit complicated because Ellis likes to think that it is so comprehensive that it embraces everything. He has labeled it a cognitive therapy, a humanistic therapy, a constructivist therapy, a brief therapy, and a behavior therapy (Ellis, 1996, 2001), so the title keeps expanding.

People sometimes have difficulty separating Ellis from his theory. He presents himself as a thoroughly authentic, down-to-earth, honest, and crusty fellow. He also swears a lot, which puts off some members of his audiences. He has been unapologetic in attacking religious rigidity as a form of cognitive disturbance. And he is a bit full of himself as many prominent people can be. In speaking about other theoreticians at a conference at which he was presenting, he expressed with his usual mischief and irreverence that he didn't much care about what others thought of him. With humor and a twinkling smile, he gestured toward his co-presenters and announced: "They hate my telling them that I am—of course!—right and that they are—indubitably!—wrong. In my youth, I would have stupidly bothered myself about that, would have shown a dire need for their approval, and would have told them that they were great guys or gals and scholars. . . . What, me honest and impolite? Never!" (Ellis, 1997, p. 69).

Well, you get the flavor of why some people might find him a little offensive. I count myself among those who get a tremendous kick out of Ellis's provocative nature. I enjoy his sense of humor, his playfulness, and his willingness to push the limits of what he can get away with. Yet, he has unnecessarily alienated folks who have been turned off to his ideas because he comes across so strongly. He has not always been the best salesman for his own ideas whereas others (Bernard, 2001; Neenan & Dryden, 1999; Wolfe, 1993) have been more persuasive, at least with different audiences he couldn't reach.

Background of REBT

There are two aspects of Ellis's background that deserve mention in understanding his approach. The first is growing up as an awkward, shy, insecure, self-described "social phobic." The second was reading as much philosophy as he could from adolescence onward, searching for ideas that might bolster his inner strength and give him courage to overcome his fears. Specifically, he devoted himself to reading about what makes people happy.

As a form of self-therapy, Ellis began reading the works of ancient philosophers such as Confucius, Epicurus, Epictetus, as well as rational thinkers such as Spinoza, Kant, and Santayana. He immediately seized on the idea that he could cure himself of his excessive worries if he tried to think more encouraging thoughts. For instance, when he received rejections by girls and magazine editors (an endless source of misery in his adolescence and early adulthood), he learned to tell himself that he wasn't a lousy person or writer just because someone didn't select him or his work.

■ ■ ■ ■ ■

FOR PERSONAL APPLICATION

Talk about ways that you keep yourself on "probation." You consider yourself worthy only to the extent that you act in accordance with your highest, perfectionistic standards. If you should make mistakes, mess up, or in any way act less than perfectly, you judge not only your behavior but also who you are as a person.

What would it mean, for example, if you received a grade on your next assignment, test, or paper that is less than you expect? What would you tell yourself about what this would mean?

From these humble beginnings, Ellis began his training as a psychologist, studying the works of both psychoanalysis and behaviorism, finding helpful ideas in both systems. From his reading of psychology and philosophy, as well as the great novelists, Ellis settled on the idea that happiness comes from two main sources: (1) unconditional self-acceptance irrespective of any specific performances, and (2) a high frustration tolerance to deal with disappointments. Once he combined these basic ideas with the importance of cognition in determining people's perceptions and subsequent emotional responses, Ellis had the makings of a new system of therapy (Ellis, 1962).

Basic Ideas

Originally, Ellis (1962) listed almost a dozen distinct irrational beliefs that are worth mentioning even though they have now been distilled into a few basic themes (Ellis, 1996). As was mentioned earlier in the discussion of Beck's cognitive therapy, one of the keys to using this approach is being able to recognize readily the most common ideas that get in people's way.

The five "biggies" that you should be most familiar with are listed next. Each of these is summarized in Table 6.1 alongside Beck's nominations for most dysfunctional beliefs. In each case, I have also supplied an example of how the idea might be presented to a client.

1. *"Life isn't fair."* What is it that strikes you about this that is irrational? Well, clearly life is *not* fair. If it were, you wouldn't have to lock your doors and everyone would treat you just as you feel you deserve. In truth, people live by different rules than you do. It is one thing to wish that other people were more like you and that life would give you just what you deserve; it is another thing to expect it.

TABLE 6.1   Comparison between Beck and Ellis's Dysfunctional Beliefs

BECK'S COGNITIVE THERAPY	ELLIS'S RATIONAL EMOTIVE THERAPY
Overgeneralization	Absolute Judgments
Personalization	Masturbating and Shoulding
Dichotomous Thinking	Awfulizing
Mind Reading	Life Isn't Fair

2. *"It's awful."* Things may be disappointing, frustrating, annoying, but almost never terrible. "Awful" represents the worst possible thing that could ever happen, usually a gross exaggeration of the situation. If something is *merely* disappointing, or *only* a setback, then it doesn't become a major catastrophe, just a minor challenge. When people are "awfulizing" they are making themselves upset by distorting or exaggerating what is occurring.

3. *"I can't stand it."* In truth, you can stand almost anything except death. It may sometimes feel as though life is difficult, but it is always something you can handle once you keep things in perspective. Remember, for example, those times when you have had to go to the bathroom *very* badly? It didn't seem like you could make it to the nearest toilet, but somehow you were able to tolerate the pain. The same holds true with emotional suffering. It may not seem as though you can stand it, but once you stop whining and feeling sorry for yourself, you can almost always bring things back under control.

4. *"I must get what I want."* It is one thing to want something, quite another to demand that you get it. Ellis calls this "masturbating," a form of "self-abuse" in which people use "shoulds" and "musts" to communicate their belief that they are special and deserving of whatever they think they need most.

5. *"I'm incompetent."* People often make absolute judgments about who they are based on a sample of their behavior. It is irrational to label oneself as shy, or stupid, or incompetent just because one (or more) times you acted that way.

■ ■ ▪ ■ ■

FOR PERSONAL REFLECTION AND HOMEWORK

In his original list, Ellis identified thirteen irrational beliefs. For each one of them, think about what it is about this internal statement that is not based in reality. In other words, why is each of these thoughts irrational?

- ■ "Everyone must love and appreciate me all the time."
- ■ "I must be competent in everything that I do in order to feel okay about myself."
- ■ "Some people who are different from me are bad and should be punished."
- ■ "It is terrible when I don't get what I want."
- ■ "Other people and events cause me to be unhappy and I have little control over this situation."

- "If I keep dwelling on something awful, maybe I can prevent it from happening."
- "It is easier to avoid difficulties in life rather than having to face them."
- "I need someone stronger than I am in order to take care of me."
- "What has happened in the past determines how I must be in the future."
- "I should become upset over other people's problems."
- "There is a perfect solution to every problem and it's possible for me to figure out what it might be."

Some of these statements might not immediately strike you as irrational or illogical. Circle the ones that seem like reasonable assumptions to you and then read some of the REBT literature to find out what it is about them that distorts or exaggerates reality.

The ABC Theory

One of the most useful ideas from this theory is its model of emotions that helps explain the process by which people become emotionally disturbed, as well as the means by which to dispute those irrational beliefs. In this ABC theory, the usual scenario unfolds as follows.

A—The Activating Event. A particular situation or precipitating event is believed to cause the emotional suffering. In this first step, you simply describe what it is that bothers you and the situation that you believe is causing the problem. Let's imagine, for instance, that you receive a grade on a class assignment that is less than what you hoped.

B—The Irrational Belief. According to this theory, it isn't the situation that causes your emotional pain as much as it is whatever you are telling yourself inside your head. If, for example, you were thinking to yourself, "Oh, well, so what if the grade isn't what I wanted. I'll do better next time," then you would hardly be upset. But if, on the other hand, you were thinking the following thoughts, you'd be very distraught:

- "I can't believe I blew this assignment *completely*. I'm such an idiot!"
- "This means I'll *never* be a good therapist."
- "This is the *worst* thing that ever happened to me. I'll *never* recover from this."
- "It isn't *fair* that the teacher graded the assignment the way she did."
- "I *should* have been treated differently than this."

If you note the italicized words, you'll see clues as to the parts of these internal statements that are illogical or irrational. One good way to determine whether a thought fits this criterion is whether it is based in reality. You should also look for:

- exaggerations ("This is the *worst* thing that *ever* happened to me.")
- dogmatic demands ("I *must* get what I want.")
- self-evaluations ("I *am worthless* because I performed less than satisfactorily.")

C—The Emotional Consequence.   This is the result of the irrational thinking, the emotional symptoms that result from the internal beliefs. Distinctions are made between unhealthy emotional responses and those that are reasonable given the circumstances. There is a big difference, for example, between sadness and depression, or annoyance and rage.

In this case, the student who was telling himself the foregoing thoughts would most likely feel upset. As a therapeutic procedure, the client is often asked to rate on a 1–10 scale just how upset he feels. It is at this point that you might choose to borrow reflective listening skills from the humanistic approach to draw out and reflect the client's feelings.

The following ratings provide a baseline for measuring progress after the cognitive interventions.

Depressed	5
Anxious	8
Frustrated	9
Discouraged	9
Angry	6
Confused	7

D—Disputing the Irrational Beliefs.   Going back to the irrational beliefs, the actual therapy takes the form of challenging the thoughts that exaggerate or distort the situation. This complete process, summarized in Table 6.2, continues by asking a series of questions:

- Where is the evidence that this is true?
- Who says that this must be the case?
- Does the response seem logical and reasonable, given the situation?
- If a witness or videocamera were observing this scene, would this person or device record things exactly as you report them?

In the preceding example, the distraught student might be asked to explore questions such as:

- "Who says that this assignment must represent a fair and accurate assessment of what you learned?"
- "Who says that your grade should be fair?"
- "Where is the evidence that because you got a grade lower than you expected this means you are hopeless as a potential therapist?"
- "So what if you got a grade you don't like. What are you telling yourself that really means?"
- "Did you really blow the assignment completely, or rather did you merely perform less well than you had hoped?"

E—New Emotional Effect. If the cognitive interventions have been successful, there will be a different emotional outcome. Sometimes the goal isn't to eliminate completely all emotional distress. Who, after all, is going to feel nothing at all after a disappointment or upsetting situation? But it is reasonable to expect that you can reduce significantly the magnitude of the emotional arousal, basing it more in reality.

In our example, the student rates his feelings again but this time with numbers that are more than half what they were previously. Now he is telling himself the following:

> Well, it is a little disappointing that I didn't do as well as I had hoped. And I do think that the assignment was rather unclear and inconsistently graded. But that is the way things sometimes go in this imperfect world. Just because I didn't perform perfectly doesn't mean I won't do better on the next assignment. Even if I don't improve, these tasks in class don't even reflect how well I will do in the field. But they do provide useful feedback that I can use to improve my knowledge and skills. So this is hardly a terrible disaster, merely a very minor setback.

TABLE 6.2   Steps in the REBT Process

1. Start with the activating event by asking the client what is most bothersome.
2. Plot the emotional consequences that are experienced, rating them in their levels of intensity.
3. Identify the irrational beliefs that are the real culprits in producing negative emotions.
4. Dispute these irrational beliefs by challenging assumptions and encouraging clearer reasoning.
5. Assess the effects of the interventions. If necessary, repeat the process.

■ ■ ■ ■ ■

FOR PERSONAL APPLICATION

Among all the theories in the text, I have always found REBT to be among the most easily personalized in daily life. In fact, there is not a day that goes by that I do not challenge my own irrational, exaggerated thinking when I am aware of feeling the least upset. Somebody cuts me off in traffic. I get disappointing news. I burn the chicken on the grill. I feel slighted by someone's actions. These and a dozen others each day provide the opportunity to examine what we are saying to ourselves about these events.

Think of something going on in your life right now that you are upset about. Starting with the activating event (what you believe created the discomfort), proceed through the steps previously covered in which you identify your irrational beliefs, describe the emotional consequences, and then dispute those thoughts and assumptions that are exaggerated, distorted, or not based in reality.

Obviously, if this is what you chose (and it *is* a choice) to say to yourself, you would feel very differently about this situation than if you ranted and raved internally, blaming the instructor, yourself, and the conspiracy of the universe to make your life miserable.

Disputing Strategies

There are two parts where beginners often get stuck applying the REBT method. Identifying irrational beliefs takes a fair bit of reading in which you familiarize yourself with the patterns that are most common. I hear little bells ringing in my head any time I hear someone say "should," or "must," or "fair." Likewise, when I hear someone say something such as "He really made me mad," or "That really hurt me," I automatically make the conversion in my head to "You made yourself mad over what he said" and "You really hurt yourself when you chose to think that this action was all about you."

These examples lead into the most difficult part of the therapeutic process in which you dispute the client's irrational beliefs. The trick, however, is to do so in a way that you shake old ideas loose without alienating the person in the process. There are two such rhetorical styles for teaching alternative ways of thinking (Walen, DiGiuseppe, & Dryden, 1992; Ellis, 1996).

In the *didactic method*, you adopt a tutoring sort of style, explaining the logical method and generating alternative ways of thinking.

You have been talking at length about what a lousy student you are, but I hear this self-assessment is based almost totally on your grades in this one class. You have also mentioned dozens of other classes in which you did quite well. I'm confused by this discrepancy. It seems as though you are overgeneralizing from one situation to make a total evaluation of your performance as a student in every other setting. Another way of thinking about this same scenario is to remind yourself that you are a fallible human being who doesn't always function at the optimal level.

In the *Socratic method*, a more questioning, challenging approach is used to dispute a client's irrational beliefs.

Where does it follow that because you got what you think is a low grade—and I don't necessarily agree with that—that this means you are stupid? Where is the evidence to support that conclusion? I'd like to see those data, because frankly, it's all in your imagination.

I wonder what you could tell yourself instead about this situation, keeping your attention purely on what is reasonable and rational in these circumstances. Let's assume for a moment that you did "totally blow the class," a gross exaggeration in its own right, so what does this say about you? Where is the evidence that this means you are stupid and that this is the "worst possible thing that could have ever happened."?

You can see in both disputing strategies, and in others called logical, philosophical, empirical, and functional, that it takes skill and practice to become proficient at these methods. In one example illustrated by Ellis and MacLaren (1998) they describe how they took one basic irrational belief of a depressed client—"I absolutely must do well and be approved of by others"— and were able to identify dozens of derivative irrational beliefs such as:

- Awfulizing: "It's absolutely terrible when someone criticizes me or disagrees with me."
- Overpersonalizing: "When she says she is too busy to do something with me, it really means she doesn't like me."
- Perfectionism: "I can't believe I made such silly mistakes. It's not like me to do that."
- Disqualifying: "She did give me a good assignment to do, but that's only because nobody else was around who could do it."

Apart from the specifics of these disputing strategies, notice the general style of the interventions. Your job is to (1) listen carefully to what the person says, (2) decode the underlying thinking that is represented in the verbalizations, (3) identify the core irrational beliefs implicit in the statements, and (4) challenge the validity of assumptions that are clearly the result of distortions and exaggerations. In addition, the use of humor helps to reduce the extent to which people take themselves, and their problems, too seriously (Neenan & Dryden, 1999).

If that seems like quite a lot to do, the good news is that this is one of those therapeutic approaches that works equally well with yourself as it does with your clients. The better you get at recognizing and correcting your own irrational beliefs, the more skilled you will be to do so with those you wish to help.

■ ■ ■ ■ ■

FOR A CLASS ACTIVITY

Get together in groups of three, with one person agreeing to work on a current problem that lends itself to disputing irrational beliefs. Ideally, this would be an issue that is not terribly serious but one that matters to that person. With two of the partners acting as team helpers, take your "client" through the following steps:

1. With what are you struggling? Collect background information on the nature of the difficulty, specifically identifying the precipitating event (A) and the emotional consequences (C).
2. What are you feeling? List at least a half dozen different feelings because rarely is there only one reaction.
3. Rate each feeling on a 1–10 scale according to how upsetting it is. A 10 represents an extreme reaction, whereas a 1 is minimal and a 5 about moderate.
4. What are you telling yourself about this situation that is making you upset? Help your partner label each of the irrational beliefs that is the source of the difficulty. Look especially for the following themes: shoulds, musts, absolute judgments, demands, exaggerations, and overpersonalizations.
5. Where is the evidence to support these beliefs? Dispute the irrational self-statements.

Being Provocative

Rational Emotive Behavior Therapy shares many of the strengths and weaknesses of Beck's theory presented earlier. It is perhaps a more confrontive approach, one that requires the therapist to challenge actively the client's irrational beliefs. After all, people don't usually give up their cherished assumptions easily, especially when they get a lot of mileage out of remaining stuck.

It would be extremely important with this approach, perhaps more so than with most, that you don't just follow a formula but personalize the theory and techniques in such a way that they fit with your unique style. Of course, in order for you to do this effectively, you will first need considerable practice in applying the methods to yourself.

DONALD MEICHENBAUM AND COGNITIVE BEHAVIOR THERAPY

Meichenbaum (1997) tells the story of how he first developed his theory while sitting at his dinner table as a child. It became the custom of his family that each person would tell a story about something that happened during the day and include all the accompanying thoughts and feelings as part of the "dinner menu." It has since occurred to him that his whole career was shaped by continuing to ask others how they talk to themselves inside their heads in response to events that happen in their lives. It is, thus, not the situations themselves that matter, he reasoned, but how people perceive them and how their core beliefs influence these impressions (Meichenbaum, 1977).

Evolution of His Ideas

Meichenbaum (1993) has since left the exclusive family of cognitive therapists and moved on to embrace constructivism as well (presented in Chapter 8). What this means is that he is no longer concerned with only cognitions but also with the larger scope of the ways that people create meaning in their lives. As such, he is not willing to make judgments about what is irrational and rational, nor is he interested in vigorously challenging those beliefs. Instead, Meichenbaum prefers to help clients examine how their thinking patterns developed and to help them to reconceptualize their situations in more helpful form.

Specifically, this means taking the following steps (Meichenbaum, 1997):

1. Develop a solid relationship with the client.
2. Help the client to tell his or her story.
3. Provide helpful information relevant to the presenting complaint.
4. Develop an alternative, more constructive way of viewing things.
5. Assess and supply needed coping skills.
6. Encourage practice and rehearsal.
7. Reinforce progress and assign responsibility.
8. Prevent relapses.

You will notice that these steps are both fairly logical and also generic to almost all contemporary approaches. Meichenbaum combines the best of behavioral, cognitive, and constructivist theory; at the same time he acknowledges the value of the therapeutic relationship.

Stress Inoculation

One unique contribution Meichenbaum has made to the family of cognitive therapies is his program for preventing relapses. As you are well aware, often the easy part is making the initial changes; the really difficult part is making the changes last. This subject of enduring change is one that has been given scant attention in the literature largely because we aren't very good at maintaining the momentum that is begun in therapy (Kottler, 2001).

In order to help clients continue the hard-won gains in their sessions Meichenbaum (1985) designed a program consisting of cognitive restructuring, rehearsal of anticipated crises through both imagery and role-playing, and lots of self-monitoring. Clients are taught to recognize the first signs they might be backsliding and especially to keep an eye on stress levels that may provoke a relapse.

■ ■ ■ ■ ■

FOR A CLASS ACTIVITY

Think of one time in which you were able to maintain changes throughout your life and another instance in which you had repeated relapses and found it difficult to keep progress going. This could have involved a bad habit that you tried to conquer, a series of dysfunctional relationships, or any behavior that was troublesome for you.

Talk to each other about what has made the biggest difference in your life in maintaining changes that you have initiated. What contributes most to losing progress? What has been most helpful to you in making changes last?

ARNOLD LAZARUS AND MULTIMODAL THERAPY

The most eclectic of cognitive therapists, Arnold Lazarus could as easily have been covered in the chapter on integrative approaches. He also could have fit into the chapter on behavior therapies because he owes much of his allegiance to this approach. Lazarus has worked hard to combine his early training as a behavior therapist into a systematic model for assessing and treating problems (Lazarus, 1971, 1989).

Although today his theory retains its strong behavioral roots with its emphasis on behavior assessment and homework assignments, he has since added other human dimensions that include affect, imagery, relationships, physiology, and especially cognitions. If the danger of eclecticism is that it can become a mishmashed jumble of techniques, Lazarus prefers the term *technical eclecticism*, which involves applying a systematic, consistent framework to choosing interventions (Lazarus, 1995).

Foundational Ideas

Multimodal therapy has at its core an assessment process that includes most facets of human experience. In this BASIC I.D. model, each of seven different modalities plays a role in the diagnosis and treatment process. You will notice that cognitive and behavioral components are included, naturally, but Lazarus also takes pains to include other aspects of functioning that might play a part in the presenting problem and its resolution (see Table 6.3).

TABLE 6.3   Profile of BASIC I.D.

CODE	MODALITY	DESCRIPTION	EXAMPLE
B	Behavior	Observable behavior that includes habits and actions	Drinking and smoking too much; acting aggressively
A	Affect	Feelings that result from thinking and behavior	Depression; helplessness; anger; loneliness
S	Sensation	Body sensations or anything significant from the five senses	Numbness; sense of isolation; disconnection from outside world
I	Imagery	Fantasies, dreams, or any strong images	Suicidal ideation; fantasies of lashing out; poor body image
C	Cognition	Thinking processes	"I'm stupid." "I'll never beat this thing." "Nobody likes me."
I	Interpersonal Relationships	Relationship problems; interactions with others	Conflict with coworkers; estrangement from family; isolation
D	Drugs/ Biology	Medical or physical conditions; medications or drugs used	Headaches; high blood pressure; excessive drinking

You can appreciate just how clearly and systematically a therapist can map out a client's presenting problems with this model, not only related to the original complaint but also any other factors that might be relevant. Just as you would use this profile to make a thorough assessment of the client's issues, your treatment plan would also follow the same format. Based on the identification of areas in Table 6.3, a treatment plan would similarly be designed as follows:

Behavior	Curtail drinking and smoking. Apply assertiveness training to change behavior to more appropriate responses to stress. Begin exercise program.
Affect	Acknowledge and work through anger. Talk about sense of helplessness and powerlessness. Use therapeutic relationship to work on intimacy issues.
Sensations	Spend time outside to reconnect with natural world. Work on fuller engagement with others to reduce numbness.
Imagery	Substitute fantasies with others that are more positive and optimistic. Practice imagery rehearsal of constructive actions that can be taken.
Cognition	Dispute irrational beliefs. Confront exaggerations and overgeneralizations.
Interpersonal Relations	Reduce conflicts at work. Reach out to others. Initiate new friendships.
Drugs	Reduce stress levels. Find alternatives to self-medication. Get a physical exam to rule out organic causes.

In this form of eclectic practice, you can see how easy it is to use almost any method you want to address client issues. The theory is heavily steeped in behavioral and cognitive facets, but you would certainly be allowed to borrow interventions from any other model. In the case described previously, for example, the man's disconnection from others, from nature, and from himself suggest the application of Gestalt or existential methods to help him look at the isolation, lack of freedom, and fear of responsibility in his life. The really great part of this multimodal framework is that you can integrate any combination of features or techniques you want.

■ ■ ■ ■ ■

FOR A CLASS ACTIVITY

Get together in groups of three. One person role-plays a client who has a host of personal difficulties. The other two partners, working as a team, ask a series of focused, pointed, open-ended questions designed to elicit as much information as possible in the shortest period of time (fifteen to twenty minutes).

After you have conducted this intake interview, all of you work together to create a BASIC I.D. profile for the client, listing symptoms present in each area (ten to fifteen minutes).

There will be considerably more discussion on other integrative systems in Chapter 12, but for now it might occur to you that it is daunting enough to think about mastering one theory, much less the expectation in this approach that you would have reasonable fluency in several of them. This is a system that is, therefore, best for more advanced practitioners after you have had considerable training in multiple approaches.

ADLERIAN THERAPY

Alfred Adler is a chameleon in that he appears to change form depending on the background against which he stands. I don't mean that this camouflage was deliberate on his part; quite the contrary, he did his best to communicate in a manner that was as clear and cogent as possible. But practically every other theory now claims him as a grandparent. Likewise, he could have easily been placed in the chapter on psychoanalytic theory, brief therapy, integrative approaches (Dinkmeyer & Sperry, 2000), and constructivist theory (Watts, 1999).

Background

In summarizing Adler's important contributions that have influenced current practice, many would now strike you as rather obvious because they have formed the basis of so many other theories. Because he was so much more pragmatic and flexible than Freud, Adler was able to reach a different constituency by introducing the following ideas:

1. the importance of thinking processes on feelings (he was the first cognitive therapist)
2. the impact of early family experiences and birth order on present behavior (he was among the first family therapists)

3. the value of constructing specific plans of action (he was the first to emphasize action strategies to follow insights)
4. the construction of an egalitarian, collaborative counseling relationship (moving far afield from the psychoanalysts who stressed neutral authority figures)
5. an assessment of lifestyle issues and social behavior as they affect personality development

Adler's theory of individual psychology is enjoying tremendous popularity these days. Quite a number of writers (see Carlson & Slavik, 1997; Dinkmeyer & Sperry, 2000; Grey, 1998; Sweeney, 1998; Watts & Carlson, 1999) have adapted the original theory to a variety of other applications and settings, each of which brings the original ideas into a fresh package.

Whereas Freud was (overly) concerned with biological factors and psychosexual development that influence a person's behavior, Adler (1931) took a far more holistic perspective. Freud may have been a fatalist (some would say a pessimist) but Adler viewed people as essentially goal directed with the capacity for being creative and responsible for their own choices. (You will recognize this philosophy in reality therapy that follows in the next section.)

Adler introduced one of the first structures for conducting an intake interview, the standard clinical assessment method used to collect background information, form a diagnosis, and create a treatment plan. He approached this task by conducting a thorough exploration of a person's lifestyle, especially a detailed family history, occupational record, love relationships, and social competencies.

Adler was himself a sickly child, subject to frequent bouts of a respiratory disorder, vitamin deficiency, pneumonia, and even several near fatal accidents. No doubt these early experiences with feeling helpless led him to think a lot about a person's internal sense of inferiority or superiority. (He was the one to first coin the term *inferiority complex*.) This would help explain how Adler ended up compensating for his own early health problems by becoming a physician himself or how the great philosopher Demosthenes developed himself as an accomplished public speaker after overcoming chronic stuttering as a child (Sharf, 2000).

In other words, Adler had great faith in the human capacity for overcoming disabilities. This belief served him well, not only in breaking away from Freud's charismatic influence but also in supplying him with the confidence and resilience he would need to sustain his work in the face of mounting criticism, both in his native Austria and abroad. Once he first opened a medical practice specializing in nervous diseases, Adler ended up specializing in some rather unique client groups: circus performers, tailors, and other working-class people. He also became quite involved in the social rights movements of his day, advocating for better working conditions for the poor, school reform, sex education, and being a vocal leader in equal rights for women. In so many ways, he was obviously far ahead of his time.

Like Freud and Fritz Perls, both nonreligious Jews, Adler escaped his homeland just prior to the outbreak of Nazi domination and immigrated to America (Freud left a bit later for England). Using New York as a base for his clinical and lecturing activities, Adler spent the latter part of his life promoting his theory, eventually recruiting others (Ansbacher & Ansbacher, 1956; Dreikurs, 1967) to carry on his work.

Rudolph Dreikurs founded the first Adler Institute in North America as a way to introduce his ideas to professionals who were enamored with traditional psychoanalytic thinking. Needless to say, it was tough going because Adler was often branded as a traitor to the master's original teachings. It would certainly be accurate to say that Adler did indeed directly contradict the orthodoxy of Freudian theory, although he was quite consistent in crediting his mentor with promoting the role of early childhood experiences, bringing attention to the meaning of dreams, and suggesting that symptoms served some useful purpose (Mosak, 1995).

The Basic Concepts

Like Freud's original concepts, so many of Adler's ideas have become part of everyday use. He was the one to talk about inferiority or superiority complexes as the primary style in which a person presents himself or herself to the world. He first brought up lifestyle issues as the background from which people make life decisions. He was among the first family systems thinkers by asking clients to examine the constellations and patterns of their early home relationships. He has been called the first cognitive therapist as well because be looked at the origins of dysfunctional thinking that led to what he called "basic mistakes." Finally, because of his innovative, experimental orientation, many of his early therapeutic techniques resemble what later developed into Gestalt therapy. Perhaps you can, therefore, appreciate why Adler is so difficult to pin down.

Birth Order

You most likely take it for granted that birth order affects the ways a person might develop, but Adler was among the first to observe that sibling position might be a critical variable to consider. Clearly, an eldest child does not grow up in the same family, nor have the same parents, as would younger brothers and sisters. During the earliest stages of a family, parents are insecure and unskilled. They lavish attention on a first-born child, sometimes spoiling him or her rotten. By the time subsequent offspring arrive on the scene, parents have calmed down a bit. This results in middle or youngest children developing in ways that could be very different from their elder sibling.

FOR PERSONAL APPLICATION

Make a chart of your position in the structure of your family, noting the ages of each sibling, and the relative space separating each of you. Consider how your birth order has affected the ways you have developed as a person. What would most likely be different if you had been born earlier or later in your family's history?

The Helping Process

According to an Adlerian approach, therapy proceeds along a series of progressive stages that will strike you as quite logical.

Establish a Collaborative Relationship.   This is an empathic, supportive relationship but one that is based on democratic principles and essential equality. The therapist uses all the regular skills favored by any other professional at this stage, using well-timed questions and reflections of feeling and content, in order to build a solid alliance. Like most other approaches you have studied, it is now considered standard operating procedure to use empathy and support to establish a sense of trust. If that doesn't happen first, subsequent therapeutic efforts are likely to be less than successful.

Lifestyle Assessment.   A thorough history is explored, including family background, belief system, cultural heritage, personal goals, and other facets of being human. Basic questions are directed toward the person's early family constellation ("What was it like for you growing up?"), social relationships ("To whom are you closest?" and "What is most satisfying to you about your friendships?"), work life ("How do you feel about your job?"), sexuality ("How satisfying are your intimate relationships with a partner?"), and sense of self ("How do you feel about who you are?"). In addition, like any other form of treatment, clients are asked standard questions:

1. "What would you like help with?"
2. "What are you expecting or hoping that I might do for you?"
3. "How would you like things to be different after our sessions are over?"

4. "What have you already tried in your efforts to take care of your concerns?"
5. "What support is available to you during this difficult time?"
6. "What are some of the strengths and assets you bring to our relationship?"

These are the sorts of questions that you would bring up in a session with a new client regardless of your theoretical orientation. They help you to efficiently and quickly gather background information, assess preliminary expectations, and find out what the client has already tried before.

■ ■ ■ ■ ■

FOR A CLASS ACTIVITY

Practice doing an intake interview with a partner. Using the six questions as a guide, take about ten minutes each to conduct the initial phase of a first session. When acting in the role of a client, it doesn't matter whether you present yourself as you really are or role-play someone else. In reality, even when you pretend to be another person, you are still being a part of yourself.

During the interview, take brief notes on what you learned, but don't let your writing distract you from maintaining good attending and listening behavior. Concentrate only on asking these open-ended questions and inserting a few encouraging probes, perhaps reflecting feelings and content as appropriate. When the ten minutes are over, regardless of how far down the list you have gotten, summarize what you have heard your partner say.

Give each other feedback on what you liked best and least about the interview. If an observer is present to serve in that role, then invite him or her to debrief you.

Interpreting Early Recollections. A type of family constellation questionnaire is often used to gather relevant information on family experiences. The goal at this stage is to assess which early events were most influential on current patterns. This inquiry would begin by asking the names, ages, and occupations of parents, as well as the sibling positions. The client would also be asked to supply the most dominant personality characteristics of each family member.

A number of other questions would be introduced:

"Who was your mother's favorite child?"
"Your father's favorite?"
"What did your parents expect and want for each of their children?"

"Which parent did you resemble more?"
"To which sibling were you closest?"
"What were your conflicts about in your family?"

Other questions would be used to explore earliest recollections:

"What is your earliest memory?"
"Describe your first sexual experience."
"Which incident in school stands out as being most significant to you?"

■ ■ ■ ■ ■

FOR A FIELD STUDY

Ask several people you know to tell you about their earliest memory. Direct them to tell you the story of what happened and how they felt about it. Make sure they don't get lost in the details but concentrate instead on their personal reactions to the event. Discover what stands out as being most significant to them about this early recollection.

In order to rehearse this field study, it would first be a good idea for you to complete the exercise yourself in a journal. After you have written out the narrative and identified the central themes, give the recollection a name at the top. For example, my earliest memory is carrying my brother home from the hospital on my lap in the back of the car. I remember being terrified by the responsibility of having this living, squirming thing in my arms and being afraid that I might drop him or hurt him. I would, thus, give this story the title of "Fearful of Responsibility."

Exploring Mistakes.　Find out what the person believes he or she has done wrong in life. Identify thought disturbances and core fears that get in the way. Because Adlerian therapy is classified as a type of cognitive therapy, practitioners are inclined to explore with clients their self-defeating thinking patterns that contribute to distorted perceptions (Mosak, 1995):

■ *Overgeneralizations.* "Because I didn't do well on this exam I have no aptitude at all for this subject."
■ *False goals.* "It is my job in life to make everyone happy."
■ *Misperceptions.* "I never get any decent breaks."
■ *Denial of worth.* "I'm shy. I don't deserve the promotion."
■ *Faulty values.* "You have to do whatever it takes to get ahead, even if that means taking advantage of others."

You will recognize that many of these dysfunctional beliefs are also found in the cognitive theories previously described. Each of the approaches might have slightly different names for the thinking patterns, but they all address basically the same themes. One area in which Adlerian theory has been especially helpful is identifying and addressing core fears.

Core Fears

An Adlerian lens can be used to examine the most common fears presented by clients. Those that have been identified most often include the following areas (Dinkmeyer & Sperry, 2000; Shulman, 1973):

Fear of Being Imperfect. It is one of our deepest, darkest secrets that each of us is a fraud. In part, we may even gravitate to this field as a way to reassure ourselves that we are not nearly as defective as we really feel inside. To make matters worse, as therapists we aren't often allowed to show our vulnerabilities and failures. Our clients and the public demand that we appear poised, confident, in control, and thoroughly perfect. This only contributes to the unrealistic expectations that we can't possibly meet.

Fear of Being Vulnerable. The more you reveal yourself authentically and honestly, the more likely that others will discover you to be inept and unprepared. We spend our lives pretending to know and understand far more than we really do. With compete genuineness, we also risk greater intimacy—and rejection.

Fear of Disapproval. Everyone wants to be loved and appreciated by everyone else almost all the time. That may not be possible but it is still part of the eternal search. The more you risk showing yourself as a real person, disclosing your true and authentic self, the more you put yourself at risk for deep hurt.

Fear of Responsibility. We have each made lots of mistakes in our lives, giving us lots of reasons for regret. If only you could do things differently. If only you could make up for past errors in judgment. If you could start over again.

Moving from insight to action, the client is helped to make new choices that are more consistent with desired goals. The first step in his phase is to identify clearly what it is that the client wants most. These goals must be realistic and reasonable.

■ ■ ■ ■ ■

FOR PERSONAL APPLICATION AND A CLASS ACTIVITY

Which of the core fears hit you particularly hard? As you review each of them, consider recent, specific times in your life in which you have struggled with these issues.

Get together in small groups of classmates—or if you are particularly daring—with family or friends. Talk to one another about your most deeply held fears, especially those that you rarely allow yourself to explore.

A Plan of Action

Almost any of the contemporary problem-solving methods might be used next in an Adlerian approach. Essentially, you would progress through the following steps:

- What are some possible ways that you could meet your goals? Among the alternatives, which one would you like to try first? Which one do you think is the best option?
- What plan of action could you follow that will get you going in the desired direction?
- What do you think about the results of your effort? To what extent has your plan produced the desired outcome?
- What would you like to do next that will get you even closer to your goal?
- What has been getting in your way and compromising your efforts to be more effective?

Because the Adlerian approach is both insight and action oriented, the therapist would not be shy in helping clients to convert their self-declared goals into specific homework assignments or tasks that can be completed between sessions. Throughout every step in the process, a collaborate, supportive relationship would be used as leverage to keep the client motivated and making progress.

It is not so much that Adler himself tried to make his theory into something for everyone as it is his followers who have found ways to do so. You can find within this theory a little bit of everything that you will recognize from other approaches. One reason for this, of course, is so many other therapists have borrowed and adapted Adler's ideas for their own purposes. Nevertheless, you could get the distinct impression from studying this model that it seems to wander all over the place, from attention to the past to a focus on the present, from a cognitive to a behavioral to an affective approach. This is quite a good thing actually because the Adlerian theory gives you an overall framework from which to use a host of other methods that might appeal to you.

Some might be inclined to criticize Adler's theory because it is another that looks too much at the development of the self rather than the self in relationship to the larger culture and a person's subcultures. Although it is a method that clearly values the role of the past in present behavior, it is somewhat narrowly focused on the influence of one's nuclear family and especially one's siblings. Although this might be especially important for some individuals, others might be far more influenced by peer relationships, school or early work relationships, or the larger popular culture of computer games, movies, and television.

REALITY THERAPY

Reality therapy is big on personal responsibility. Everything in this theory is about three main questions:

1. What do you want?
2. What are you doing (or not doing) to get what you say you want?
3. What are the consequences of the choices that you have been making?

When William Glasser (1965) first wrote about his "control theory," later renamed "choice theory," he was a practicing psychoanalyst just like Albert Ellis and many of the other writers mentioned in this book. Just as Ellis got sick of listening to people whining all the time about how miserable their lives were, Glasser became impatient and frustrated listening to patients in the veteran's hospital blame others for their plight. He tried his best to help them to accept responsibility for their own problems by interrupting their endless ruminations and asking them instead to look at what they were doing and what results this behavior was producing.

After moving into the area of juvenile delinquency, Glasser found another difficult population with which to experiment by helping law-breaking teenagers to be more responsible for their actions. He decided that schools in general would be far better off if they focused on a success rather than failure orientation (Glasser, 1969). Next, he moved on to another tough problem of irresponsibility, perhaps the most difficult one of all: addictions. Glasser (1976) believed that some type of addiction in humans is inevitable given our propensity for instant gratification, but he felt that positive addictions such as noncompetitive exercise and meditation could be reasonably substituted for negative addictions such as drugs or alcohol (Glasser, 1976).

There are aspects of this approach that are clearly existential (emphasis on freedom and responsibility), behavioral (focus on specific outcomes and consequences), client centered (importance of an accepting, nurturing environment), as well as cognitive (clarification of internal reasoning processes). What is singularly unique, however, are the specific underlying assumptions of the approach, as well as the structured therapeutic program that is followed.

There are several main ideas that form the background for reality therapy that have been summarized by Wubbolding (1988, 1991, 2000) here and in Table 6.4.

■ People are driven to satisfy their universal needs for safety, comfort, freedom, belongingness, power, and fun.
■ People are also highly motivated to fulfill their personal desires, which are unique to each person.
■ People become frustrated when what they are getting out of life is less than what they want or perceive they need.
■ People behave in such a way to meet their needs and wants, making intentional choices that have particular consequences.

People don't get what they want in life because of a lack of commitment and follow-through. At the most minimal level of commitment, a person is asked how badly he or she wants something and says, "I don't know." At the next level, the person might say, "I do want it, but I'm not sure I want to invest the energy it would take to get it." The next level of commitment leads one to say, "Okay, I'll try it and see how it works out." One step further would mean a person declaring, "I'll do my best," and the ultimate level of commitment would be, "I'll do whatever it takes." Obviously, in the process of therapy, your job is to help people who are at the tentative stages ("I think this is what I want" or "I'll see what I can do") to move to a deeper level of personal responsibility for their outcomes: "I want this more than anything and I will do whatever needs to be done to make sure I get it."

TABLE 6.4 **Steps of Reality Therapy in the WDEP Model**

W—Explore basic Wants.
D—Find out what you are Doing.
E—Evaluate whether it is working.
P—Formulate a new Plan.

Does It Work?

Similar to strategic and problem-solving therapists you will read about in a later chapter, Glasser was fond of asking people if what they were doing was working for them. He noticed the phenomenon that people keep repeating the same self-defeating behaviors over and over and over again even though they were not producing desired results. It is, thus, extremely helpful to ask clients:

1. Is what you are doing helpful to you?
2. Is it getting you want you want?
3. Are you abiding by the rules?

This last question is especially important for those clients who are consistent rule breakers, who have been acting irresponsibly or otherwise engaging in troublesome behavior. Quite often people are inclined to make lots of excuses for why they didn't manage to do what they say is so important. In this approach, clients are not permitted to blame others, nor are they allowed to use any excuse for not following through on declared goals. Either you want to do it or not: the proof is in the outcome.

■ ■ ■ ■ ■

FOR PERSONAL REFLECTION

In this excuse-making exercise, make a list of all the reasons you can think of why people would not have been able to accomplish objectives that they claimed were important to them. Imagine, for example, that you declared that you wanted to devote a significant amount of energy and time into learning the material in this book and class. When pushed to put your actions behind your words, you agreed that you would spend a minimum of an hour, four times per week, to reading about theories that interest you. (Okay, this was an ambitious goal.)

Now picture that you might have a number of excellent reasons (remember, you are smart so any excuses you come up with would be good ones) for why you weren't able to accomplish what you said you wanted to do. Consider the following excuses as possibilities:

■ "I didn't have time."
■ "I meant to do it but got distracted."
■ "I couldn't help it."
■ "Something came up I couldn't control."
■ "I'll try to do better next time."
■ "Procrastinating runs in my family."
■ "I've always been this way."
■ "It was just bad luck."

Now imagine that the very next time you amended your declared assignment, you committed yourself to the notion that there could be no legitimate excuse for not doing what you say you want to do.

The Therapeutic Process

Reality therapy has become a favored approach in schools, not only because Glasser (1969, 1990) has written about applications for this setting but also because the approach is rather simple to learn. He believed that if you could design educational institutions in such a way that they radiated a warm, accepting, supportive climate and at the same time you absolutely required people to be responsible for their choices and behavior, you could remove much of the punitive atmosphere that students find so pervasive. This would contribute to what he described as a "success identity" rather than the usual sense of failure that problem children experience.

There are basically four sequential steps to his helping process (also summarized in Table 6.4).

1. Ask the client what he or she wants. Explore the person's personal desires, goals, and wants.
2. Figure out what the person is already doing.
3. Evaluate the results of this action. Is it working?
4. What is a new plan that can be constructed that is more likely to produced desired results? The best such plans are highly realistic, specific, and completely within your own power to control (so there are no possible excuses).

FOR PERSONAL APPLICATION

Apply reality therapy's process to your own life by asking yourself the following basic questions.

1. What is it that you want?
2. What are you doing to get what you want?
3. How is this working?
4. What excuses are you using to explain why the consequences are not as desirable as you would prefer?
5. What could you do instead?

Limitations of This Approach

Although like the proponents of every other approach, reality therapists enthusiastically believe that this theory works with almost everyone almost all the time, there are some aspects of its philosophy that you might find to be culturally and gender biased. Notions such as freedom, personal responsibility, and control are distinctly Western ideals, often synonymous with the dominant male values of our culture. In other parts of the world and among indigenous peoples, values such as cooperation, interdependence, and shared responsibility are considered far more important than the North American emphasis on rugged individualism.

In the past, ingredients of therapeutic relationships have been downplayed, whereas the idea of transference or personal therapist reaction has been all but ignored. Also, like any of the approaches that emphasize behavior in the present moment, the impact of the past is minimized. Perhaps you might agree that the way we act now is deeply rooted in the patterns we learned as children in our families of origin. This doesn't mean that we must be controlled by the past, as some theories have suggested, but that we are certainly strongly influenced by the ways we were raised and the experiences to which we were exposed.

■ ■ ■ ■ ■

FOR HOMEWORK

Taking action or putting ideas into practice is an integral part of reality therapy. As in a few other approaches, there is a strong belief that what you do outside sessions is far more important than what you do in sessions. There are people who can talk and talk, complain and whine, and state all their preferences and good intentions but never actually *do* anything to change their predicaments.

1. Focus on some aspect of your current behavior that needs work.
2. If your client was engaging in such self-defeating behavior, what would you say?
3. What excuses do you consistently use to avoid taking greater responsibility?
4. What is a realistic plan you have for getting your needs met more effectively?
5. What will you do when things don't work out as planned or when you feel discouraged?

If you were to make comparisons between reality therapy and other cognitive approaches, you might be struck by the emphasis on the external consequences to behavior rather than the internal ones. In cognitive therapy and REBT, you will recall that people are asked to examine how thinking in a particular way will influence the way they feel inside. The reality therapist, however, pays less attention to internal cognitive states and far more to asking clients to predict what will happen if they make particular choices. The two approaches share the strong belief that outside forces don't cause personal discomfort, and that the past doesn't control the present, but they differ in that cognitions are viewed by the reality therapist as only one aspect of experience. "The reality therapist emphasizes choice as a means to more effective living, rather than requiring a change in thinking as a prerequisite" (Glasser & Wubbolding, 1995).

Because the leaders of each theory interact with one another on a regular basis and also read one another's material, there is little doubt that many of the approaches are converging. Just as the cognitive therapists have been strongly influenced lately by constructivist paradigms, reality therapists have been incorporating those ideas, as well as cognitive principles, into their work. During actual sessions, it is becoming increasingly difficult to identify which approach a practitioner might be using because so many of the models may come into play.

■ ■ ■ ■ ■

FOR PERSONAL REFLECTION

You are probably struck by the sheer number of choices available to you when faced with most therapeutic situations. No matter what a client says or does in a session, you can pick a half dozen possible interventions depending on which theory you are using and on which facet of the interaction you want to concentrate.

A client says to you, for example, "I just feel so lost I don't know what to do next. I just can't seem to make a decision."

The client-centered therapist might respond with something such as, "You are feeling out of control and overwhelmed not only because you are afraid of making a mistake but also because you can think of so many options, any one of which might be the right one."

A REBT practitioner would concentrate on the person's internal state by mentioning, "You are feeling lost because you are telling yourself that there is a right choice and, furthermore, that it's possible for you to figure out what that might be. No wonder you are feeling so much pressure with that kind of absolute, unrealistic demand on yourself."

Now imagine that you want to select an intervention from reality therapy to respond to the part of the communication that gets at accepting responsibility for the reluctance to make a choice. As a hint, remember to ask the person what he or she really wants and what he or she is doing (or in this case avoiding) in order to meet stated goals.

As one further reminder, connect the nature of this exploration with the existential theory you studied earlier. Imagine ways you might combine ideas from reality and existential approaches to encourage your client to consider the meaning behind the avoidance of responsibility and anxiety related to freedom. Because there are also limits to a purely insight-oriented approach, also think through how you might confront your client to take action based on what is understood.

SUGGESTED READINGS

Beck, A. T. (1999). *Prisoners of hate: The cognitive basis of anger, hostility, and violence*. New York: HarperCollins.

Bernard, M. E. (2002). *Rational emotive therapy with children and adolescents*. New York: Wiley.

Carlson, J., & Slavik, S. (Eds.). (1997). *Techniques in Adlerian psychology*. Philadelphia: Accelerated Development.

Cormier, W. H., & Cormier, L. S. (1998). *Interviewing strategies for helpers: Fundamental skills and cognitive behavioral interventions* (4th ed.). Pacific Grove, CA: Brooks/Cole.

Dinkmeyer, D., & Sperry, L. (2000). *Counseling and psychotherapy: An integrated, individual psychology approach* (3rd ed.). Upper Saddle River, NJ: Merrill.

Dryden, W. (1995). *Brief rational emotive behaviour therapy*. London: Wiley.

Ellis, A. (1995). *Better, deeper, and more enduring brief therapy: The rational emotive behavior therapy approach*. New York: Brunner/Mazel.

Ellis, A. (2001). *Overcoming destructive beliefs, feelings, and behaviors: New directions for rational emotive behavior therapy*. New York: Prometheus.

Glasser, W. (1998). *Choice theory: A new psychology of personal freedom*. New York: HarperCollins.

Grey, L. (1998). *Alfred Adler: The forgotten prophet*. Westport, CT: Praeger.

Lazarus, A. A. (1997). *Brief but comprehensive therapy: The multimodal way*. New York: Springer.

McMullin, R. E. (1999). *The new handbook of cognitive therapy techniques*. New York: W. W. Norton.

Sweeney, T. J. (1998). *Adlerian counseling: A practitioner's approach* (4th ed.). Philadelphia: Accelerated Development.

Wubbolding, R. E. (2000). *Reality therapy for the 21st Century*. New York: Brunner/Routledge.

■ ■ ■ ■ ■ ▬▬▬▬▬▬▬▬▬▬▬▬▬▬▬▬▬▬▬▬▬

CHAPTER 7

WHAT IS LEARNED CAN BE UNLEARNED

Behavioral Approaches

You probably remember something about Ivan Pavlov and his animals salivating to the sound of dinner bells, John Watson and his phobia-conditioned rats, and B. F. Skinner's prowess in teaching pigeons to play Ping-Pong or mice to run mazes. What, you might ask, does any of this have to do with helping people? Well, theories of intervention were developed as a direct outgrowth of experimental studies of how animals learn behavior, as well as how they are conditioned to act in particular ways. If we understand the ways that behavior is reinforced, we can design treatment programs to increase the frequency of fully functioning behaviors and discourage those that are self-defeating.

HISTORY OF THE BEHAVIORISM MOVEMENT

As with any of the other theoretical families that are presented in each chapter, there is almost as much diversity within the behaviorist school as there is between it and other models. Even at the very beginning of its inception as a therapeutic approach, there was great heterogeneity in the diverse paths taken from that of systematic desensitization (Joseph Wolpe), applied behavior analysis (B. F. Skinner), social influence (Albert Bandura), and later the cognitive behavior therapies (O'Donohue & Krasner, 1995). Nevertheless, behavior therapists have always favored an objective, empirical approach to predicting and managing behavior, one that favors controlling the external environment as much as possible.

Ivan Pavlov and Classical Conditioning

Pavlov was a Russian physiologist interested in studying the digestive processes of dogs, so it seems particularly ironic that he ended up launching the behavioral movement that was to have such a profound impact on psychology and education. If you know anything about the ways great discoveries were made, so often they resulted from accidents and serendipitous encounters. Columbus thought he had arrived in India only to find that poor navigation and misguided beliefs landed him on a whole other continent. Everything from X rays and many drugs to Post-it notes were similarly discovered by sheer accident. So perhaps it isn't surprising that the study of digestion would lead to behavior therapy.

Like any good scientist, Pavlov was a keen observer. During his investigations into the physiology of metabolic processes, he noticed that his subjects began salivating before he even presented them with their dinner. Just the sound of food being prepared was enough to spark a strong anticipatory emotional response. In other words, the dogs became conditioned to respond in a particular way just at the sight of food or the sounds associated with its delivery.

Pavlov began pairing the presentation of food with other cues, such as a flashing light or a ringing bell, simply to prove that he could condition the dogs to salivate in response to almost any neutral stimulus. He was, thus, able to demonstrate most convincingly how animals and humans learn to like, or even fear, certain relatively innocuous occurrences in the environment. Depending on your prior experiences, and whether they were rewarding or punishing, you may develop strong preferences or aversions toward things you once encountered.

John Watson and Learned Neuroses

Following Pavlov's work, John Watson has been credited as being the founding parent of behaviorism. He conceived of the new science of psychology, launched a few years earlier by his contemporary William James, as a purely objective enterprise, one that is directed toward predicting and controlling behavior. In his famous credo, Watson (1924) crowed: "Give me a dozen healthy infants, well-formed, and my own specified world to bring them up in and I'll guarantee to take any one at random and train him to become any type of specialist I might select—doctor, lawyer, artist, merchant, chief—and yes, even beggar-man and thief, regardless of his talents, penchants, tendencies, abilities, vocations, and race of his ancestors" (p. 104).

■ ■ ■ ■ ■

FOR PERSONAL APPLICATION

What are some of your greatest fears, phobias, and neuroses? Assuming that you were not born with particular aversions to these things, how were these attitudes conditioned in you?

Well, Watson certainly didn't lack any confidence in himself! Yet he did have evidence from his animal studies that it was indeed possible to control behavior. Once he began experimenting with humans, he discovered that he could both create phobic reactions as well as take them away by using principles of behavior modification. In his classic case of "Little Albert," Watson demonstrated that he was able to condition an 11-month-old infant to develop a fear of a white rat and eventually to generalize that fear to anything that resembled the hated object (piece of cotton, mitten, Santa Claus beard). The implications of this study were profound for it showed how neurosis and psychological symptoms might develop as a result of conditioning processes. Furthermore, once it is understood how maladaptive behaviors are elicited and reinforced, similar methods can be used to countercondition the symptoms. Unfortunately, Little Albert's mother yanked him out of the experiment before Watson had a chance to undo the psychological damage.

B. F. Skinner and Operant Conditioning

If Watson was the specialist in classical conditioning, employing the method first discovered by Ivan Pavlov to elicit certain responses by presenting particular stimuli, then B. F. Skinner became the master of instrumental conditioning, or reinforcement theory, in which stimuli were used to increase or decrease target behaviors. This later became known as behavior modification.

Skinner envisioned a world in which people would be reinforced systematically for their good deeds that benefit society, writing about a utopian world in *Walden II* that encouraged people through shaping and maintaining their behavior. Following the philosophy once articulated by British philosopher John Locke, Skinner believed that people are indeed born as "blank slates" upon which experience writes its impressions. As you may recall, he set out to support this thesis by demonstrating all the ways that pigeons, rats, and people could be conditioned to behave in certain ways according to various schedules of reinforcement. With several colleagues (Lindley, Skinner, & Solomon, 1953), he was also the first to use the term *behavior therapy* as a means of treating hospitalized schizophrenics.

The First Behavior Therapies

The disciples of Watson and Skinner concentrated mostly on exploring the ways that humans and animals learn, spawning a whole set of new theories to explain memory, knowledge and skill acquisition, and forgetting. It was a South African psychiatrist, Joseph Wolpe, and an English psychologist, Hans Eysenck, who began applying behavioral principles to the practice of therapy.

At this particular time in the middle of the twentieth century, psychoanalysis was supreme, practically the only legitimate form of therapy. A whole bunch of disgruntled ex-analysts were in the process of setting up their own schools of thought, but at that point in time the main option available was long-term, insight-oriented excavations into the unconscious.

Wolpe (1958) developed a method he called systematic desensitization, a kind of counterconditioning method that used relaxation strategies to help clients suffering from anxieties and phobias to learn alternative ways to respond to threatening stimuli. Wolpe first began experimenting with cats, demonstrating that they could be "taught" to develop anxiety neuroses by shocking them and then curing them of their symptoms by using counterconditioning methods. He was actually the first brief therapist, demonstrating that he could rid animals and people of their symptoms in just a few sessions rather than the usual number of years that were required in psychoanalysis.

If Wolpe was the supreme innovative clinician, then Eysenck (1952) was the scientific genius interested in applying empirical methods to measure the objective effects of therapy as it was practiced at the time. The bad news was that he found that people didn't improve in therapy any more quickly than they would have if they had received no treatment at all. The good news, well . . . there wasn't a lot of good news. But he did bring a *lot* of attention to the objective measurement of therapeutic outcomes, which is one of the foundations of the behavioral approach.

A decade later, Albert Bandura (1969), spurred on by the challenge to develop reliable intervention methods that could be verifiably measured, developed a handbook of behavioral principles that used as their core neither the operant theory of Skinner, nor the classical theory of Watson and Pavlov, but rather the concept of modeling or social learning. Bandura believed that people can learn and be reinforced not only directly but also through observational learning. He, thus, loosened up behavioral theory considerably, adding to its methodology an appreciation for cognitive, verbal, and observational features in the change process.

■ ■ ■ ■ ■

FOR HOMEWORK

In looking at the process of modeling, Bandura noted that influencing others emanates from a sense of personal power. People pay attention to others whom they perceive as powerful. There are many different kinds of personal power that give you the ability to command attention in others' eyes. There is the obvious physical power, that is, an imposing physical presence. There is also the kind of power that comes from being seen as an expert, a source of nurturance, an icon of prestige, or a sex object.

Advertising companies understand this phenomenon all too well, designing their commercials in such a way that they display one or more of these modeling processes. Thus, the spokespeople for products tend to be celebrities (prestige), dressed in white lab coats (expertise), sexually alluring (models), or physically commanding (athletes). They know you are far more likely to be influenced by such a commercial, or enjoy a music video or computer game, if the dominant figures radiate one or more varieties of power.

Look at the advertisements on television or in magazines to find samples of the various kinds of modeling power that are intended to influence consumers' buying habits.

Fishman and Franks (1997) review the forces that led to behaviorism as a second therapeutic force to counter the psychoanalytic theory that was so dominant at the time. Summarizing points made earlier by Krasner (1971) and others, they identify the following influences:

1. Rational philosophy during the eighteenth-century Age of Enlightenment and British empirical philosophers set the stage. John Locke, in particular, was among the first to talk about humans as being born as "blank slates" written on by experience.
2. Wilhelm Wundt was the first experimental psychologist. All psychology students memorize that in 1879 Wundt established the first psychological laboratory in Leipzig. This gave a scientific foundation to the field.
3. Ivan Pavlov's studies at the turn of the twentieth century demonstrated the ways that organisms learn behavior through classical conditioning.
4. John Watson demonstrated experimentally the ways that classical conditioning is applied to individuals' dysfunctional behavior.
5. B. F. Skinner and other learning theorists demonstrated operant conditioning in which behaviors are reinforced or extinguished by certain stimuli.

FOR A CLASS ACTIVITY

One easy way to remember the differences between the two learning modes is that classical conditioning involves stimulus-response learning (taking out your appointment book signals that a session is over), whereas operant conditioning involves response-stimulus learning (the client reports on successful homework and receives a big smile from the therapist).

In small groups, talk about other ways that these two forms of conditioning might operate in therapeutic relationships. In other words, what examples can you think of in which particular therapist behaviors elicit desired responses in clients, and when therapists might reinforce or extinguish client behavior?

6. Learning principles were applied to address a number of human problems, such as the use of reward and punishment systems to encourage or discourage particular behaviors.
7. Scientific and empirical methods were applied to psychology, social work, medicine, and education.

BASIC PRINCIPLES

Like many of the other theories that have been around for a while, many behavioral concepts have become co-opted by other therapeutic systems. In fact, behavior therapy rarely stands alone in contemporary practice but is often combined with the cognitive approaches presented in the previous chapter.

Reinforcement

One major application of behavioral theory is the systematic use of reinforcement (rewards and punishments) to increase or decrease target behaviors. On the most subtle level, therapists use smiles and frowns to indicate their relative approval of what is going on. Other verbalizations can be more direct as illustrated in the conversation that follows.

Client: It was so much harder than I thought. I had no idea . . .

Therapist: But the important thing is that you did it! I know how difficult that was for you.

Client: Yeah, I guess you're right about that.

Therapist: [Smiles and nods her head, offering encouragement]

Client: It was one of the hardest things I've ever tried.

Therapist: You can sure say that again.

Client: But I still think that maybe I shouldn't move so fast, maybe I should wait a while before I go any further.

Therapist: [Shakes her head] I can certainly understand how you would feel hesitant, but I'm not sure I agree with you.

Client: Well, maybe it's not as bad as I think it is.

Therapist: Absolutely. You'd be surprised how strong you can be.

On one level, it appears as if the therapist is just being supportive (and she is). She is also being quite systematic in using both nonverbal and verbal reinforcement strategies to encourage optimistic statements and discourage those that are filled with doubt. Because the therapist's approval is so important to the client, subtle cues lead the course of the interaction in directions the therapist believes are most helpful.

Shaping

Learning does not usually occur in one single dose of reinforcement but rather develops in successive approximation toward the ultimate goal. You don't just start out waiting for the right behavior to occur, and then attempt to reward it, or you may end up waiting a very long time. Instead, you pick a series of little goals, each one leading to the next stage, eventually ending up at the final objective. Like a hunk of clay, the intention is to shape its form through a series of small, incremental movements.

Let's say, for instance, that you have a client who persists in communicating in a rather annoying, counterproductive manner. He rambles constantly, talking to fill up space. You have wondered if this style is not intended to avoid real intimacy and keep people from getting too close, but regardless of its purpose, it makes working with him very difficult. Furthermore, you suspect that his dysfunctional interpersonal style is responsible for many of his other problems that occur at work and with his few friends.

You have tried waiting for an instance when he abandons his talkativeness in favor of brevity so you can reward this behavior, but you have not yet recognized a single opportunity to intervene. From the moment he walks in the door until the time he leaves, he talks nonstop. You could confront him, of course, but the behaviorist recognizes clearly the disadvantages of any intervention that might be perceived as punishment. It is far preferable to use positive reinforcement whenever possible.

Because you can't reward the target behavior that is your final objective, your job instead would be to shape his behavior in desired directions through a series of little steps. When the client pauses to catch his breath during a particularly long-winded story, you immediately jump in and tell him how lovely it is to enjoy a companionable moment of serenity with him. A little later, when he is momentarily distracted by a sound outside the room, you use that opportunity to tell him how much you like the way he speaks with his eyes as well as his mouth. You even find a rare occurrence when he manages to tell a relatively brief story (completely irrelevant to the work in therapy, of course) and you jump all over that by thanking him for being so concise and how much easier it is to hear and understand him when he speaks in shorter periods.

In each of these examples, you are using your own approval as leverage to shape the client in a particular direction. Although Rogers and other humanists have called this unduly manipulative, Skinner once responded in a debate that he thinks all teachers and therapists subtly shape the behavior of others by selectively rewarding some behaviors over others. When Rogers hears an expression of feeling, he immediately lights up and reflects what he understands, yet if the client intellectualizes, Rogers would be inclined to ignore that response. This is called extinction and is designed to discourage those behaviors that are not thought to be useful.

Measurement

Behaviorists are very big on measuring outcomes as objectively as possible. They want to know from clients exactly what they are going to do, how often they are going to do it, and what will happen if they don't do what they say (as in reality therapy, consequences are very important). Ideally, behaviors are a lot easier to measure if they are observable actions. This is consistent with behavior therapy's preference for dealing with actions that can be seen rather than internal processes.

The emphasis on measuring outcomes is one of the enduring influences that behaviorism has had on our field, establishing the practice of therapy as both a science and an art. To some extent, all practitioners are now required to evaluate the impact of their interventions and demonstrate that their methods are indeed effective.

It's Action That Counts

Although it is no longer the only approach that concentrates on what the client is doing rather than thinking, sensing, or feeling, behavior therapy was certainly the first theory to promote changes through action methods. The behaviorist doesn't dwell long on what people are feeling inside but rather moves things along toward what needs to be done.

Unlike its main competition at the time, psychoanalysis, behavior therapy concentrates on the present rather than on the past. Likewise, insight is minimized with the rationale that understanding why you are so messed up doesn't necessarily change anything in your life. If you have known people who have been in therapy for years, without any apparent, visible changes in their behavior, perhaps you are sympathetic to this argument.

To summarize the main points, behavior therapy remains in the present rather than the past. It minimizes the role of insight in the change process, instead focusing on specific actions that can be taken. It plays down the importance of relationship and affective variables, preferring to create a therapeutic connection that is business-like, collaborative, and problem oriented. Rather than investigating underlying causes of behavior or unconscious motives, the behavior therapist sticks with presenting complaints and observable symptoms. You would have a lot of company if you thought this might be a gross simplification of the human experience.

BEHAVIORAL TECHNIQUES

The behavioral approach is just loaded with practical, concrete strategies that you can use in sessions regardless of your favored theoretical orientation. Many of these techniques are so universal that they are employed by most therapists when the situation calls for it.

■ ■ ■ ■ ■

FOR A HOMEWORK ASSIGNMENT

Find an organization in your community that operates a behaviorally oriented treatment program to manage daily life. This might be found in a local psychiatric hospital, a group home for adolescents or the elderly, a classroom environment, or perhaps a correctional facility.

Spend some time observing the way this behaviorally oriented program is managed. Note the special kinds of reinforcers that are used to increase and decrease target behaviors. If possible, talk to members of the staff, as well as the clients, about how they experience the system.

Remember that not every client presents the sort of problem that lends itself to specific treatment objectives and objective measurement of outcomes. If someone comes to see you and wants to stop some annoying behavior, learn to become more assertive, or work on some particular goal, the behavioral approach is ideal for those circumstances. At other times, clients won't even know what is bothering them, or they don't feel ready so much to change behavior as they just want to be listened to and heard. Or perhaps clients want to understand some aspect of their lives a little better. They may eventually be ready to make the kinds of changes that lend themselves to behavioral intervention, but remember that like any of the models, behavioral techniques are ideally suited to some circumstances but not to others.

Goal Setting

This a *very* nifty, useful method that helps clients to translate their concerns into specific therapeutic tasks. There was a funny movie a few years ago called *What About Bob?* (unfortunately, there are lots of movies that make fun of therapists) in which Richard Dreyfuss employed a strategy with his clients called "baby steps." The method was ridiculously simple but no less valid: changes are often best brought about when people are encouraged to take small, successive steps in the direction they wish to go.

A behavioral approach to counseling incorporates into its procedures the expectation that clients will complete homework assignments in between each session. If you think about it, the actual therapy represents less than 1% of the person's waking time during the week. Even if the person came for sessions three times per week, that would still be just a drop in the bucket compared to all the rest of the time that the person spends engaging in the same dysfunctional behaviors. So therapists in general, and behavioral practitioners in particular, are always looking for ways to help people apply what they are learning in their real lives where things matter the most.

It is one of the most frustrating parts of this job that some people will come in and talk your ear off and yet they don't actually *do* anything in the world to change their patterns. They come in week after week, report on how wonderful they feel, perform like circus animals jumping through all your hoops, but they still engage in the same self-destructive behavior. This isn't their fault, of course. Transfer of learning, or generalization of learning, from one situation to another is the most difficult challenge of change processes. You've got to help people to start applying new changes in their lives outside of sessions, where it matters most. The best goals are those that meet the following criteria.

Mutually Developed Goals.   One mistake that beginners make is in assigning or prescribing homework assignments to their clients. This is a recipe for disaster because people tend to not feel committed to goals that they didn't come up with themselves. Imagine that your client returns the next session and says to you: "Gee, I'm sorry. But I wasn't able to do that assignment we talked about. I was just too busy." Then the client looks you directly in the eyes as if daring you to say something.

If, however, the goals are mutually constructed, then you have the leverage to say to the client:

> **Therapist:**   Okay, I guess what you said last week wasn't so important after all.
>
> **Client:**   Well, that's not true. It *is* important.
>
> **Therapist:**   This is your life we're talking about, not mine. You were the one who came up with this homework assignment, and then you decided not to do it after all. That's fine with me. You will do it when it finally matters more to you than anything else that you allow to get in the way.

Developing mutual goals involves negotiating with the client a therapeutic task that is consistent with the work you've been doing and helps him or her to take one baby step in the right direction. You typically end the session with a statement such as:

"So, maybe you could summarize what you understand we did today and what you've agreed you will do before we see each other next time. I heard you say that you very badly want to change the pattern of trying to get approval from your boss. To make progress in that area, you've said that you will limit yourself to visiting her office to once per day instead of the usual two or three times."

Specific Goals.   Consistent with behavioral principles, it is important to declare goals that are concrete, observable, and measurable. Ideally, you want to help the client to come up with a homework assignment in which it is clear exactly what will be done, how many times this will take place, where and with whom the action will occur, and what the consequences will be for doing (or not doing) the assignment.

Realistic Goals.   During your negotiations with clients over what they will do in between sessions, it is extremely important that the assignment is reasonable. Contrary to what you might imagine, clients tend to want to do too much. They declare homework assignments that are way beyond what is probably manageable. Because it is so important to build in success experiences, you want to make sure that the goals are realistic.

Imagine you are working with someone who wants to begin an exercise program for a number of good reasons. This isn't only about physical health and lifestyle issues but also is related to the person's work on self-image and practice of self-control. The dialogue sounds like this:

Client: So what I'm going to do this week is go to the health club I just joined and work out every day for an hour. [This is very good in meeting the criterion of specificity, but not in being realistic.]

Therapist: Let me get this straight. In the previous week, and every week before that, you haven't worked out a single time. And now you are saying you are going to do it every day for an hour?

Client: Do you think that's too much? [Because mutuality is important in these negotiations, the therapist doesn't want to take too strong a role in telling the client what to do. Instead, efforts are more indirect.]

Therapist: Well, what do you think? I certainly don't doubt your commitment. And you probably will visit the club most days just like you want to, but maybe it would be better to start out a little more modestly.

The therapist already has in mind a goal that he or she thinks is realistic, say, three times per week for half an hour, but he or she will take the slower route to negotiate a goal that is definitely manageable, with no excuses possible. It may turn out that this client does work out every day as he intends, but the declared goal should be modest to make certain it can be achieved.

Relevant Goals. In the zeal to translate discussion into some sort of action, therapists often make the mistake of reducing a very complex issue to a goal that is specific but hardly pertinent to the main themes. Resist the urge to push clients to work on goals prematurely, or to bite off the most irrelevant part of the problem just because it lends itself to a homework assignment.

A client has been struggling with feelings of hopelessness and despair. He feels worthless and incompetent—in school, with his friends, and at home. During the conversation, he casually mentioned that he hadn't been completing all his school assignments. Because the therapist feels so helpless and sad for her client and wants to do something constructive immediately, she jumps on the school assignments as the place to concentrate their attention. This turns out to be very conducive to a specific therapeutic task that can be completed, but lost in the dust were all the other important feelings that were just beginning to be explored. This client was just discouraged from talking about his feelings, something with which he is already extremely uncomfortable, so that they could both work in territory that both find easier going.

■ ■ ■ ■ ■ ▬▬▬▬▬▬▬▬▬▬▬▬▬▬▬▬

FOR A CLASS ACTIVITY
OR HOMEWORK ASSIGNMENT

Work with a partner to help him or her negotiate a specific goal that can be accomplished within a reasonable period of time. Start out by using your active listening skills and a few open-ended questions to find out what the problem is. It would probably be advisable to start out with something relatively minor.

Negotiate with your partner to devise a goal that meets the criteria that have been discussed. One way to remember them is to use the pneumonic device *SPAMMO* in which each of the letters signals one of the things to keep in mind.

1. Specific.
2. Pertinent.
3. Attainable.
4. Measurable.

5. *Mutual.*
6. *Observable.*

After you are done, your partner should have written down exactly what he or she is going to do, how often, and under which circumstances. You should then make plans to talk again within a specified period of time so there is some accountability.

One final criterion to keep in mind when helping clients work toward goals is to make sure they are ethical. What if, for instance, someone wants help to become more exploitative of others? Or what if a drug dealer feels guilty because of his chosen profession and wants your assistance to reduce this annoying side effect? Or what if someone comes to you requesting help with an activity that is immoral or illegal?

As you have no doubt learned in other courses, the practice of therapy is fraught with moral dilemmas and ethical conflicts. You will want to discuss thoroughly with your clients the consequences of their choices and decisions about which goals they want to accomplish.

Relaxation Training

This is another generic strategy that has become mainstream in the field. You are most likely already familiar with it in which a person is taught to relax various muscles systematically as an attempt to control inhibiting stress or anxiety. The instructions resemble a kind of hypnotic trance induction method in which the client is invited to get as comfortable as possible and to close his or her eyes.

You begin with breathing, asking the person to concentrate completely on the process of drawing in and exhaling a breath.

> With your eyes closed, listen to the sound of my voice and allow it to help you relax. Notice that with each breath you take you can feel your chest rising, and falling, and rising. [*Time the cadence of your voice to the actual rising and falling of the client's chest.*]
>
> Each time you exhale, I want you to just think the word *relax*, say the word *relax* to yourself. As you do so, with each breath you take, you will find yourself becoming more and more calm, more and more relaxed. Just spend a minute enjoying how good it feels to breathe deeply and think the word *relax*. Just follow your breath as it originates deep inside your chest, gathering together all the toxic air in your body and bloodstream, and then as your chest contracts you can feel all the used air exhale out through your mouth and your nose. As you exhale, you think the word *relax*. Then you breathe deeply and slowly taking in fresh

oxygen, nourishing your body and your mind. Just let your breathing help you to relax.

After a few minutes of teaching the person how to use deep breathing as a relaxation exercise, directions are now used to help the person to go to a much deeper state of serenity. This is often done through imagery in which a particular scene is created on the beach, or floating on a cloud, or walking through a quiet meadow. You can even ask the client to go to the place in which he or she feels most safe.

Next, deep muscle relaxation is often introduced. The client is asked to imagine that each muscle in the body is stretching itself, all the tension draining away.

> Beginning with your feet, I want you to picture each of the tiny, little muscles in your feet beginning to relax. From the tips of your toes, up your instep, around your ankles, at your heel, you can feel each of the muscles stretching out like rubber bands. Imagine as you lie there, so relaxed, concentrating on your breathing, thinking the word *relax* as you exhale, that your feet are becoming light as feathers, almost able to float of their own accord. And now you can feel this warm sensation of relaxation and stretching begin to move into your calves and lower legs.

The client is continually directed to concentrate on breathing, thinking the word *relax,* and to imagine each and every muscle in the body—from the legs, to the abdomen, to the chest, down the legs, into the hands, and fingers, up into the shoulders and back, into the neck, the face, and all the tiny little muscles around the eyes and nose and mouth, moving into the scalp. This whole process might take half an hour the first time. Throughout the exercise you are watching carefully for the least sign of tension and, if detected, you back up a little and keep working until the person is ready to move on. Most people find this experience to be incredibly refreshing and relaxing.

Depending how deeply you want to take the person, or how much tension he or she is carrying, you can include further imagery.

> You lie there completely relaxed, with every muscle in your body stretched out and drained away of tension. I'd like you to picture an escalator that is going down, down, down. I'd like you to step onto the escalator and, as it takes you lower, I want you to feel yourself become even more deeply relaxed. You are continuing to move down, and with each descent of a floor, you can feel yourself become more profoundly relaxed, almost as if you could float away.

If this resembles some sort of hypnotic procedure, that is because it is. Relaxation methods are favored induction methods to put people into hypersuggestible states. There is no magic to this; you are simply helping the person to let go of defenses, tension, and inhibitions.

■ ■ ■ ■ ■ ▬▬▬▬▬▬▬▬▬▬▬▬▬▬▬▬▬▬▬▬▬▬▬▬▬▬▬▬▬▬

FOR HOMEWORK OR A CLASS ACTIVITY

Working with a partner, practice using an abbreviated form of relaxation training. Start out by asking the person to close his or her eyes and concentrate on breathing for a minute or two. Each time the person exhales, repeat the word *relax*, inviting your partner to repeat this with each subsequent breath.

For this exercise, you will concentrate solely on one region of the body—the chest. Ask the person to visualize that all the muscles in the chest are loosening, stretching, and expanding, making it progressively easier to breathe. Encourage your partner to take deep, cleansing breaths, each one bringing a greater sense of serenity and relaxation.

Suggest that your partner imagine himself or herself resting in a special or favorite place that feels especially safe and relaxing. This could be lying on a beach, sitting in a favorite chair, or swinging in a hammock—wherever the person associates a place of peace and quiet.

Remind your partner to keep concentrating on breathing deeply and calmly, thinking the word *relax* on each exhale, and picturing himself or herself resting in that special place.

After a few minutes of this process, ask your partner to talk about what the experience was like, as well as to give you feedback on what worked best and least effectively.

If time and the situation permit, reverse roles so that each of you has a chance to practice.

The beauty of this method is that, once learned, the client can use it whenever he or she is confronted with stressful situations. By thinking the word *relax*, and taking a few deep breaths, the person can bring back the same feelings of self-control and serenity.

The relaxation method is a relatively simple procedure to learn, although as with any therapeutic strategy, supervision and feedback are required from more experienced practitioners. There are several different scripts that you can learn, each one adapted to specific type of presenting concern (Smith, 1999).

Sensate Focus Exercises

In the field of sex therapy, various behavioral homework assignments are combined with other forms of therapy to help couples make steady progress eliminating sexual dysfunctions. Most such problems, from orgasmic difficulties in women to erectile problems in men, are caused in part by inhibiting thought processes. How can one possibly have an orgasm if you are constantly thinking to yourself: "I wonder if I'll come this time." How can one maintain an erection if you are continuously thinking, "I wonder if it will stay or whether I'll lose it again." It is, thus, a kind of performance anxiety that creates or exacerbates most such sexual problems.

To combat such self-defeating thinking, and to build in a series of successful experiences, therapists often use a series of progressive homework assignments for couples. Essentially, all sexual dysfunctions are conceived as a systemic rather than individual problem (more on that theory in Chapter 9). What this means is that although it may appear that the man or the woman has the sexual problem, it is actually the result of interactive dynamics between them. A man who has premature ejaculation may be expressing anger unconsciously to his partner: "Ha, ha, ha. I got off and you didn't." A woman who doesn't have orgasms with her partner may be saying: "You aren't good enough to excite me." Quite often, individual sexual problems are signs of some other relationship difficulty that must also be addressed.

The sensate focus exercises are intended to use behavioral strategies to reduce "spectatoring," to remove internal pressure, and to create positive, successful, loving experiences in bed. The exercises begin with each partner directed to pleasure the other one through a full body massage, but without touching one another's genitals. This removes all pressure to perform. In the case of a premature ejaculator, he might be directed to try brief penetration and then to immediately withdraw. In the example of erectile dysfunction (that is not organically based), he might be specifically ordered *not* to have an erection (this is called a paradoxical directive and will be discussed in Chapter 10). With a woman experiencing orgasmic difficulties, her partner may be directed to pleasure her in ways that have nothing to do with eliciting sexual arousal.

■ ■ ■ ■ ■ ▬▬▬▬▬▬▬▬▬▬▬▬▬▬▬▬▬▬▬▬▬▬

FOR PERSONAL APPLICATION

This might very well be the most fun exercise in the book. Tell your spouse, lover, or partner that you have a homework assignment for school. (If you don't have a partner, your first job is to find one.)

Turn off the phone and create complete privacy with no interruptions.

Take a bath or shower together.

Take turns spending a total of 30 uninterrupted minutes pleasuring your partner (without leading to sex or orgasm) while he or she remains relatively still and passive. Have your partner verbalize what he or she enjoys most.

This assignment is often a variation of the first step in behaviorally based sex therapy in which couples are taught to reduce performance anxiety associated with lovemaking.

Very slowly and progressively, partners are given other assignments that involve behavioral principles of reinforcement and changing the automatic stimulus-response patterns. Such therapeutic strategies are incredibly effective, by the way, demonstrating cure rates well into the 90% range (if there is no underlying physical problem involved such as side effects from blood pressure medication or a neurological disease).

Contingency Contracting

This is another excellent structure that you already know about and use in your life intuitively. As it was originally conceived, the idea was to control better the reinforcers of target behaviors. After goals are specified and a plan of action is constructed, the final step includes identifying the agreed upon consequences. When you declare to yourself that you will allow yourself a dessert if you are able to stay within your scheduled diet for the day, you are using this strategy. If you tell a reluctant client that she can stop coming to sessions if she manages to stay out of trouble for two weeks, you are also employing contingency contracting.

Recall that behavior can be increased in two ways according to the behaviorist:

- *Positive reinforcement.* This is also known as rewarding people when they do something desirable. Common examples include smiles, verbal encouragement ("Great job!"), and prizes (candy).
- *Negative reinforcement.* This is another kind of reward in which you remove something that the person finds undesirable. Four example, you might take away some dreaded chore once the person does what has been agreed upon.

There are also two ways to decrease the frequency of behavior:

- *Punishment.* This involves applying some stimulus that the person finds noxious or undesirable. When someone doesn't do what he or she is supposed to, the person is punished by doing extra chores. Keep in mind that punishments (and rewards) are perceived differently. Some kids actually enjoy negative attention and other individuals find what you consider to be a punishment to actually be enjoyable in a perverse way. Also remember that punishment has its side effects in that it often produces defensiveness, anger, or withdrawal.

■ *Reinforcing incompatible behavior.* Another way to decrease the frequency of certain behaviors is to reinforce other behaviors that are incompatible with it. This is the strategy behind relaxation training, for example, because you can't be anxious when you are also feeling calm.

Depending on the situation, the individual, and the desired goal (to increase or decrease behavior), you would design a personalized contract that includes the following components:

1. Which behaviors do you wish to change and in what direction?

   I want to increase the amount of time I spend with my family members and decrease the time I spend at work.

2. What is your plan of action?

   I agree to spend a minimum of thirty uninterrupted minutes with my husband five out of seven nights. I plan to spend at least two hours on the weekend with my two children doing just what they want to do. Furthermore, I will not bring work home with me more than three nights per week instead of the five nights that I have been currently doing so.

3. What might get in the way?

   Regarding the first goal with my husband, he might not always cooperate because he also has his own commitments. As for the second goal with my children, it has been easy in the past for me to let myself get sidetracked when the phone rings. The third goal is the most challenging of all because I can't control my workload; my boss may assign me tasks that have to be completed within a deadline.

4. How do you propose to overcome these obstacles?

   First, I will kidnap my husband if necessary, even if we have to get out of the house to go for a walk so we make sure we take the time to debrief one another. If he still won't cooperate on a regular basis, I will follow through on our getting marital counseling to address the issues. The same goes for my children: I will take them and leave the house to do something together so we aren't interrupted or distracted. As for the situation at work, I intend to have a conversation with my boss and explain the new limits under which I will be working. I realize he will try to circumvent and sabotage my efforts, but it is completely within my power to enforce what I say I will do.

5. What are the contingencies that will be put in place?

   Well, much of this new behavior is self-rewarding and intrinsically pleasurable. But I know myself well enough that I need some incentives. If

I manage to do what I say I'll do with my husband and children for three weeks in a row, then I will schedule a family trip to Disneyland to celebrate. If I don't complete these family goals, I will cook dinner and clean up an extra night each week for a period of four weeks. With respect to my work goal, my reward will be to have my children cook dinner an extra night each week because they will enjoy more of my company. If I don't follow through on this plan, then my punishment will be to not spend any money on clothes or luxury items until such time that I can maintain this new pattern for three weeks in a row.

In constructing contracts, either for yourself or clients, it is generally a good idea to work on one behavioral goal at a time. When developing a reward system, keep in mind that it is better if they can be delivered immediately and if they may be applied frequently to small, successive steps toward the ultimate goal (Gilliland & James, 1998).

Often contracts such as this might be signed and witnessed as a powerful form of accountability. People are far more likely to do what they say they want to do when they have made public commitments about their intentions. Try putting the contract on the refrigerator where everyone in your household can see it, and you must face it every day, and then try to weasel out of your agreement.

CONTEMPORARY DEVELOPMENTS

Behavior therapy was the first treatment method designed to be short term, symptom oriented, and concerned with reaching specific, identified goals. No wonder, then, in today's climate of managed care that this approach is so popular among insurance administrators who like its emphasis on accountability, precise measurement of outcomes, and efficiency. It is cost-effective from the standpoint that if it is going to work with a given case, there will be observable results in a relatively short period of time.

There are now over a dozen different journals devoted to the practice of this brand of therapy. Consistent with its heritage, the focus of much of the research is on empirically validating specific methods with particular client complaints such as eating disorders (Tobin, 2000), attention deficit disorders (Novotni & Petersen, 2000), or family-mediated psychiatric disorders (Mueser & Glynn, 1999).

Quite a number of technological advances have also made it possible to deliver reinforcers through remote devices or to communicate with therapists via the Internet. Record keeping and evaluating outcomes are also much easier with the use of portable devices. These innovations make it possible for people to keep much more accurate records of their progress, as well as to make adjustments as needed.

The most contemporary development of all in this approach is the way that its practice has been incorporated and synthesized into so many other methods.

Limitations of This Approach

Obviously, human beings are made up of far more than observable behaviors. We are thinking beings and also feeling beings. Although in recent years behavior therapy has been all but swallowed up by the cognitive-behavioral approach, there is still a suspicion of anything that is too nonempirical, unobjective, and illogical. As such, this is a relatively mechanistic approach.

Behavior therapy downplays the importance of insight in the change process and also minimizes the importance of the therapeutic relationship. That is not to say that contemporary behavior therapists don't spend time working on their alliances with clients, just as they also explore issues related to self-understanding, but the theory has not emphasized these factors much. This is changing rapidly as behavior therapy becomes subsumed under the larger family of cognitive behavior therapies described in the previous chapter.

The stance of the therapist in this approach is that of an expert who designs strategies in collaboration with the client. There is, thus, a danger of manipulation and abuse of power when the inequality of roles is emphasized. Again, in practice, behavior therapists may operate very differently from this style, but the original theory implies that it is the professional's job to figure out what the problem is, to design a treatment strategy, to implement that program, and then to measure the outcome. This has contributed much to the status of the field, especially with regard to developing empirically validated treatments for specific disorders.

If you are the type who especially values spiritual issues and the role of feelings and internal processes in daily experience, this is probably not the best approach for you. Nevertheless, you will still find much of value in terms of techniques that you can adapt for your clients' needs.

SUGGESTED READINGS

Bandura, A. (1969). *Principles of behavior modification.* New York: Holt, Rinehart, and Winston.

Gottman, J. M., & Silver, N. (2000). *The 7 principles for making marriage work.* Three Rivers Press.

O'Donohue, W. (Ed.). (1998). *Learning and behavior therapy.* Boston: Allyn and Bacon.

Scotti, J. R., & Meyer, L. H. (Eds.). (1999). *Behavioral intervention: Principles, models, and practices.* Baltimore, MD: Paul H. Brookes.

Skinner, B. F. (1948). *Walden two.* New York: Macmillan.

Spiegler, M. D., & Guevremont, D. C. (1998). *Contemporary behavior therapy* (3rd ed.). Pacific Grove, CA: Brooks/Cole.

Smith, J. C. (1999). *ABC relaxation training: A practical guide for health professionals.* New York: Springer.

Thorpe, G. L., & Olson, S. L. (1997). *Behavior therapy: Concepts, procedures, and applications* (2nd ed.). Boston: Allyn and Bacon.

Watson, D. L., & Tharp, R. G. (1997). *Self-directed behavior: Self-modification for personal adjustment* (7th ed.). Pacific Grove, CA: Brooks/Cole.

Wolpe, J. (1991). *The practice of behavior therapy* (4th ed.). Elmsford, NY: Pergamon.

CHAPTER 8

ALL IN THE FAMILY

Systemic Approaches

It will probably come as no surprise to you that there are as many different theories of family counseling as there are those designed for individual or group settings. That means, of course, another barrage of names and terms with which to familiarize yourself. The good news is that approaches to family therapy have more in common than they have differences; family therapists tend to be much more cohesive as a group than do their colleagues in other specialty areas.

THINKING IN CIRCLES RATHER THAN IN STRAIGHT LINES

Representing a radical departure from the traditional approaches to helping, systemic theory sees human interactions as resulting from circular rather than linear influence. In other words, the usual way of understanding situations is that:

1. the husband did something that aggravated his wife, or
2. the teacher expected too much from the student, which caused him to overreach his capacity, or
3. the boss yelled at her subordinate, which made him feel inadequate.

Notice in all three of these examples, the verbs that describe what happened—"did something," "expected too much," and "yelled"—imply that the actions of one person *caused* the behavior of another. In truth, human interactions are a *lot* more complex.

If you think in circular interactions rather than straight lines of cause-effect relationships, then the dynamics of what takes place between people become a matter of continued reciprocal influence. This kind of thinking, in which behavior is examined in terms of mutual effects and underlying, hidden forces, is an important part of all the theories mentioned in this chapter.

■ ■ ■ ■ ■ ▬▬▬▬▬▬▬▬▬▬▬▬▬▬▬▬▬▬▬

FOR PERSONAL REFLECTION OR A CLASS ACTIVITY

Take each of the three examples and convert them into scenarios that represent mutual effects and influences over one another. Instead of imagining that the husband aggravated the wife, picture instead that when the husband came home from work and plopped his feet up on the table, the wife took this as a personal affront. Although he had hoped for, and expected, a warm greeting from his wife, she appeared cold and withdrawn. Before you blame her as the cause for their conflict, consider that she had been harboring some residual hurt from their lovemaking the previous night when the husband had made a comment that caused her to feel unattractive. Just before his remark, however, she had appeared unresponsive to something he had been doing to arouse her, making him feel inadequate. And then . . .

Well, you get the point: It is virtually impossible to trace back who is at fault or the cause of the problem because each participant in the process is both the cause and the effect of the other's actions.

Make up situations to explain how the other two examples might have resulted from circular dynamics.

SYSTEMIC THINKING

There are several different disciplines that have contributed to the systems approach, making it the most integrative of all the frameworks studied so far. Many of the contributions come not so much from traditional social sciences as from biology, physics, and mathematics.

Natural Science

Lewis Thomas is a cellular biologist who specialized in studying ant and termite colonies, as well as writing a series of essays on the mysteries of science. In particular, he has made observations about the ways cells are organized according to the same design as the larger planet (Thomas, 1974). In his musings about the ways that cells are structured, Thomas noticed that each of a cell's various parts—mitochondria, nucleolus, chromatin, endoplasmic reticulum—has a striking similarity to the components of a planetary body such as Earth. He wonders if our planet is not just a cell in a larger organism and whether we are not just bits of floating protoplasm. Such wonderings have led Thomas to make similar comparisons between the ways that termites and ants communicate with one another, as if they are not separate beings but all part of one neurological system operating as a single, purposeful entity. These apparently whimsical hypotheses are all part of a general philosophy that led scientists to look beyond their own narrow disciplines to the underlying structures of physical forces. This is the same motive that drove Albert Einstein to devote his life to searching for general laws to account for physical forces.

Mathematics

Of all fields of study, you would think that higher-order mathematics would be the most linear of all. Numbers line up so purely and logically in straight lines in which A leads to B, which leads to C. Everything you ever learned about geometry, algebra, and calculus only confirms the belief that the universe is orderly and linear.

It took a mathematician, Norbert Wiener (1948), to observe that not everything in the physical world does indeed proceed in a linear manner. Take the regulation of a thermostat, for instance, the favorite metaphor to explain circular causality. The heater is set at a particular temperature. When it receives information that the warmth has dropped below a threshold level, it kicks in to reestablish a stable environment. This kind of feedback mechanism, which also operates in the biological world of organisms (equilibrium), helps explain what happens in families as well. Any nonverbal gesture, expression, or action within the family acts as both a cause of others' behavior, eliciting responses, and also the effect or result from others' behavior. There is continuous, self-regulating feedback loops, which Wiener called "cybernetics," from the root Greek term that describes the person who steers a boat.

Chaos Theory

We will study this theory in greater depth in Chapter 10 but, for now, you should know that it seeks to understand the hidden order of things. James Gleick (1987), who wrote the first popular book on chaos theory, and Edward Lorenz, a meteorologist who helped found the field of chaoplexity to describe the complex, interrelated ways that weather patterns are affected by apparently remote incidents, are among those who call themselves chaos or complexity theorists (see Horgan, 1996; Waldrop, 1992). This is a scientific approach that studies apparently random, unpredictable behavior, searching out underlying patterns and order.

You may see obvious similarities between the role of the chaos theorist and what family therapists do. Clients enter in the throes of their own apparently random, chaotic, disordered interactions. It is your job to help them to sort out and make sense of what is producing undesirable outcomes and what can be done instead.

Physics

Quantum physicists (see Capra, 1975; Zukav, 1979) discovered two important ideas in their work that sharply contrasted with the traditional ideas of Sir Isaac Newton. First is that everything is connected to everything else; you can't study one little aspect of the world without including all the interconnected parts and the underlying patterns. Second, you can't study an object without influencing and becoming part of the phenomenon you are investigating.

Again, there are rather clear parallels between quantum physics and the work of therapists. The systems approach also believes that you can't look at anyone's behavior without considering all the interconnected parts. Likewise, once you enter the system to study what is going on, you also become a part of the family.

Systems Theory

There was a great scientific revolution in which some theoreticians such as Von Bertalanffy (1968) attempted to think beyond their parochial disciplines and unify all knowledge, especially with regard to all living systems. He believed that when studying any sort of living organisms such as humans it was necessary to look at the bigger picture rather than just individual actions. Once you expand your window of observation, it becomes far more apparent that the behavior of any single unit is affected by the actions of others within that system. The whole is, thus, far more important than the parts (Patton & McMahon, 1999).

Evolutionary Psychology

This was another big framework, like systems theory or cybernetics, that looked at individual behaviors of animals and humans on a much larger scale. We are not only part of the larger community of organisms and forces in the present but we are also influenced by our evolutionary history in the past.

First launched from the work of Darwin (1859) and then Edmund Wilson (1975), the theory was later popularized for a lay audience (Wright, 1994) and for students in a text on the subject (Buss, 1999). There is even a whole system of therapy based on the principles (Glantz & Pearce, 1989).

According to this theory, all behavior represents an attempt by individuals to increase the likelihood of perpetuating their own genetic material. Of course, because genetic programming for our survival instincts was established tens of thousands of years ago, and the ancestral environment for which we were originally designed (a savanna) no longer exists in the civilized world, behavior must be understood in terms of its original functional value.

Take fear or anxiety reactions, for example. At first, they seem like totally useless, destructive impulses that create nothing but heartbreak and dysfunction for humans. You are merrily minding your business, and wham, a panic attack. Or you are about to give a public speech or walk out on a high balcony, and you are virtually incapacitated by anxiety, barely able to function. What possible functional value could such responses have for our survival?

The original environment for which our nervous systems were designed was a very dangerous place. Individuals were constantly in jeopardy of being eaten by a predator, picked off by an enemy, or stumbling off the edge of a cliff. The "fight or flight" reflex is what arranged for our bodily systems to engage in the most appropriate state of readiness to deal with whatever might come up. In the case of facing a raging snaggle-toothed tiger, there were two viable options: One is to run away as fast as possible and the other is to hold your ground and do battle. In both cases, the ideal state for your body would be to increase oxygen flow to muscles and brain (heavy breathing and hyperventilating), increase heart rate to circulate more oxygen (pounding chest), cut off blood flow to extremities so you don't bleed to death if injured (numbness), and close off bodily functions such as digestion that you won't be needing to save energy (fluttery stomach, dry mouth). In addition, we are hardwired to overgeneralize and overreact to *any* potential for danger because it is far more adaptive to have false alarms than not to be prepared at all (Buss, 1999).

Now consider what fears, phobias, and anxiety are all about. We no longer face many life-threatening dangers in daily life that require a "fight or flight" reaction. In just a few generations, the ancestral environment has become rather placid, devoid of opportunities to use the system for which we were designed. Nevertheless, we are still calibrated to respond to the slightest potential danger even though we often misinterpret or exaggerate signals. Some people's emergency response systems are so out of whack that they have panic attacks (just another name for mobilizing resources), debilitating anxiety, or fear.

■ ■ ■ ■ ■

FOR PERSONAL APPLICATION

Evolutionary psychology provides an interesting framework for making sense of others' behavior. Basically, whenever you are puzzled by someone's actions, ask yourself the questions: How is this behavior helping this person in ways that may not be immediately obvious? Even though this behavior seems self-defeating and counterproductive, how might it once have served a useful purpose a long time ago in human evolution?

For example, you accidentally cut someone off on the highway and the person becomes enraged by this perceived challenge to his manhood and territorial space. He begins tailgating you and you can see in the rearview mirror that he is screaming and swearing. Even though this behavior seems ludicrous, what is it about this behavior that may be adaptive, meaning that it contributes to a greater likelihood that he will produce offspring who will survive?

Psychoanalysis

It was Alfred Adler (1931) who first expanded Freud's theory to include family dynamics in the understanding of a problem. Nathan Ackerman (1937), another psychoanalyst and one of the earliest proponents of family therapy, also drew attention to the power of families to shape the directions taken by individuals. Just as with almost every other theory you have studied, the first generation of practitioners were mostly psychoanalysts who abandoned this approach for others they believed were more useful or at least better suited to their work and personalities.

Anthropology

You will recall that Gregory Bateson (1979) was mentioned earlier in reference to his work studying schizophrenic families as the context for those hospitalized patients who ended up "crazy" as a way out of an untenable situation. With training in anthropology (he was also married to Margaret Mead), Bateson noticed that communication patterns represented the ways that systems functioned. Furthermore, he did not see that certain behavior caused particular reactions in a linear way but rather that a more circular process was involved. He noticed that very subtle nonverbal and verbal cues acted as both causes and effects of others' behavior. *Linear causality* is, thus, based on the behavioristic idea that one event or action elicits a particular response. In *circular causality*, however, influence moves in multiple directions at the same time.

Bateson gathered together a group of researchers to study the communication patterns of families that produced schizophrenic children (Bateson, Jackson, Haley, & Weakland, 1956). Composed of a cultural anthropologist (Gregory Bateson), communications theorist (Jay Haley), chemical engineer (John Weakland), and psychiatrist (Don Jackson), this eclectic group of scholars tried to decode the complex patterns of interaction that take place in families with a schizophrenic member. They noticed, for example, some intriguing mixed messages embedded in the communications between a parent and psychotic child. Labeled as a *double bind*, the following scenario unfolds:

1. A mother warmly greets her hospitalized son: "Oh, honey, I've missed you so much! Come give me a hug!"
2. The son approaches as directed.
3. The mother squeals in indignation after being touched: "Not so hard! You'll mess my hair."
4. The son backs away and starts to withdraw.
5. The mother punishes: "Now what's wrong? Why must you always act so crazy? Don't you love me?"

Under such circumstances, becoming schizophrenic is practically a logical escape from an untenable situation. Putting aside genetic and biochemical predispositions to psychotic disorders that we now understand are so influential, this theory had wide application to many other areas.

Goldenberg and Goldenberg (2001) supply another example of this process in which a mother is accused of being a bad parent who produced sick children (and she believes this). Unhappy and disengaged from her husband, the mother becomes overinvolved in her relationship with her son, excluding her younger daughter. The teenaged girl begins to act out for attention, while the son becomes more independent. The mother feels even more helpless and depressed, believing that the problems really stem from the absent father. He turns resentful and angry, withdrawing even more. This influences . . . Well, you get the point. Rather than a simple cause-effect situation, each member of the family becomes the instigator for each other's behavior. It is virtually impossible to assign blame or even identify who is the real problem. Furthermore, it is not useful to do so.

■ ■ ■ ■ ■ ▄▄

FOR A CLASS ACTIVITY

Working in pairs, take a few of the following cases of linear causality and make up scenarios to explain the more complex interactions that might really be taking place as part of a circular causality phenomenon.

1. "My instructor is a real jerk. She terrorizes us with her unrealistic demands and ridiculously difficult assignments."
2. "My father abandoned us emotionally. He was just never around because he didn't care about us. That's why I have such trouble today sustaining relationships with men."

3. "I did well in the competition mostly because of the quality of the instruction and coaching I received."
4. "I'm just not good at math or any sort of quantitative task because of the way I'm built. I've just never had a head for numbers. Nobody in my family does."

In the next chapter on brief therapies, you are going to learn about a technique called reframing in which problems as presented by clients are redefined in such a way that they may be more easily solved. For example, you would have great difficulty addressing the issues described earlier because of the ways they imply that the solution is to fix the lousy instructor, traumatic past, or bad math genes. Go back and try to reframe these presenting complaints so that they lend themselves far more easily to therapeutic intervention.

PRINCIPLES OF SYSTEMIC THINKING

I have no intention of confusing you further by adding another dozen theories to your already bulging list. After all, there are whole other texts devoted to this subject (see Becvar & Becvar, 1999; Gladding, 1998; Goldenberg & Goldenberg, 2001; Nichols & Schwartz, 1998). Nevertheless, it would be helpful for you to become minimally familiar with the basic concepts that are universal among most of the approaches.

Circular Causality

As already discussed, the basic idea is that you think in circles instead of in lines. Instead of assuming that one person is the cause of a conflict, look at the way conflict occurs in the context of others who are pushing one another's buttons. This means that conflicts are always the result of several parties and almost never the result of one scapegoat. In addition, when one person comes in for help, this client might be the one designated as the identified problem, but therapists should assume that the difficulty is part of interactive struggles.

Whenever a parent calls for an appointment for his or her child, I always begin by asking both parents to come in first to give me background information. I tell them that I'd like to get their perspective on things before I meet with their child. Although this is true to a certain extent (okay, it's not really true at all), I've noticed that more often than not, I don't see the child at all. It often turns out that the child's problem in school or at home was the excuse that brought attention to other issues in the family. So I start talking to the parents about their child's problems, and then I ask what seems to be an innocent question:

"So, tell me a little about yourselves."

They usually look at me quizzically and suspiciously, as if to say, "Why do you want to know about us?"

"It's just that I'd like to get to know you a little better to get some family background that will help me when working with your child."

This makes perfect sense to them so we begin talking about their relationship, and before long we often drop the pretense that they are really there to talk about their child when it is apparent that they are the ones with the primary difficulty.

Even when the child really is the one with the greatest needs, it would still be useful to work on this issue within a family context because the child's behavior is likely affecting others in the household. The child's behavior is also being influenced by others in the family.

Rules of Relationships

Every family (and human system) has rules that guide behavior. Some of these rules are made explicit (e.g., Take off your shoes when you come into the house) and others are subtle (e.g., Don't talk to your parents right after they get home from work because they are often in a bad mood). Some of these rules are very helpful in organizing family behavior, whereas others are extremely toxic and dysfunctional. When rules become so restrictive and rigid that they limit the options available and keep families stuck (called the redundancy principle), then there is often trouble afoot.

As part of the rules that develop in families, a structure evolves that includes various subsystems or coalitions in which some members align with siblings or one parent in opposition to others. It is often easy to see these coalitions establish themselves as soon as a family enters a session for the first time.

During most family interviews, you will spend a lot of time studying and identifying the family rules with respect to the following areas:

- *Power.* Who's got it and who doesn't? You may want to realign the structure of the family, empowering members who have been marginalized or scapegoated.
- *History.* What are the family legends, myths, and history that still live within the family? Every family has narratives that were inherited from previous generations. Many themes from one generation play themselves out in subsequent generations. It is common to use a genogram (a pictorial representation) to map out the history of a family, including mention of any ancestors who had particular problems (see McGoldrick, Gerson, & Shellenberger, 1999).
- *Coalitions.* Who is most closely aligned with whom? It is helpful to create a family map, which plots out the various subsystems, the

levels of engagement or conflict among members, and the relationship of one coalition to others.

- *Hierarchy.* What is the pecking order of those in control? Power isn't only centralized in one alpha member, but everyone in the family has an assigned order in the overall structure.
- *Roles.* Who is assigned to which "jobs"? Members often end up in consistent roles as the "rescuer," the "distracter," the "troublemaker," or the "helpful one."

■ ■ ■ ■ ■ ▬▬▬▬▬▬▬▬▬▬▬▬▬▬▬▬▬▬▬▬▬▬▬▬▬

FOR A FIELD STUDY

Get together with a classmate, volunteer, or partner to conduct a family assessment. Limit the session to sixty to ninety minutes in which you attempt to gather information about as many of the areas listed here as possible, including family structure, history, hierarchy, power, coalitions, roles, boundaries, communication patterns, and so on. Practice using open-ended questions, reflective listening, and other skills to learn as much as you can.

▬▬▬▬▬▬▬▬▬▬▬▬▬▬▬▬▬▬▬▬▬▬▬▬▬▬▬

- *Boundaries.* How easily does the family allow interactions with others? Some boundaries are permeable, permitting influence and interaction from outside the system; others resist any sort of outside interference (making the therapist's job very difficult).
- *Enmeshment.* How overdependent are some members on others? Members sometimes fuse with one another, losing their separate identities in the process. There is a difference between healthy interdependence and overdependence (keep in mind cultural differences).
- *Culture.* What is the dominant cultural identity of the family and the members? This involves not only ethnicity but the family members' religion, socioeconomic class, career paths, social circles, and other influences.
- *Communication.* How do members relate to one another and what are the rules for these interactions? Note not only the surface interactions but also the metarules, or what people are really saying to one another beneath the surface.
- *Life cycle.* At what developmental stage is the family functioning? The tasks of a family with an infant are distinctly different than one with a child about to leave home.
- *Metaphors.* What are the symbolic interactions that reveal underlying issues? Communication and interactions often are expressed

as metaphors that can be unraveled. A wife can make her husband a dinner of successive appetizers as an expression of her desire for more foreplay in bed.

Obviously, this is quite a lot to attend to in a first family session, especially considering that you already have enough to do just keeping everyone on track and behaving themselves. That is one reason why family therapists like to work in pairs so each partner can track different aspects of the session and then compare notes afterward. This also gives you a sense of how much harder conducting a family session might be, which is why it requires additional training and supervision beyond basic practice.

■ ■ ■ ■ ■

FOR PERSONAL REFLECTION AND A CLASS ACTIVITY

Family therapists often use drawings or maps (called genograms) to represent the relationships and interconnections that exist in a family system. During the initial interview, the therapist might ask a series of questions about historical legacies (family of origin themes), who is aligned most closely to whom (coalitions), who has the power (hierarchy), and sources of conflict (boundaries).

In one family of four, for example, it is determined that the mother enjoys a close relationship with her son and a very dependent (enmeshed) relationship with her younger daughter. The father is in continual conflict with his son and is often estranged from his wife, but he enjoys a solid relationship with his daughter. The maternal grandmother is also involved in the family a lot, resents her son-in-law, and sides constantly with her grandson and daughter against the father. Because family systems are very complicated, this is only a small part of the picture but it could easily be graphically represented in a drawing.

Make two drawings of your own family system, one representing the family you were part of as a child (pick an age that is most easily accessible), and the other depicting your family now.

Get together with several classmates and talk to one another about what you learned as a result of this exercise.

A QUICK REVIEW OF THE OPTIONS AVAILABLE

Although I promised I wouldn't overwhelm you with more names and theories, it might be helpful for you to at least learn about the leaders in the field and the names of their theories (summarized in Table 8.1). Then when you come across these terms or names in the future, you will at least have some familiarization with them.

Psychoanalytic Approach

I mentioned before that the first family therapists applied psychoanalytic ideas to sessions with multiple family members present. Murray Bowen, Nathan Ackerman, and James Framo were among the first to look at family history as a significant influence on present family problems.

Just as you would expect, a psychoanalytic approach looks at the way influences from the past shape present family dynamics. Murray Bowen, for example, examined the ways that couples' patterns of interrelationship are transmitted from previous generations. This was one reason he developed the use of a genogram to plot and trace family history in a systematic way.

TABLE 8.1   Summary of Systemic Approaches

SYSTEMS THEORY	PROPONENTS	FOCUS POINTS
Psychoanalytic	Murray Bowen, Nathan Ackerman, James Framo	Family of origin issues; transgenerational legacies; enmeshed relationships
Humanistic	Carl Whitaker, Virginia Satir	Present experiences; fostering growth and development; authentic relationships
Structural	Salvador Minuchin	Family subsystems, power, and coalitions
Strategic	Milton Erickson, Jay Haley, Cloe Madanes	Interaction sequences and communication patterns
Multicultural	Derald Sue, Paul Pedersen, Allen Ivey	Cultural worldviews and identity; marginalization and oppression
Constructivist	Kenneth Gergen, Michael Mahoney, Michael White	Societal influences; subjective reality; language and narratives

Humanistic/Existential Approaches

Certainly you would imagine that there would be applications of this framework to family situations. Individuals such as Carl Whitaker and Virginia Satir developed approaches that emphasized their relationships with family members. They presented themselves as warm, engaging, and playful. They followed the basic humanistic principle of fostering growth through a series of stimulating experiences.

Structural Approach

The ideas contained in this theory developed by Salvador Minuchin and others are now so basic that they have virtually become part of the standard knowledge base of the field. Practitioners following this theory look at the underlying structure of families and seek to initiate adjustments to help members function more effectively.

Strategic Approach

If structural theory examined the underlying patterns of the ways that families organize themselves, then the strategic approach developed by Jay Haley and Cloe Madanes was concerned with interactional and communication styles and how they could be altered. Because this theory is also covered in the next chapter on brief therapies, I will only mention here that this is another model now universally used. After identifying the interactional sequence between family members, the goal is then to interrupt this pattern in favor of another means to communicate. The therapist is highly active, directive, and even manipulative, doing whatever it takes to promote changes.

Multicultural Approaches

Although not intended as a *family* systems theory, there is a significant movement in the field to look at the change process on a much larger scale, which takes into consideration the societal forces of marginalization, oppression, and ethnic identity. If psychoanalysis was the first force in the field, behaviorism the second force, and humanism the third force, then multiculturalism has clearly been the fourth force (Baruth & Manning, 1999; Lee, 1996; Sue, Ivey, & Pedersen, 1996).

The multicultural movement means taking into consideration cultural worldviews as the context for whatever help is offered (Sue, Ivey, & Pedersen, 1996). Related to our present subject, this means that factors such as ethnicity, gender, and other wider cultural influences are part of the system to which any given client belongs. Diversity is, thus, looked at not only in terms of an individual's developmental evolution when compared to others in that age and stage of life but also among others who share similar cultural backgrounds.

■ ■ ■ ■ ■ ▬▬▬▬▬▬▬▬▬▬▬▬▬▬▬▬▬▬▬▬▬▬▬

FOR HOMEWORK AND A CLASS ACTIVITY

Identify the most prominent cultural groups that are likely to be repre-sented in your client population. At the very least, you will want to ex-plore the most common minority groups in North America: African Americans, Native American groups, Asian American groups, Latin American groups, and groups that have been subject to oppression and discrimination (gays and lesbians, women, the economically disadvan-taged). Among these various populations, select three that you know the least about in terms of their basic values, dreams, identity development, and unique issues that may bring individuals from these groups to ther-apy. Interview several representatives of each of these groups, concen-trating particularly on what they would look for most in a good therapist and what negative experiences they have had in the past with helpers.

Get together with classmates and exchange information about what you learned.

Develop some guiding principles from this research and discussion to guide you in your efforts to be more culturally sensitive and responsive.

From a practical point of view, all therapy has now become multi-cultural in its application. Regardless of the particular theory you em-ploy in sessions, you must explore and respect carefully the client's cultural background, adapting methods to fit the person's ethnicity, re-ligious beliefs, sexual orientation, gender, and other cultural factors.

CONSTRUCTIVIST THEORIES

Rather than looking only at family systems, constructivists examine an even larger context for understanding human behavior: society and its influences. This means that we are not only products of our families but we are also strongly shaped and influenced by our gender roles, the media, cultural identity, language, and the stories we have learned about who we are and where we come from.

One of the best attempts to explain a constructivist approach is of-fered by Anderson (1990) in his highly readable introduction, *Reality Isn't What It Used to Be*. Three baseball umpires are sitting around having a beer after a game, talking about their approaches to their job. "There are balls and there are strikes," says the first one with great authority and confidence, "and I call 'em the way they are." The second umpire frowns and shakes his head, offering his approach: "There are balls and there are strikes and I call 'em the way I see 'em." The third umpire scoffs at both of his colleagues and says, "There are balls and there are strikes, and they ain't nothin' until I call 'em."

The third umpire is what could be called a radical constructivist. He does not acknowledge objective reality except as it is perceived differently by each person. Balls and strikes are creations of each person's imagination, and although we can agree on a general strike zone based on operational criteria, they don't really exist as things. The second umpire, a more moderate constructivist, also views balls and strikes as extensions of his own perceptions. With humility and flexibility, he also acknowledges that others might see them differently. The first umpire, however, believes that things such as strikes and balls actually exist in the world and that everyone would agree what they are.

In a nutshell, the approach taken by constructivist practitioners and scholars is closely aligned with the second and third umpires. The theory is steeped in a philosophy in which all knowledge is viewed in the context of the language and perceptions of each person. That is an especially helpful stance for therapists to adopt because it keeps us humble, respectful of different experiences, and flexible enough to look at things from multiple viewpoints.

Several writers (see Gergen, 1985; McAuliffe & Eriksen, 1999; Neimeyer, 1995) have summarized the basic principles of constructivist thinking as it would be translated into therapeutic practice. Constructivist approaches could easily be located in the chapter on brief therapies but constructivism is often classified more as a systems approach because its emphasis is on how an individual's problem is part of the narratives that evolved in the family. Michael White, Tom Andersen, and others have been instrumental in developing this approach.

Narrative Therapy

Like the strategic approach covered in the next chapter, one constructivist theory, narrative therapy, is exerting major influences on the field because of its innovative ideas. For this reason, we will look at this theory in greater detail.

At first glance, it will not appear much different from other theories you have studied. It seems phenomenological in that it looks at people's inner experience. It is existential in that it searches for personal meaning. It is language sensitive such as the approaches taken by cognitive and Gestalt theories. It is often considered a feminist theory as well because it looks at the ways that people are "colonized" and marginalized as a function of their gender and ethnicity. Yet it also integrates many of these ideas and makes them more contemporary by including them under the label *postmodern.*

The narrative therapy approach, originally developed by Michael White and David Epston (1990), has since been described in a number of sources (see Eron & Lund, 1998; Monk, Winslade, Crocket, & Epston, 1997; Parry & Doan, 1994). Most authors talk about a significant shift in the paradigm that therapists use to conceptualize their work. Such a transformation takes the following form (Lindsey, 1998):

MOVING AWAY FROM . . .	MOVING TOWARD . . .
• treatment	• collaborative conversations
• theoretical superiority	• co-construction of theory
• client inadequacy	• client expertise
• therapist responsibility for change	• therapist responsible for guiding conversations
• social control	• respect for client reality
• clients who are wrong or misguided	• clients who are doing the best they can
• diagnosis and labeling	• curiosity toward understanding
• problems exist in reality	• problems exist in language
• objective reality	• subjective perceptions
• reality is internal and private	• reality is public and interpersonal
• therapist knowing	• therapist not-knowing

As you can see from this brief summary, narrative therapy takes a very different approach to helping. I have been taught my whole life (and taught generations of therapists) that the goal of therapy is to teach clients to accept responsibility for their problems rather than blaming external factors outside of their control. Following the assumptions of theories such as reality therapy, Gestalt therapy, and Rational Emotive Behavior Therapy, I believe that there is a certain sense of empowerment that comes from taking charge of one's own life, ignoring what is outside of one's control, and focusing on only those things that are within one's power to change. This strategy has worked well in my own life and with my clients. I love saying to people, for instance, "You can't do anything about the past, the weather, your skin color or appearance, or other people's behavior, but you can do a heck of a lot to alter the way you choose to think and respond."

Sounds pretty good, huh?

Then along comes narrative therapy and turns everything upside down. In this approach, rather than teaching people to internalize their problems, the goal is to *externalize* them. This means that instead of saying to yourself, "I choose to be upset about this situation because of the way I am thinking," you would instead distance yourself from the blame. This separates the person from the problem, reduces guilt, counteracts labeling, and assists the client in joining with other family members and friends to defeat the problem (Monk, Winslade, Crocket, & Epston, 1997). The therapist would, thus, ask the client, "How did it happen that these upset feelings managed to first come into your life?"

If you understand the basics of theories already covered, then you can appreciate just how strange and counterintuitive this strategy must appear. Yet externalizing problems is at the heart of what narrative therapy is all about.

Stages in the Narrative Process

Among all the constructivist approaches, narrative therapy is perhaps the most well developed in terms of an operating system.

Externalizing Conversations.   The first step is to help the client develop an externalizing conversation in which all the family members are enlisted to join forces against the annoying problem. For example, a young girl is having difficulties with her eating habits, refusing to eat anything except white foods—mashed potatoes, turkey, bread, white chocolate (but no milk!). The therapist approaches the situation by asking the girl, and everyone else in attendance, "When did the white foods start to take over your eating?" By implication, the message is that this is not the girl's fault nor anyone else's fault. Instead, efforts can be directed toward understanding and solving the problem.

Mapping the Influence.   This clever strategy helps the family to explore all the effects and outcomes that result from having the problem (Remember: The identified client is not the only one who "owns" the problem; it belongs to everyone). This conversation helps the client to feel heard and understood by everyone else, as well as invites each person to talk about the ways they have been impacted by the situation.

Therapist: I am wondering, Laurie, how the white food restricts your life.

Laurie: Well, I can't go to many restaurants. And when I go to a friend's house, I usually have to bring my own food (white bread with mayonnaise and white cheese).

Therapist: Uh huh. How else does it affect your life?

Laurie: My mom gets mad at me a lot. I guess I understand but I can't help it.

Therapist: I know you can't. That old white food just takes over so that you can't eat anything else.

Laurie: [Nods her head]

Therapist: What about you, Mom? How does the white food control your life as well?

The therapist will continue to track the influences the problem has on each person in the family. At the end of this stage, each person will feel more understood by others and also have a better grasp of the ways that they are all in the same trouble together.

Unique Outcome Questions.   Other theories call this "looking for exceptions." The client is asked to think about those times when she has managed to overcome or ignore the problem. In other words, the participants are encouraged to focus on the times when they were not controlled by the white foods. This logically leads to asking the follow-up question: "How did you manage to fool the white foods into leaving you alone so that you could eat the red gelatin?" This, of course, encourages people to examine the ways they have experienced success and focuses them on what they have done that works.

Unique Possibilities.   Continuing the style of "curious questioning," clients are asked to consider what things would be like if they no longer had the problem. "If you managed to defeat the white foods and make them cooperate with all the other colored foods, how would your life be different?"

This strategy helps clients to visualize a time in the future when the problem is resolved. It is also a subtle way to get clients to suggest their own solutions when they are asked to picture a time when they no longer have the problem and then are asked what they did to make it go away. (More on this "miracle question" in the next chapter.)

Restorying.   All of these questions and therapeutic conversations are designed to help people change their narratives about who they are and how they got to be where they are. This is similar to cognitive therapies in that the focus is on altering perceptions of events. However, unlike these theories that concentrate mostly on internal dialogue, the narrative approach more broadly examines how reality is interpreted. As far as techniques employed, whereas REBT uses confrontation and challenging strategies ("Just because you have always done it that way doesn't mean you have to continue to do so"), narrative therapy prefers the use of questions ("What did that mean to you?" "How did you manage to resist the temptation?").

Clients are helped to develop an alternative story about their lives. Rather than naming the client's experience, using interpretation and reflective listening, attempts are made to draw out the person's own story, using his or her unique language. Throughout this process, the therapist adopts a stance of curious questioning, a position that encourages the client to create new narratives.

■ ■ ■ ■ ■

FOR PERSONAL APPLICATION AND A CLASS ACTIVITY

Write down on a piece of paper (or in your journal) the dominant story of your life. This means the main theme that seems to guide your life, the one that is the greatest source of your self-identity but also that which restricts your freedom and options.

Where did this story come from? Who wrote it? How did it come to so dominate your life?

In small groups, share your narrative with classmates. Practice using the stance of curious questioning to draw one another out. For the sake of this exercise, do *not* rely on skills of interpretation and active listening that you might use with other theories.

The Problem Is the Problem

The narrative approach is somewhat unique, even among the systemic theories covered in this chapter. Each of the models covered in this text, as well as those from other disciplines (science, philosophy, religion, social science), have different ways of looking at the problems that clients present in therapy. Several of the most common assumptions are presented next, each compared with the narrative approach at the end (Monk, 1997).

THEORY	BASIC ASSUMPTION
Common Sense	The person is the problem.
Religious View	The weak spirit is the problem.
Biological Approach	The disease is the problem.
Psychoanalytic Theory	The past is the problem.
Behavioral Theory	The reinforcement contingencies are the problem.
Sociological Approach	The family is the problem.
Anthropological Approach	Cultural practices are the problem.
Narrative Approach	The problem is the problem.

■ ■ ■ ■ ■

FOR A CLASS ACTIVITY

Using the contrasting viewpoints chart as a guide, structure a case conference in which each participant presents a different set of assumptions in looking at a case that is presented. Case conferences are usually both a means of quality assurance and supervision for staff. They are usually conducted by the senior clinician or chief administrator. All new cases are presented by those who did the intake interviews and then everyone shares input about what they think might be going on and how this case might best be treated. In ideal circumstances, there is a lively exchange of ideas and then a consensus is reached about how to proceed with the case in the future. In less than optimal situations, heated arguments, power struggles, posturing, and showboating take place. After all, therapists have very strong opinions about the ways they think therapy should be done. And as you already know, there is not exactly universal agreement on the best way to operate.

For the purposes of this exercise, assume that you are all relatively respectful of one another, even though you have very different viewpoints. One person should be the client and tell his or her story about what is going on in his or her life and with what he or she is struggling. Then each "staff member" will take one of the viewpoints in the chart and present his or her perspective on what he or she thinks the problem is and what needs to be done.

In the narrative approach, like many other brief therapies, the presenting complaint is treated at face value as the problem to be addressed. There is no assumption that the therapist is the expert in deciding what is wrong, what needs to be fixed, and how this should best be accomplished. I hope you can appreciate just how different this approach is compared to the others you have studied.

A UNIFIED FRONT

Just as you would expect, there are behavioral, Adlerian, cognitive, Gestalt, and other approaches to family and couples therapy. In addition there are several other schools of thought that are only designed for this type of work. Nevertheless, all these models agree on the following:

1. Problems should be understood in the context of their family systems rather than in terms of individual experience alone. Individual problems represent larger family dysfunctions. This means that presenting complaints should be treated in a family rather than an individual context. Most often it is done with members of the nuclear family present, although some approaches work with the whole extended family or even larger networks that include everyone who is considered important in the person's life. Even those who work with only one person at a time still employ leverage to influence the whole system via this identified person.

2. Change in any one part of the system will affect others who are interconnected.

3. It is more expedient to involve all family members (or as many as you can recruit) in treatment. There are exceptions to this as well. Some practitioners even prefer to conduct one session with everyone present to decide who has the most or least power in the system. Then the therapist works exclusively with that client in order to alter the whole family.

4. All therapy is family therapy because even when you work with only one person present, you are still interested in altering the whole system to which the client belongs.

5. Just as the individual goes through a life cycle (toddlerhood, adolescence, etc.) so does a family progress through predictable stages (courtship, beginning family, infant family, etc.).

6. What you experienced in your family of origin while growing up shapes the way your family evolves in the present. Discipline strategies, communication styles, decision-making methods, and even family rituals were all once modeled (for better or worse) in your earliest experiences.

■ ■ ■ ■ ■

FOR PERSONAL APPLICATION

Look at your current (or last) intimate relationship with a partner, spouse, or lover. Consider the ways you relate to one another, how you make decisions, what you disagree about, how you resolve differences, and what you share as life priorities. Look at some of your daily habits and rituals that have evolved over time.

Now compare your relationship to the ways your parents interacted with one another. Before you protest that things are completely different, try to ignore some of the obvious things on the surface and look more deeply at the underlying structures.

7. Families (and other human systems) organize themselves in order to maintain stability. I have mentioned earlier how this takes place around coalitions, in which boundaries and hierarchies of power determine who has power and who does not.

8. Family structures exist in a cultural context, reflecting the participants' ethnicity, socioeconomic background, religious preferences, and other identified cultural identities. Two partners in a relationship must negotiate their respective differences, coming to some mutual accommodation. Their offspring represent a blending of the cultural heritage.

■ ■ ■ ■ ■ ▬▬▬▬▬▬▬▬▬▬▬▬▬▬▬▬▬▬▬▬▬▬▬▬▬▬▬

FOR A CLASS ACTIVITY

In small groups, talk to one another about your own cultural identities (note plural) that shape your family life. This includes not only your ethnic background but also your gender, sexual orientation, socioeconomic class, religion, geographical origins, leisure interests, profession, and family legacies. Discuss the negotiations that take place in trying to reconcile your cultural heritages with those of your partner.

▬▬▬▬▬▬▬▬▬▬▬▬▬▬▬▬▬▬▬▬▬▬▬▬▬▬▬▬▬▬▬

9. Human behavior is often triangular, meaning that invisible others are often covertly involved in conflicts between two warring parties. When two people are in conflict, look for a missing third part of the triangle who may be meddling, controlling, or otherwise involved in the struggle.

■ ■ ■ ■ ■ ▬▬▬▬▬▬▬▬▬▬▬▬▬▬▬▬▬▬▬▬▬▬▬▬▬▬▬

FOR PERSONAL REFLECTION

Think of a time recently when you were involved in an argument or conflict with someone else—a family member, friend, coworker, or classmate. It seemed as if the problem was only between the two of you, but assume for a moment that this disagreement was really part of a larger systemic issue. Neither of you operates independently, nor do you function without being part of other behavioral patterns.

Going back to this interpersonal difficulty, think about how you may have been triangulated into a struggle that really involved others. For instance, just today I found myself getting mad at my son for not cleaning up his stuff when I really could have cared less about the situation (I have learned to stay out of his room). Upon reflection, I realized that I was really speaking for my wife who had been telling me earlier that she felt hurt that our son wasn't confiding to her about things he had been telling me about. In a sense, my argument with my son had nothing to do with his messy room but I was acting as a surrogate for my wife.

Back to *your* problem, however: Think of a time when you are fairly certain that conflict occurred in your life because of someone else's stubbornness, attitude, or behavior. Identify, as closely and specifically as you can, exactly what this other person did that caused you so much grief or aggravation.

Now, this next part will really stretch you a bit, so be prepared for some resistance. Pretend that *you* had as much to do with this problem as the other person did. I know you don't believe this yet, so just imagine that this is the case. Picture that this conflict developed not because of what this person did to you but rather because of what you did to one another. Put fault and blame aside for a moment and concentrate on the circular pattern of influence that developed between you.

In the particular conflict that you are considering, avoid focusing on what the other person did that annoyed or hurt you and instead look at what you each contributed to the problem. Do this without placing blame. Simply make objective observations just as a mediator might do who was asked to step in and sort things out.

Notice how different the struggle looks when you move away from your usual vantage point and instead adopt a more systemic perspective.

---

10. Families and other systems get stuck in repetitive patterns that restrict their freedom and options to develop more fully functioning ways of interacting with one another and making decisions. Called the redundancy principle (Jackson, 1965), this set of metarules keeps families stuck and dysfunctional. In the course of identifying such family patterns, it is then possible to encourage needed adjustments.

FOR PERSONAL REFLECTION AND A FIELD STUDY

What were some of the metarules in your family? Make a list of some of the unstated laws of your household that were never actually acknowledged overtly. For instance, my brothers and I were told not to fight with one another, but the real rule was just not to fight when our father was around. Next time you get the chance, talk to your siblings in order to compare notes on the unstated rules in your home.

---

11. Symptoms that emerge in families are often useful and functional, operating to maintain a state of equilibrium and stability. Often there is a designated client, the family member who "volunteers" to have the problem in order to rescue or help others. A child, for example, may develop problems in school as a way to keep his or her parents from arguing with one another over their marital conflicts. A wife will become depressed as a way to punish her husband who needs to feel in control all the time. A grandparent will have recurrent physical maladies as way to keep his or her family together. In each case, these are not conscious or manipulative ploys; rather, individual presenting complaints are examined in the context of what good they are doing—for the individual as well as the family system.

■ ■ ■ ■ ■

FOR A FIELD STUDY

Interview several people you know (or classmates) who are experiencing some personal difficulty. Start with the assumption that there is something useful about their symptoms, that they are serving some function (or they wouldn't continue). These "payoffs" were often observed by nurses in their patients who didn't improve rapidly after surgery. It was discovered they were actually enjoying the benefits of being sick, liking the attention they were getting, and wanting to remain helpless so they could avoid returning to lives that were less than satisfactory.

Most commonly, people might "enjoy" their problems because:

1. In a perverse way, it gives them a sense of power and control. ("I am destroying things on my own terms.")
2. They are allowed to avoid responsibility. ("It isn't my fault. Do you think I enjoy being in pain like this?")
3. They are able to procrastinate, put off action, and avoid taking risks. ("I prevent you from getting close and distract you from my issues.")

Help your interviewees to identify what benefits or secondary gains they might be getting out of their problems.

Try applying this same method to yourself when you become aware of some annoying symptom. Ask yourself what payoffs you (or your family) might be enjoying as a result of the problem.

Doing Family Therapy

The experience of conducting a family session is a little like running a circus with two, three, or more different acts going on at the same time. I have seen lots of videotapes of famous folks doing sessions and I am here to tell you that they look nothing like my work. I'd prefer to think that's because they handpicked their best families for demonstration purposes. (Surely, they wouldn't show potential true believers in their system an example in which the family stormed out or started throwing things at one another.) I also think there are certain advantages to doing family work in a training center or university clinic (where they have videotape equipment to make these demonstration videos) when your pals are watching from behind a one-way mirror and can jump in to offer help when it's needed most.

In my experience, I've done a lot of family therapy alone—without the benefit of a co-therapist and a "reflecting team" behind the one-way mirror. And it isn't pretty.

There is a certain elegance to an individual session that is only possible because of the control you can exert. Even in group therapy (which is its own exercise in chaos), it is entirely possible to maintain a semblance of order. But families . . . Let's just say that they can be *very* passionate and expressive. In spite of your best efforts, they will scream at one another. Little kids will scoot about the room and paint on your walls, and all the while their parents watch indulgently. Sometimes combatants must be physically separated from one another in order to make sure that nobody gets hurt. And it is not uncommon that one or more participants will storm out of the room, slamming the door so hard your favorite picture will fall off the wall.

It doesn't sound as though I like this sort of therapy, does it? Or maybe it seems as though I'm trying to scare you off. On the contrary, the wild and wacky world of family therapy is the future of our field. Most therapy will some day be offered in this way. It is more consistent with the preferences of most cultural groups. It often produces results in far more dramatic and brief intervals of time. It is also very exciting and stimulating. I like it a lot, even though I come out of each session exhausted.

From this disclosure (which is quite different from the ways that other professionals might feel), you might deduce the following about doing family therapy:

1. The first thing you have to figure out is with whom you are going to work in the family. Generally, it is best to recruit as many members as possible, but sometimes this isn't practical or desirable. You can even include extended family and friends.
2. You have to join the family in order to make a difference from within. You must earn the trust of all participants, a tricky proposition when each person is competing for your approval.
3. You have to be careful you don't take sides (or are perceived that way) and walk a fine line so that you are seen as fair and objective.
4. You must maintain control over the session or you will quickly lose any credibility and leverage to initiate changes.
5. You must help members to redefine or reframe the problem so that the focus is not only on one problem member but also is located within the whole system.

6. You must be highly active and directive in order to implement interventions.
7. You must look not only at individual dynamics and behavior but also constantly assess interactive patterns within the context of the family's rules and structure.
8. You have to keep things moving. Especially with children present, you can't spend all your time just talking about things. You've got to do stuff, act out issues, and keep everyone involved and engaged.
9. You must get more than the usual amount of supervision with family cases because things are definitely more complex and volatile. Ideally, you will want to work with a more experienced co-therapist when you are first learning the method.

Stages in the Process

Most approaches to family therapy proceed according to a consistent plan that is similar to what you would do in individual sessions but may also be applied differently. You must remember at all times that because there are multiple persons in the room, all with their own agendas, all communicating with each other at all times through nonverbal and verbal means, that the process and dynamics of what unfolds are as important as any content that is discussed.

First Contact.   A lot of information is transmitted during those first minutes of an initial session. Both the therapist and participants form first impressions that shape subsequent sessions so it is very important to be perceived by clients as accessible, knowledgeable, confident, and calm. At the same time that you are busy establishing that first contact with family members and connecting to each person in a way that is intimate and meaningful, you are also observing carefully where they sit in the room, with whom each person interacts the most and least, and what it feels like to be part of this group.

Joining the Family.   The next stage involves developing relationships with family members to build trust and confidence in your work. Unless you can join the family, you can't intervene in a way that will be very influential. This is a difficult challenge because each family member is hoping you will side with him or her and is watching you very carefully to see whom you favor or agree with. It is almost as if you are the new parent who has been "hired," and everyone is watching you cautiously and suspiciously to see what you will do. In this stage you use your warmth, authority, and interpersonal skills to build as many connections as you can with participants.

■ ■ ■ ■ ■ ▬▬▬▬▬▬▬▬▬▬▬▬▬▬▬▬▬▬▬▬▬▬▬▬▬▬▬▬▬

FOR A FIELD STUDY

Interview several clinicians who specialize in family therapy. Find out how they like to work and how they take care of the challenges that have been previously mentioned. How do they maintain control in the room? What do they do if someone confides a secret but forbids them to tell anyone else in the family? How do they handle a family that is so enmeshed that some members are never allowed to express themselves? Find out what they like most and least about family work.

▬▬▬▬▬▬▬▬▬▬▬▬▬▬▬▬▬▬▬▬▬▬▬▬▬▬▬▬▬▬▬▬▬▬▬▬

Assessment.   This is where you form your diagnostic impressions of the family system, as well as that of each member. You check out coalitions, power hierarchy, communication channels, undercurrents, dysfunctional behavior, all in addition to the individual assessments of each person's strengths and weaknesses. What does it feel like to be part of this family? How do they behave together? How do they solve problems? Who seems to be in charge, and who is really in charge? What goals does each member have for a successful outcome? These are just a few of the questions you might consider.

■ ■ ■ ■ ■ ▬▬▬▬▬▬▬▬▬▬▬▬▬▬▬▬▬▬▬▬▬▬▬▬▬▬▬▬▬

FOR A CLASS ACTIVITY

Just for fun, do a simulation of a family session. Organize yourselves in groups of six. Three members of your group will get together and decide the roles they will play (mother, father, adolescent, or single parent with two young children, or grandparent, parent, child) and the issues they will present in session.

Two other group members will act as co-therapists. Your job is simply to help the family members to talk about why they have come for help. You are not to intervene in any way with this "family" but merely to experience what it's like to work with multiple clients who all have their own agendas. You will need to keep people on track and stop them from interrupting one another. Help each person to be heard and tell his or her version of what is going on. You will also be doing a preliminary assessment.

The sixth group member will be an observer outside the group. Your job will be to take notes on the process of what occurs. Pay attention to the structure and dynamics of the family, the roles each person plays. Note the ways the co-therapists work as a team. Write down impressions you have about the session, being as supportive as you can. When the session is over, your job is to debrief everyone and lead a discussion about what transpired and how each person feels about the experience. Remind the co-therapists that they were not supposed to do a "good" job but merely to gain some experience doing a family session in a reasonably safe setting.

Reorientation.   Depending on the theory, this stage might be called a number of different things—reframing, reconceptualizing, redefining the problem, reeducating, accentuating the positive—but what you are actually doing is presenting your initial impression of what you believe is going on. This is a really tricky task because if there is significant disagreement with your assessment, you will be fired. Remember also that there are many different opinions in the room, each of which conflicts with the others. You also have to present your image of what is going on in such a way so that you can actually do something about it. Your first major intervention really is redefining or reframing the problem in such a way that it conforms with what you think is most constructive and lends itself to be resolved most easily.

Let's take as an example a family that comes in consisting of a single mother, her own mother, her youngest sister who also lives with her, and two children, ages 8 and 14. The younger daughter, Kalie, has been identified as the problem: She skips school and hangs out with gang members. When each person is asked what the problem is, they say something such as:

Mother: I work hard so I've not been around as much as Kalie needs me. She just needs more supervision and there's nobody around to give it to her.

Grandmother: Excuse me, dear, but I am in that house more than anyone. What this girl needs is a good whupping. She's just got no discipline. You never taught her nothin' about taking care of her business. You just let her run wild.

Older Sister: Well, I'd have to agree with you, Mother. But I also think that I'm sort of to blame as well. Kalie, we've always been close to one another and, ever since you were little, you've seen me out partying all the time. I think you're just trying to be like me.

Mother's Youngest Sister: Ya'll just bother Kalie too much. You should leave her alone and not make her do this. She's strong and she can fix this on her own. Besides, she ain't the only one with a problem in this family.

Kalie: You got that right! Sure, I got a few problems, but so do the rest of ya'll. Mama, you've been bringing that lowlife home. He's just a drunk and he's gonna beat you like all the others.

And you, Grandmama, you just sit around the house and watch TV all day. You got nothin' to do but worry about others.

Grandmother: You hush now. You show me respect.

Kalie: This lady asked me my opinion so I'm just tellin' it.

Therapist: Go on, Kalie, and finish.

Kalie: I'm tryin' to, if I didn't get interrupted. Nobody else got interrupted. See, that's the thing. They're always on *my* case. . . .

I'm sure you've got a sense of the challenges involved in offering some sort of reorientation of the problem that everyone will accept. You want to move the focus off Kalie and spread the responsibility around to everyone. You want to stop each person from blaming herself or anyone else. And you want to define the situation in a way that you can do something about. In this example, the therapist would, therefore, wish to make the following points:

- "You are a strong family who really cares about one another." Build on strengths and reinforce positive features.
- "You are all concerned about Kalie and her association with older kids who are getting in trouble. Kalie, you've admitted as well that if you don't start going to school, you're going to have a lot more problems." The presenting problem is acknowledged.
- "I also agree with you, Kalie, that this isn't just about you, that all of you are involved with one another and trying to help one another. For instance, earlier Mrs. _____ , you remarked that every time Kalie gets in trouble, it takes your mind off your own troubles. In that way, she's kind of helping you." The focus is widening, taking attention off Kalie, and redefining the problem in a more systemic rather than linear way. This will win Kalie's approval because she doesn't want to be seen as the problem.
- "I'd like to suggest that we start working together, not only by looking at what Kalie has been doing, but how all of you fit into this. That way, we pull together to help Kalie and all of you as well." Notice the use of *we* to emphasize the joined effort.

Structural Realignments.   It is often necessary in dysfunctional families to make some changes in the ways family members interact with one another. This can have to do with the way decisions are made, the way communication takes place, or the underlying power structure of the family. With the family previously mentioned, you can see immediately in the ways they position themselves that there is some structural work to be done. The grandmother sits on one side with the older child. The mother sits with her sister. And Kalie sits by herself.

■ ■ ■ ■ ■

FOR PERSONAL REFLECTION

If you were the therapist, how would you ask the family members to re-seat themselves in a way that would be more consistent with healthy functioning?

Intervention. The relationships have been established. Assessments and treatment planning have been made. Now it is time to do something therapeutic. In family therapy, perhaps even more than in individual therapy, it is critical to take action. This can involve therapeutic activities in the session as well as homework assignments. Depending on which theory is adopted, the intervention can involve an interpretation, a paradoxical directive (you tell the person to do the opposite of what you really want), a family sculpture (having members act out their typical interactions), or an assortment of other strategies. The key here is that you are beginning to help family members communicate with one another in more constructive ways and to initiate changes in the ways they deal with one another.

In Conclusion

Family therapy is more difficult than individual or group sessions. It requires more training, more preparation, and more supervision. The theories are distinctly different from those that evolved from models of individual practice, even though they have the same shared professional history.

When individuals need to separate and individuate from their families, it is often not as helpful to work with the whole family as the single client. Similarly, there are times when family members can't abide by the most basic rules of civilized conduct and the situation is too volatile to conduct family sessions.

There are practitioners who are licensed as family therapists in some states and believe that this is the way to go with every case. There are also clinicians who do family work only occasionally, believing that it is best suited for those situations in which the nature of the presenting problem is particularly systemic in origin. There are still other therapists who almost never see couples or families together, believing that you can do your best work seeing one person at a time. Some have said that all therapy is family therapy, no matter who actually attends the sessions, because when you change one person, you end up influencing the whole system.

It is beyond the scope of this chapter to cover all the facets of systemic theory and their applications. That is one reason you will likely receive specialized training in family therapy, marriage counseling, sex counseling, and organizational development, depending on your career goals and professional interests. You will find it useful to consult additional sources at some later time to familiarize yourself more completely with the theory in this important discipline (see Brock & Barnard, 1999; Gladding, 1998; Goldenberg & Goldenberg, 2001; Nichols & Schwartz, 1998).

SUGGESTED READINGS

Anderson, W. T. (1990). *Reality isn't what it used to be.* San Francisco: HarperCollins.

Baruth, L. G., & Manning, M. L. (1999). *Multicultural counseling and psychotherapy* (2nd ed.). Upper Saddle River, NJ: Merrill.

Becvar, D. S., & Becvar, R. J. (1999). *Family therapy: A systemic integration* (4th ed.). Boston: Allyn and Bacon.

Family Therapy Networker. Washington, DC: Family Therapy Network.

Gladding, S. T. (1998). *Family therapy: History, theory, and practice* (2nd ed.). Upper Saddle River, NJ: Prentice-Hall.

Goldenberg, I., & Goldenberg, H. (2001). *Family therapy: An overview* (5th ed.). Pacific Grove, CA: Brooks/Cole.

McGoldrick, M., Gerson, R., & Shellenberger, S. (1999). *Genograms: Assessment and intervention* (2nd ed.). New York: W. W. Norton.

Napier, A., & Whitaker, C. (1978). *The family crucible.* New York: Harper and Row.

Neimeyer, R. A., & Mahoney, M. J. (1995). *Constructivism in psychotherapy.* Washington, DC: American Psychological Association.

Nichols, M. P., & Schwartz, R. C. (1998). *Family therapy: Concepts and methods* (4th ed.). Boston: Allyn and Bacon.

Rosen, R. C., & Leiblum, S. R., (1995). *Case studies in sex therapy.* New York: Guilford Press.

Sue, W. S., Ivey, A. E., & Pedersen, P. B. (1996). *A theory of multicultural counseling and therapy.* Pacific Grove, CA: Brooks/Cole.

Winslade, J., & Monk, G. (2000). *Narrative mediation: A new approach to conflict resolution.* San Francisco: Jossey-Bass.

Young, M., & Long, L. (1998). *Counseling and therapy for couples.* Pacific Grove, CA: Brooks/Cole.

CHAPTER 9

PROBLEMS AND SOLUTIONS

Brief Approaches

Any theory that you have already studied most likely has an abbreviated version that is designed for brief intervention. Even those approaches that were originally conceived as long-term therapies have since been recast as more efficient models that can make a difference in a matter of weeks rather than years. As the most dramatic example of this, psychoanalytic approaches have traditionally taken years of treatment in order to be considered effective whereas now there have been models designed to produce results in a matter of months or even weeks (Bellak, 1992; Book, 1998; Borden, 1999; Davanloo, 1980; Horowitz, 1988; Malan, 1976; Mann, 1973; Sifneos, 1987; Wolberg, 1980). The same pattern has followed course for other insight-oriented and relationship-steeped approaches.

At one time it was thought that in order to do "good" therapy, meaning the kind that deals with underlying issues and long-term gains, the process must necessarily take considerable time. In many cases, however, dramatic and enduring results are possible within a matter of weeks rather than years. Sometimes, even a single encounter can be life altering.

In the story of how he went through profound structural changes as a result of a session with Milton Erickson, Mahoney (1997) describes the process he experienced as a result of a relatively brief interaction that has had enduring effects throughout his life. He believes that core changes in his being took place primarily because of his own readiness for such a transformation. "In my session with Milton Erickson, the life-changing potential of our meeting was almost guaranteed by the fact that I was facing an imminent career decision, the consequences of which were neither clear nor calculable" (Mahoney, 1997, p. 35). Thus, he points out that the amount of time that people actually need to change depends much less on the length of therapy than it does on the exact pattern and form that those treatment moments take.

■ ■ ■ ■ ■

FOR PERSONAL REFLECTION

Think about a time in your life in which you were irrevocably changed as a result of a single conversation or encounter. One minute you were merrily going about your normal life, doing the same things you always do, and then—wham!—things no longer seemed the same.

What was it about this experience that was so impactful, not only in the short run but over the long haul? How was it possible for you to make changes in your life in such a short period of time?

BRIEF THERAPY DEFINED

What is considered brief to some can seem interminable to others. To someone in prison, whether metaphorically or physically locked in a cell, each minute passes with excruciating slowness. The prospect of waiting months, or even weeks, for relief of symptoms may seem like a life sentence with no hope of parole.

Any number of therapists and counselors may promise to do brief treatment, but their claims may be based on a relative standard that depends on their own perceptions of swiftness. A certain practitioner of self-psychology, a contemporary revision of Freud's work, sees clients for an average of six months to a year, which represents considerable brevity when compared to his own seven-year analysis while in training. Another clinician who favors a cognitive approach considers three to six months to be about average for successful treatment but also applies an abbreviated method aimed at ten to twelve sessions.

■ ■ ■ ■ ■

FOR A CLASS ACTIVITY

In small groups, get together and plan a brief version of this class. Imagine that rather than having a whole semester to complete the material and learn all the theories, you must complete this assignment in a mere three sessions (four hours each) spread out in monthly intervals. Before you scoff that this is impossible, consider that for a period of time therapists and counselors didn't even take a class in this subject at all.

It would also be helpful to think outside the usual conventions of traditional educational methods. Throw out what you think you already know about the way therapist training takes place and start over in such a way that you can capitalize best on your limited structure and time allocated.

Construct a curriculum, a class structure, and plan of action that is both realistic and yet ambitious. Keep your goals within reasonable limits. Define what you would need to do differently in such a format. Discuss the advantages as well as disadvantages of such a program.

Brief therapy is defined not so much by the exact number of sessions (ranging from three to thirty) but whether the time limit is established from the outset. In addition, these two conditions are usually followed (Messer & Wachtel, 1997):

1. There are a specific focus and defined treatment outcome.
2. Clients are usually screened carefully as to their suitability for limited treatment. Brief therapy works best with acute, specific symptoms rather than chronic conditions.

Any theoretical approach can be abbreviated according to these preconditions. How quickly you operate depends on your own inventiveness and the client's willingness and openness to change.

Changing Landscape of Practice

When I first began practicing a few decades ago, most middle-class individuals had health insurance that paid for 50 percent, 75 percent, or even 90 percent of whatever was charged for therapy. This included up to fifty sessions per year with no lifetime limit! Today a person is lucky to be approved for a dozen sessions, and even that requires heaps of paperwork and begging.

In today's climate, practitioners have been forced to operate more efficiently, to justify and defend their treatment plans, and to demonstrate the effectiveness of their interventions. This has not been an altogether bad development in the field. We are now held to be more accountable for our actions, to support our efforts with solid research, to follow best practices that have been established, and to meet the needs of consumers. We are now forced to adapt the concepts of any sound business and to be cost-effective in our services. This means that we can help a much wider range of people, and we can do so reliably and swiftly.

On the other hand, some of us mourn the loss of those days when we could do relationship-oriented, insight-focused work for those who wanted to come to terms with their past or who wished to better understand themselves and their behavior. They may have arrived in our offices originally because of some disturbing problem, but they often remained after the symptoms were addressed in order to examine the core issues or find greater meaning in their lives. This was a time when the average length of treatment was six months to a year, and it was not at all uncommon for even working-class clients to attend sessions for three years or longer. There were days when school counselors were actually allowed to do counseling for as long as they deemed necessary and when clinicians in agencies were permitted to decide for themselves, in conjunction with supervisors, how long treatment should last.

We now live in a time in which review boards, quality assurance committees, and managed care providers decide what you can do and how long you can do it. Depending on the diagnosis you report, you may be allocated three, or five, or perhaps eight sessions in which to alleviate symptoms. Furthermore, you may be mandated to apply a particular treatment approach that has been found successful in the past with this type of problem and situation.

No matter where you work, what sort of specialty you develop, and what your career goals might be, it is clear that you must become proficient in some form of brief therapy. Regardless of what your employer and profession may require of you in the future, it is your clients who feel most grateful if you can, under the right circumstances, intervene quickly and effectively to alleviate their suffering.

The Theory behind Brief Therapies

Not all the proponents of brief methods are enamored with the value of theory, which some find gets in the way of more pragmatic, innovative methods. If you remember, however, that a theory is not an exact blueprint but rather a rough guide to follow, you can appreciate that everyone needs such a model in order to make good decisions about what you believe is going on, what you think needs to be done, and how you might best go about taking care of business. Although some of the brief models examined here tend to downplay theory in lieu of best practices that work, you would be well advised as beginners to do more than merely learn a set of clever interventions and techniques.

Any of the theories previously presented in this book could be useful to you as a guiding framework, combined with any others reviewed later. Of course, you will notice some contradictions among them, as well as some outright opposing forces, but these can be worked through if you keep an open mind and nimble attitude.

■ ■ ■ ■ ■

FOR A FIELD STUDY

Identify several practitioners who do mostly long-term work, meaning that they see people for longer than a few weeks and sometimes up to several years. You will find these professionals mostly in private practice, but some may work in mental health and community agencies that have a flexible policy or more disturbed client populations. You will also find them more among psychiatrists, psychologists, and social workers than you will among family therapists and counselors, but much depends on their type of job and training.

In spite of their preference for doing long-term therapy, it is likely that they are also frequently called upon to do brief interventions with clients who can only come for a few sessions. Find out how they adapt their theory and methods to fit the demands of this type of work.

Rather than just speaking hypothetically, ask for specific case examples in which someone came in for only one or two sessions, and this was the plan agreed upon from the beginning. How did the clinician reconcile this brief relationship with his or her dominant theory?

In this chapter we review only those therapeutic models that were originally designed as brief treatments. Each of these frameworks provides the practitioner with a fairly detailed and structured plan for what to do with clients when time is very limited. They are certainly not appropriate for every person who walks in, but even if you must (or choose to) do longer-term work, you will still find many of the strategies to be useful.

Each of the approaches to be covered holds in common the following premises:

- Therapy and counseling need not take a long time in order to be helpful.
- Treatment objectives tend to be specific, limited, and realistic.
- The clinician needs to take a fairly active, directive role in designing and implementing interventions.
- Practitioners adopt flexible, experimental mind-sets that allow them to respond rapidly and decisively to changing circumstances.
- The focus of sessions tends to be on present problems rather than past events.
- The most important work takes place outside of sessions during structured homework assignments.

- Most problems are looked at in terms of their larger systemic context.
- Sessions are scheduled flexibly and strategically so as to maximize therapeutic gains.
- Insight and relationship factors are often minimized in favor of action methods.

Regarding this last point, some of the proponents of brief therapy (those of the Milton Erickson school) are quite vehement that insight is not only unnecessary but also possibly counterproductive in that it gives people excuses for avoiding change: "I can't help it. I had an unhappy childhood caused by my abusive mother and neglectful father."

In an article entitled "Insight May Cause Blindness," Watzlawick (1997) argues that in today's climate we don't have time to wallow in the reasons for our problems. Furthermore, although once a practicing Jungian analyst, he can't think of a single instance in which a client having an insight actually produced any sort of magical effect. He cites as a metaphor for the state of the more popular theories in our field the case of a man who compulsively claps his hands every few seconds. When asked why he engages in this behavior, he responds it's to keep the elephants away. It is next pointed out to him that there aren't any elephants in the vicinity, to which he replies: "See, it's working."

Watzlawick (1997) offers four possible ways that this man might be helped:

1. Establish a trusting relationship with the man until he changes his mind about elephants being a problem.
2. Analyze the man's past to discover the unconscious reasons for this symptom.
3. Bring elephants into the session to prove to him that his clapping doesn't keep them away.
4. Break one of his hands so that while encased in a plaster cast, he will be unable to clap.

Surely you will recognize some of the theories you studied in the approaches just listed. Watzlawick is quick to point out that he would never advocate breaking someone's hand in order to stop a person from clapping, but neither would he do any of the other things. At least the last one, he argues, would probably work. This might strike you as an extreme position to take with regard to the role (or lack thereof) of insight in brief therapy approaches, but it is typical of some of the more recent models that are designed for one thing and one thing only: efficient removal of a client's symptoms.

FOR A CLASS ACTIVITY

In small groups, organize a debate in which each of you takes one of the following positions:

1. Insight is a necessary condition for *real* change to take place at the deepest possible level. Unless you take care of the underlying problem and understand its origins, symptoms will just come up in another form. Those who do not understand history are doomed to repeat the mistakes of the past.
2. Insight is desirable with most clients most of the time but is usually not enough to promote lasting changes by itself. There has got to be some kind of action component as part of therapy.
3. Insight is, at best, irrelevant, and at worst, a distraction from the real work in therapy. All too often, people use their self-awareness or understanding as a defense to avoid changing.
4. Insight is actually quite dangerous. People already spend too much time thinking about their problems and blaming themselves for what happened and why. The best strategy is to forget about the past and to move on.

After each person presents an initial argument for his or her position (maximum two minutes), you are invited to spend another ten minutes debating one another. A moderator should make sure that everyone gets an equitable share of time and that no one person on the panel is allowed to monopolize the discussion.

Next, another few minutes can be devoted to members of the audience questioning positions that they find unconvincing or unsupportive.

After the debate is completed, spend time talking to one another about how your own ideas have crystallized or changed as a result of this discussion.

Some Brief History

The first brief therapists would not have labeled themselves as such. Although several of Freud's disciples, notably Otto Frank and Alfred Adler, were impatient with his slow, laborious process of delving into the unconscious, they would only have been considered brief when compared to their mentor. Yet even Freud practiced brief therapy on occasion, as noted by his biographer who documented his work with the prominent composer, Gustav Mahler. In a single, lengthy session of four hours, Freud successfully treated Mahler's impotency problem (Jones, 1961).

When other situations presented themselves, he was also known to abbreviate his therapy to a half dozen sessions (Messer & Warren, 1995).

Dozens of analysts from that first generation of protégés attempted to experiment with ways that they could shorten the amount of time needed to promote a cure. Many of the most familiar names mentioned in this book, such as Fritz Perls, Albert Ellis, William Glasser, Carl Rogers, and so on, were all committed to operating more efficiently and devised schools of thought that became influential in their own right.

From the beginning of the family therapy movement as well, its practitioners created therapeutic structures that could be implemented in shorter time periods. Murray Bowen (1966) and Nathan Ackerman (1958), in particular, launched the whole family therapy movement by emphasizing not only its greater power but also its efficiency.

Brief therapy, as we know it today, essentially began with the work of Milton Erickson (1954) and his protégé, Jay Haley (1967, 1973), who interpreted and popularized his methods. Haley had already been working with others who were experimenting with briefer methods for treating schizophrenia (Bateson, Jackson, Haley, & Weakland, 1956), when he came upon Erickson's hypnotic methods. After acting as the biographer for Erickson's strategies, Haley (1976) began developing a brief, problem-solving therapy of his own, as did several of his colleagues (Watzlawick, Weakland, & Fisch, 1974). Eventually teaming up (marrying and later divorcing) with Cloe Madanes (1981), Haley developed a strategic method for working with difficult adolescents and families that used the kinds of paradoxical techniques he learned from Erickson.

Essentially, if you ask people to do something directly (e.g., Stop eating so much) and they keep engaging in the same behavior, the next line of attack is to try the opposite: Prescribe the same symptoms that they are already showing. This paradoxical intervention, actually designed to be disobeyed, would often provoke changes in the entrenched dysfunctional patterns.

Haley also spent some time working with another family therapist, Salvador Minuchin, who was a specialist in working with inner-city families in Philadelphia. Whereas Haley had been emphasizing hypnotic methods and paradoxical directives (linguistically based) to disrupt the person's self-defeating process, once he collaborated with Minuchin, he began looking at underlying organizational structures (Cade & O'Hanlon, 1993).

Minuchin (Minuchin & Fishman, 1981) was also finding success with a brief method of structural therapy, but his approach examined and altered the hierarchies of power in family relationships. At its simplest level, he might notice that as a family entered the office, they aligned themselves according to their coalitions just by their seating arrangement. A family of four walks in the room, for example. The mother sits between her two children on one couch, while the father sits alone on the other. Minuchin would immediately rearrange this configuration, asking the two parents to sit together, thus realigning the coalitions within the family. Such strategic and structural interventions devised by Haley and Minuchin and others revolutionized the ways that therapy could be done. Rather than merely talking about problems, the clinician actually intervened to disrupt the underlying organizational structure.

Individual theorists such as Albert Ellis, William Glasser, and Carl Rogers also were experiencing success in their methods that were designed for less than a dozen sessions. With contributions from behavioral, cognitive, Gestalt, and other approaches, it was firmly established that solid, lasting changes could indeed be initiated within briefer time periods than could ever have been imagined. Regardless of the specific approach that is used, it has since been demonstrated that the majority of clients can indeed achieve their treatment objectives within five to ten sessions, especially if their therapists believe that such gains are possible and plan for such effects from the beginning (Asay & Lambert, 1999).

It's difficult to know which was the chicken and which was the egg: Did models of brief practice evolve in response to the demands of managed care, or did health organizations begin requiring shorter treatments once they became available as an option? Regardless of which preceded the other, it is now clear that we live and work in an era of managed care in which increased accountability and briefer treatments are the orders of the day (Chambliss, 2000).

Among the time-limited models that have been developed in recent years are those that fall into several main groups: (1) Ericksonian hypnotherapy, (2) problem-solving therapies, (3) solution-focused treatments, and (4) planned single-session therapy.

ERICKSONIAN HYPNOTHERAPY

There are few therapists outside of Freud and Rogers who have exerted more dramatic influence on practitioners than Milton Erickson. This was a man who rarely wrote anything and had little interest in traveling around promoting his ideas to others. Instead, people made the pilgrimage to visit him in order to learn his methods, which have been called a form of magic and wizardry.

A Typical Erickson Story

Erickson struggled with a physical handicap that confined him to a wheelchair throughout most of his life. As a young man, before beginning medical school, he decided to take some time off to canoe in the wilderness of

Canada. The paddling of a boat is no great challenge for a man without functioning legs, especially for one with such highly developed upper body strength, but portaging the canoe, or transporting it over land and across dams, is certainly a major obstacle for someone who can't walk.

Rather than asking for direct help when he encountered a dam, Erickson decided to experiment with indirect ways to solicit assistance. He wondered how successfully he could get people to offer to carry his canoe across obstacles without him having to ask them. He, thus, devised a number of routines that seemed especially effective in getting people to volunteer. From these humble beginnings, Erickson began thinking of ways he could help people with personal problems without approaching them directly. Why, he reasoned, was it necessary to deal with resistance and defensiveness if you could bypass all that and just change people at a preconscious level?

Based on the limited writings of Erickson (1954, 1964) in mostly hypnosis journals about a new technique, and later in a series of personal interviews, Jay Haley (1973) sought to chronicle Erickson's therapeutic adventures. There have since been hundreds, perhaps thousands, of stories told about the amazing things that Erickson could do with so-called hopeless cases, but perhaps one representative example involves a catatonic schizophrenic who hadn't moved a muscle in many years. He just sat there, immobile, staring off into space from morning until night.

Erickson approached the frozen patient and sat down next to him. Unlike other therapists, he didn't attempt to speak with him or engage him in conversation, which he knew would be fruitless after so many others before him had tried and failed. He just sat with the man for awhile, considering that about the only thing he was doing that could be described as a behavior was breathing. Because Erickson could not establish rapport with him, or any kind of connection, by talking to him, he decided to breathe with the patient. He simply matched the pace of his breathing to that of this bricklike human. He timed his inhalations and exhalations to the exact same rhythm of his companion.

After a period of time, Erickson gradually started to slow the rate of his breathing and he noticed an amazing thing happen: The catatonic slowed *his* breathing, too! Next, Erickson imperceptibly began increasing his rate of breathing and the man matched him as well. Now they were in a sort of collusion, even if the patient wasn't consciously aware of what was going on. They went along that way for some time, with Erickson leading their interaction, and the patient following him.

When after some hours, Erickson turned to the patient and asked him if he'd like a cigarette, the patient spoke aloud the first words anyone had heard in a long time. They had begun a dialogue with breathing and then eventually began talking with their voices. This was typical of the creative and unusual ways that Erickson would attempt to make contact with people. Dozens of well-known therapists from Virginia Satir and Michael Mahoney to Jay Haley have similar stories to tell of the miracles they have witnessed.

The Antitheorist

The major feature about Erickson is that he was really an *antitheorist*—he just didn't believe in theories. He was interested in only results, the ultimate pragmatist. He'd leave it up to others to explain what he did; he would concentrate his efforts instead on helping people to change. That turned out to be a fine state of affairs because others such as Haley (1984), Satir (1972), Bandler and Grinder (1975), and Zeig (1982, 1985) would explain and promote his ideas.

Erickson certainly introduced some very novel ideas to the practice of therapy, the most controversial of which was probably an altered therapist's stance. You will recall that most other therapeutic approaches advocate a professional role that is collaborative, open, straightforward, authentic, and transparent. Then Erickson comes along (or rather was discovered operating in the Arizona desert) and he conceived of a new sense of therapist power based on the following ideas (Gilligan, 1997):

1. The therapist knows stuff that the client does not know. As such, the therapist is an expert.
2. There are certain things the therapist knows that the client does not need to know. It isn't necessary to explain what you are doing, or even for the client to understand what is going on.
3. The therapist is entitled to use what he or she knows to influence the client in ways that are believed to be helpful, without necessarily recruiting the client's cooperation and support along the way.
4. Being deceptive or manipulative are ethical and acceptable if they are used for the client's own good.

■ ■ ■ ■ ■ ▬▬▬▬▬▬▬▬▬▬▬▬▬▬▬▬▬▬▬▬▬▬▬

FOR PERSONAL REFLECTION

Do you believe that it is moral and appropriate to manipulate or trick clients into doing things (for their own good) without their consent? How would you respond to the arguments presented that all therapists engage in such deception whether they admit it or not?

You can see just how radical a vision of therapy can be under this framework. Certainly not all brief therapists, or Ericksonian therapists, subscribe to this idea that it is okay to be deceptive, but almost all of them resort to some form of subtle manipulation to "trick" clients into changing. Furthermore, advocates would argue that even someone such as Rogers was actually being manipulative and *conditionally* accepting when he chose to lead, guide, and direct clients to talk about their feelings in particular ways while ignoring other aspects of their communication that he didn't see as important.

Fisch (1982) was most incisive in describing Erickson's contributions to brief therapy by highlighting what he did *not* do in his work. He didn't:

1. Take detailed histories or delve into the past.
2. Restrict himself to a prearranged time period for sessions.
3. Get people to talk about their feelings.
4. Interpret behavior or bring attention to resistance.
5. Oppose or argue with clients.

If this is what he did *not* do in sessions, what he *did* do was the following (Bloom, 1997):

1. Stayed with the present rather than the past.
2. Explored thoroughly the presenting problem—when, where, and with whom it occurred.
3. Looked for exceptions when the problem did *not* occur.
4. Designed arduous tasks for clients to complete that were sometimes worse than the problems themselves.
5. Prescribed paradoxical directives to clients that were designed to be disobeyed.
6. Ignored the role of insight completely, believing that it was a waste of time, if not dangerous.
7. Favored the use of hypnosis to bypass resistance.
8. Adapted traditional methods to follow the basic procedure: ask the person to do something he or she is already doing.
9. Asked the person to do something voluntarily.
10. Used metaphors to approach problems indirectly.

As you can readily see, the Ericksonian style of therapy was indeed a radical departure from other theories practiced at the time. Just as with most influential ideas in our field, the best contributions from this approach (i.e., looking for exceptions) have now been infused into almost all forms of practice.

Limitations and Contraindications

It may immediately occur to you that, as powerful as these methods might be, there are some problems associated with their application in real-life situations. First of all, when a therapist assumes complete and total responsibility for outcomes and believes that he or she knows what is best for people, there is a greater danger of casualties.

I have been to many workshops on this type of treatment (and the ones that follow). I continue to be amazed, even spellbound by the drama and magic of these interventions. I watch demonstrations in videos and on stage, showing the methods in action in which people are transformed before my very eyes. Yet I have also found that when I take the methods back to my own practice, I don't get quite the same results. Of course, one would expect this considering that I have neither the experience nor the support team to back up my efforts. It is one thing to use intrusive, powerful methods when you have a team of observers behind a one-way mirror who can call in suggestions and feedback when you get stuck. It is quite another challenge to operate in solo practice. My point is that the more powerful the interventions used, the more careful you must be to use them within the scope of your practice and with the quality and quantity of supervision available.

PROBLEM-SOLVING TREATMENTS

Continuing the work of Erickson and expanding his hypnotic methods to more mainstream practice, Haley (1963, 1984, 1987) and several colleagues (Madanes, 1981, 1984; Watzlawick, 1978) developed a systematic method for solving client problems. Eventually working under the auspices of the Mental Research Institute (MRI) in California, Haley and colleagues began looking at human problems from the perspective of their communication patterns.

Some premises of this strategic, problem-solving approach were mostly derived from Erickson's work and were combined with the burgeoning field of family systems therapy, as well as the MRI team's own creativity and inventiveness.

In this approach there was no real interest in theory but rather in the pragmatics of finding what works with a given person. Problems must be examined in terms of what they are expressing and communicating in the context of their larger system. A child who has stomachaches, for instance, may be "speaking" on behalf of others in the family. One of the effects of these symptoms is that it stops bickering parents from arguing with one another long enough to address their child's needs. Problems are, thus, seen as functional and helpful in some ways.

There are several other assumptions of the problem-solving approach:

1. There is a much greater likelihood of resolving difficulties if they are defined in a way that says they can be solved.

2. The therapist, as the expert, is clearly the one who is responsible for devising and implementing a plan of action. You will note this is a marked departure from the more collaborative models you studied earlier.

3. Small changes lead to big changes. If you can get the client to make a little adjustment in the way things are done, leverage has been created to keep the momentum going. For example, a client who can't seem to lose weight could be ordered to *gain* one pound, just to prove that weight changes are within one's control.

4. There is no such thing as client resistance in this approach because all people are seen as doing the best they can. When therapists are frustrated, because clients aren't doing what they expect or cooperating in ways therapists prefer, this is called noncompliance.

THE STRATEGIC PROCESS

There is a logical, sequential series of stages to problem-solving therapy that begins with collecting data. This is not unlike what happens in any therapeutic approach except that the kinds of information collected are specific and focused. The problem-solving therapist will not delve much into the past, except to find out when the symptoms were most and least disturbing, as well as what has worked and what has not worked before.

Reframing the Problem

Regardless of the theoretical approach you eventually adopt, reframing is one of those concepts that has universal value with almost any client and situation. As you would imagine, clients come into sessions with their own views about what the problem is and what needs to be done to fix it. I can say with confidence that usually this perspective is not only illogical, distorted, and counterproductive, but also it is almost impossible to make things better if you accept things as they are presented.

"My husband is the problem," a new client will tell you. "He's just lazy and inconsiderate." Even if this were the case that the husband did demonstrate these qualities almost all the time (which is highly unlikely because he would have a different perspective), what could you do to fix the matter? By implication, the way the client is defining the problem, you would dismiss her from treatment, bring in the husband, and then somehow make him less lazy and inconsiderate. This is extremely improbable that you would even get the husband to come in under these terms, much less change his behavior because his wife doesn't like him the way he is.

Instead, what you might do is negotiate with the client, reformulate the problem in a way that is acceptable to her, and also cast it in a form that makes it easier to change. Of course, you can't outright dismiss the client's definition or you will get fired, so you have to be somewhat clever in the ways you reframe it: "It sounds like what you're saying is that you haven't been as effective as you would like in getting your needs met in this relationship."

That is just the starting point for your reframed problem definition. The client prefers to put blame and responsibility on her husband, whereas you would like to work on an issue that is more within your power to change. Because, according to this approach, there is no such thing as resistance but only ineffectiveness on the part of the therapist in selling a particular idea, it is your job to recast things in a more helpful light.

- When a client talks about the frustration he feels in overcoming some obstacle, that can be reframed as a challenge to be overcome.
- When someone talks about her coworkers who are sabotaging her project, that can be reframed as them trying to help in ways that are different from what she prefers.
- When a man says that he is shy and that's why he doesn't have any friends, you can help him to see that he sometimes *acts* shyly (but not always).

■ ■ ■ ■ ■

FOR A CLASS ACTIVITY

Whether you ever identify yourself as a problem-solving therapist, I can't stress enough how important it is for you to master the skill of reframing. If you can't redefine the presenting problem in a way that you can do something to be helpful, your efforts are likely to be wasted. Often the simple act of offering another perspective on things has a significant impact on the client's perceptions of his or her situation.

Working with a partner, either in class or on your own, brainstorm several different ways that you could reframe the following presenting complaints:

- A kid insists that she's getting bad grades because she's stupid.
- A couple who is experiencing sexual difficulties (he is impotent, she has little sexual desire) blame one another for the problems.
- An older man tells you that he has nothing to live for because his children and grandchildren never visit him much anymore.

In each case, you are trying to acknowledge the client's view of things but are also suggesting alternative ways to look at the situation to be more consistent with what you can offer.

Advance Preparation

Because many problem-solving directives are designed to be challenging, the hardest task is to get clients to comply with the therapeutic tasks. Clients must be motivated and prepared for what they are about to do. Often subtle or playful approaches help. Following Erickson's lead, problem-solving therapists might be inclined to say something such as the following:

"I have a cure for your troubles but I sense you aren't ready for it just yet."

Of course, the client then begs for the solution, but the therapist will not give in. "Perhaps next week, if I think you are ready, I will give you the cure then."

The following week, the client comes in eager and impatient for the promised cure. "Okay, okay, so what have you got for me?"

"I still don't think you are quite ready yet," the therapist counters. "What you will have to do is very distasteful and difficult and I just don't think you are committed to follow through on what I ask you to do."

"Oh, but I am, I am," the client whines. "Please, can we do it now?"

"I want you to think about things until next week, decide just how ready you are to do what must be done," the therapist responds. Obviously, by the following week, the client is ready to do almost anything that the therapist asks—even if the tasks are abhorrent. This increases the likelihood of compliance, although it does not guarantee such cooperation.

Directives

Haley (1984) has said, more than a little facetiously, that the object of therapy is to provide experiences that are so distasteful that clients will cure themselves so they don't have to return again. He is quite serious, actually, when he orders couples who fight too much to set their alarms at 3:00 A.M. and schedule an argument for not less than forty-five minutes. The object of these ordeals is to cause levels of distress that exceed those caused by the original problem. Of course, in order for this to work, the clients must be "sold" on the method or they won't do it.

Accentuate the Positive

Many different systems of brief therapy have a policy of asking clients not only what is going wrong in their lives but also what is going right. This means looking for exceptions to those times when the person is debilitated by the symptoms.

A man complains constantly about the effects of a stroke that has left him paralyzed on one side and with numerous cognitive dysfunctions that impair his memory, perceptions, and reasoning abilities. He feels life is hopeless because he is always a victim of this terrible misfortune.

"Always a victim?" the therapist asks him softly.

"Excuse me?" the client answers.

"I asked you if you were *always* miserable as a result of your stroke. I wondered if there was ever a time, even for single minute, when you feel reasonably good. Was there a time today, for instance, when you smiled or laughed at something?"

"Well, yeah, I guess. I had a delicious meal on the way over here. And I saw my grandson. . . ."

"So, all in all, it has been a fairly pleasant morning for you. You have managed to overcome the symptoms of your stroke and act as if you are someone capable of being quite content."

Clients often think that their job is to come into sessions and tell you all the things going wrong in their lives. This includes every complaint imaginable, every injustice, and every single disappointment or setback. If you let this continue, the conversation will easily be filled up with a litany of such annoyances. The client will use therapy as a dumping ground, which can sometimes be useful but often can make things worse.

When you accentuate the positive, you attempt to reposition clients in a place where they are taking a more balanced view toward their lives. There are failures but also successes. There are disappointments but also some progress. Your job is to make that clear.

Predict a Relapse

Although there are many other strategic interventions, the last one I will mention is quite clever and also has universal application to a wide variety of situations. One of the ways that you can prevent continued relapses is to predict that they will occur so that the client is not unduly alarmed or unprepared.

Just after a client has made significant progress, I like to say something such as:

"I can see that you are really excited about what you have done and feeling really proud of your accomplishment. I applaud your efforts and think you have made wonderful progress. I must warn you, however, that the effects will not last."

This gets the client's attention in a big way. A look of worry appears, sometimes even panic.

"Just because you experience some setbacks is no big deal, however. Just as I know that you will fall flat on your face, I also know that you have the ability to pick yourself back up—if you choose to do so. The beauty of what you have learned is that you can take a step backward and still not lose sight of where you are headed. You can apply what you have learned again and again."

This pep talk prepares the client for inevitable backsliding. When you predict a relapse, one of two things will happen. Either you will seem like a magician because what you said would happen did indeed occur, or you will be proven wrong. If the former, the client has been warned and prepared ahead of time. If you are wrong, then there is really nothing lost.

SOLUTION-FOCUSED THERAPY

Also derived from Erickson's influence, solution-focused therapists such as William O'Hanlon (1993) and Steve de Shazer (1985, 1991) operate very creatively and pragmatically. One difference, however, between this approach and the previous one is that rather than taking on the role of an expert to fix the problem, the solution-focused therapist represents himself or herself as a consultant. This approach takes the line of inquiry that the client is already an expert on the problem and just needs a little help to redirect efforts in more constructive directions. The therapist functions as an assistant in the change process, helping the client to plan and implement his or her own change efforts (Chevalier, 1995).

Major Premises

The theory behind this approach is rather simple: (1) If something isn't broken, don't fix it, (2) if it works, do more of it, (3) if it doesn't work, do something else (Quick, 1996). There is no attempt to understand how and why the problem developed, only to fix it. This strategy is shared by most brief therapists who have neither the time nor the inclination to explore deeper meanings.

There is also no interest in psychopathology or individual intrapsychic dysfunction, only interactional behavior that was mishandled. It should be noted, for example, that two parents who described their 3-year-old as a "monster" got very different reactions, depending how they responded to their child when he first woke up.

Although the solution-focused approach, as well as other brief approaches, minimizes the value of theory, there are actually several implicit theoretical assumptions in its practice (O'Hanlon & Weiner-Davis, 1989; Walter & Peller, 1994):

1. It is an optimistic view of human beings and their abilities to resolve their own difficulties (similar to a humanistic perspective).
2. It keeps a positive attitude throughout, continuing to concentrate on what is going right rather than what is going wrong.

3. It remains in the present at all times, continuing to look at the presenting problem and its consequences (similar to reality therapy).
4. It sees the client's perception of reality as a constructed rather than an external phenomenon (similar to narrative and constructivist approaches).
5. It continues to address limited, concrete, specific goals (similar to the behavioral approach).
6. Because change is inevitable and continuous, the best approach is one that capitalizes on gradual shifts and small, incremental steps in problem solving (similar to shaping in behavior therapy).
7. Making a small alteration in behavior affects and leads to changes in other parts of the system (similar to any systemic approach).

Stay Flexible

The clinician adopts a very flexible approach to therapeutic work. Essentially, the following formula is followed:

- If the client completes a straightforward task, give another one.
- If the client modifies a task, offer an easily changeable task that is ambiguous.
- If the client doesn't complete homework, don't give more homework.
- If the client does the opposite of what is asked, give paradoxical directives.

In other words, stay loose and flexible, altering your interventions in response to how clients behave. This may sound logical and reasonable, yet many clinicians stick with their favorite interventions regardless of the outcome. For example, my absolute favorite strategy is to use a skill called immediacy whereby I describe and reflect what is going on in the session as it is happening. This is an extremely powerful, evocative intervention and I love the way it brings attention to the immediate moment.

I notice that a client is beginning to withdraw just as he is talking about his problems with intimacy in relationships. I smile to myself because now I know I've got him red-handed.

"I see that right this moment . . . [I pause for dramatic effect] . . . just as you are talking about your difficulty getting close to people . . . [I see a sick look on his face, which I ignore because I'm so enjoying this brilliant observation] . . . you are pulling away from me."

In response to this insightful comment, the client visibly withdraws further. He actually leans way back in the chair and wraps his arms around his knees in a protective pose. So, what do I do?

I ignore the cues that are staring me right in the face because, after all, this is my favorite intervention, and I try another use of immediacy.

In other words, I try exactly the same thing again, which clearly didn't work, because I am committed to this course of action.

"See, even now, just as I pointed out your withdrawal, you pulled away even further. You look curled up inside that chair as if I'm going to attack you."

I'm so proud of this immediacy, again I fail to notice that it is not having the desired effect. So I try again. . . .

■ ■ ■ ■ ■

FOR PERSONAL APPLICATION

Think of a time recently in which you were stuck doing something that didn't work very well. This could have been a conversation in which you were trying to get a point across. It could have involved something quite simple such as trying to unlock a door that was stuck. Examine the ways that you remained committed to a favorite course of action even though it was not producing the desired effect.

What would it take to get you to be more observant about the effects of any action you choose, changing course when what you are doing is not working?

The hallmark of any self-respecting brief therapist is flexibility and responding differently to changing circumstances. Because such practitioners don't restrict themselves to one particular ideology, except to use whatever they can find that works, they aren't hampered by purity of application. On the other hand, they may be criticized for operating without much of an organized plan, like mechanics who don't really understand the complex mechanisms and consequences of their tinkering.

Discover the Patterns and Change Them

Everything that a person does, says, or doesn't do is a form of communication. Embedded in communications are also deeper-level, metaphorical messages that can be uncovered. These patterns, however, would not be interpreted or brought to the client's attention such as in psychoanalytic treatment. Instead, they are used as templates for interventions.

The therapist seeks to modify the repetitive sequences of behavior, especially those that are dysfunctional. In order to do this, the therapist must get a complete picture of the problem by asking several focused questions (Cade & O'Hanlon, 1993):

■ When does the problem occur?
■ Where does the problem occur?

- What does it look like when the problem is occurring?
- With whom does the problem occur?
- When does the problem *not* occur?
- What are the effects of the problem on others?
- What behavioral examples of the problem does the client manifest during sessions?
- What is the client's view of how and why the problem occurs?
- What does the client expect and hope will happen when the problem is resolved?
- What has the client already done to try to resolve the problem?
- Among those things that have been tried, what has worked and what has not worked?
- How will it be known when the problem is resolved? What will be different?

■ ■ ■ ■ ■

FOR A CLASS ACTIVITY OR OUTSIDE ASSIGNMENT

Team up with a partner or find a volunteer who would agree to talk about a problem in his or her life. To make this exercise proceed smoothly, it helps if the problem discussed is one that is fairly specific. Using the problem definition questions as a guide, proceed through the list to get a complete picture of when, where, how, and with whom the symptoms are displayed. Take notes on what you were able to discover.

After you have completed the interview, which should take between half an hour and an hour, debrief one another by summarizing what was learned. Collaborate on identifying the patterns that emerged.

You can easily imagine structuring a whole interview around these core questions. Furthermore, you can probably see how constructive this systematic inquiry would be, for both the therapist and client, to get a handle on exactly what has been going on and suggesting what might need to be done.

The Miracle Question

Sometimes called a skeleton key or crystal ball, this intervention is like a broad-based antibiotic in that it often works with a variety of complaints and situations (de Shazer, 1991). Essentially, the device is used during those times when clients feel stuck or at a loss to come up with solutions to their problems. It is also commonly used as an assessment device to determine what the client sees as a satisfactory resolution of the presenting problem.

First, the client is taught a technique called time travel in which fantasy is used to go back and forth in time. "Imagine that you are living at a time when you no longer have this problem. Let me know when you have arrived at that point."

Once the client signals that he or she can picture such a scene, the next question follows: "What is different about your life now?"

Obviously, this is an invitation for the client to speak with great enthusiasm about how wonderful life is without the problem. It is likely that the person will mention things such as greater freedom and control, more contentment, and so on.

Okay, now the kicker: "Since you are now so happy and satisfied with having fixed this problem, what did you do to fix it?"

Not always but quite often the client will name exactly what needs to be done to make things better. The person solves his or her own problem by going into the future and then looking back at the present. Such a vantage point often frees people to be more proactive and innovative.

I am not saying this will work all the time, or perhaps not even most of the time, but the beauty of this approach is that you have the freedom to try lots of things until you find the right combination. Problem-solving and solution-focused therapists don't talk much about the therapeutic relationship, but the fact of the matter is that if you are able to develop a solid alliance with your clients you will give yourself lots of latitude to experiment without getting yourself fired.

SINGLE-SESSION THERAPY

What do you think about the possibility of a therapy model that is specifically designed to occur in a single meeting? Before you scoff at the possibility, consider the number of times in your own life that you have been irrevocably and permanently changed as a result of one dramatic incident.

FOR A CLASS ACTIVITY

Think about a time in your life in which you were irrevocably changed as a result of a single encounter or conversation. Perhaps someone said something to you that has stuck ever since. There was probably a time when you went on a trip, or visited somewhere, and something happened during your travels such that you were forever changed.

In small groups, talk to one another about these transformative encounters in which a single session had major therapeutic benefits. Once you have all related your experiences, find the common elements that made them such powerful episodes.

It has usually been the case that when clients don't return after an initial session, they are called dropouts or treatment failures. It is assumed that because the therapist did not meet the client's needs, he or she elected not to return. Working for a huge health conglomerate, Talmon (1990) decided to investigate this phenomenon by following up on those who didn't come back after their first session. To his amazement, he discovered that 78% of the 200 ex-clients he interviewed did not return after their one and only session because they already got what they needed! Because this result was so unexpected, and so counter to conventional wisdom, Talmon asked several colleagues to duplicate his study and they not only confirmed his original results but also found that 88% described themselves as "much improved" after their one session.

Talmon began to speculate that if so many people are helped after one session when the therapist had no awareness that such powerful gains were possible, what could be done if therapy was actually planned as a one-shot deal?

Talmon was not the first to observe the power of one therapeutic session. Even Freud once reported a cure after one meeting, as have dozens of other prominent practitioners (Bloom, 1997). Summarizing the research and clinical experience on single-session therapy, both Talmon (1990) and Bloom (1997) offer several principles to keep in mind when doing this type of work.

1. Don't underestimate the power of your own positive expectations: Expect good things and they will happen.
2. Remember that the therapy begins with the first phone call. Talmon, for example, reports telling a client during their first phone conversation: "Between now and our first session, I want you to notice the things that happen to you that you would like to keep happening in the future. In this way, you will help me to find out more about your goal and what you are up to" (Talmon, 1990, p. 19). He points out that with that single statement, he immediately accomplished several things that launched the therapy off to a flying start. First, he emphasized the importance of natural and effortless changes. Second, he focused on what would be possible in the future. Finally, he implied that the client was in charge of his own changes.
3. Talmon advocates calling the client back within twenty-four hours of the appointment, not only to prevent "no-shows" and communicate continued interest but also to plant more therapeutic messages, such as: "You've probably already noticed a difference in how you feel just since you took this important step in scheduling a session."
4. Choose candidates for single-session therapy wisely. Obviously, not everyone can benefit from one contact. When time restraints make

it impossible for someone to return, when someone has a very specific problem to work on, when someone is in crisis, or when modest goals can be quickly identified, this treatment might be ideal.
5. Decide on who should attend the session.
6. Select an issue or problem with modest goals.
7. In your zeal to get through the agenda, don't forget the power of empathy.
8. Keep track of time and structure as needed.
9. Work from the client's strengths.
10. Affirm what has already been accomplished.
11. Audiotape the session and give it to the client afterwards.
12. Schedule follow-ups via the phone or Internet.

Special Problems

It is clear that single-session therapy is not appropriate for all, or even most, people who need help. Generally speaking, it takes time to develop a trusting relationship, to gather enough information to do a reasonable assessment, and then to implement solutions. Besides, so often people come in for help in the first place not only to solve problems but also because they hunger for understanding and attention.

THE BEST CANDIDATES FOR BRIEF THERAPY

The central issue with respect to brief therapies is when and with whom to use them. Clearly during times of crisis or when time is limited, there is little choice but to intervene quickly and efficiently. Summarizing the work of Sifneos (1987), Davanloo (1980), Mann (1973), and others, Bloom (1997) lists the contraindications and best prospects of this type of treatment. You would not, for instance, want to try brief therapy with any of the following:

- major thought disorders or psychotic disturbances
- serious, chronic depression
- severe personality disorders
- substance abuse or addictions
- those who are unusually defensive, resistant, or unmotivated
- those with underlying, unresolved issues that are at the heart of their problems

Of course, Bloom points out that these would be poor prospects in *any* form of therapy, not just brief methods. So, who would be the most ideal candidates for time-limited methods? Those with:

- high motivation
- acute, specific problems
- psychological sophistication
- crisis situations
- willingness and ability to articulate concerns
- above average intelligence
- ability to form a trusting relationship with the therapist
- ability and willingness to stay on task
- early responsiveness

Again the point can be made that these type of clients would do well with most any form of therapy employed and would likely respond rather rapidly to any helping effort. Nevertheless, this chapter helps you to think not only in terms of which approach to use with any given case but also whether to use an abbreviated regimen if the situation requires it. Such would be the case with any of the following scenarios:

- A client traveled by bus from across town in a disadvantaged neighborhood. The first statements out of her mouth are how difficult and inconvenient this journey was, how uncomfortable she is leaving her young children at home with limited care, and how reluctant she is to return. It is clear that no matter how successful you are in this first session, it is going to be highly unlikely she can return for more than a few sessions.
- A managed care plan provides for a maximum of only six sessions, after which a review may extend the benefits to four more sessions.
- A person is experiencing an acute problem in an otherwise high-functioning life.
- Your own workload is such that your organization does not permit you to see clients for longer than a few months.
- A client comes in with the clear and nonnegotable expectation that treatment will occur rapidly, as in: "Okay, let's get to work. I'd prefer that we resolve this matter right away. If necessary, I can come back for another session."

Whether you are ready for it or not, brief therapy is the future of our profession. There are just too many people who need our help to allocate our services to only those who can afford it. Furthermore, as managed care continues to exert its influence on the profession, we will continue to feel pressure to operate as swiftly and efficiently as possible.

There will always be a market, however, for longer-term treatments. Therapy and counseling are more than merely solving problems and curing symptoms. They are also designed to help people understand themselves better, to work through long-standing personal struggles, to find greater meaning in life, to meet needs for intimacy, and to feel heard and understood.

Brief and long-term treatments are also not mutually exclusive. Frequently, in fact, you will work on cases in which initial presenting complaints, once resolved, lead to other issues that arise. Often clients will return to you, months or even years later, with merely an excuse to resume the relationship. What is obvious is that they just miss the ongoing opportunity to reflect on their lives, to be pushed and stimulated to go after something more in their work or their primary relationships.

Any competent therapist or counselor in today's climate must become proficient in both brief and lengthier treatments, depending on what the situation calls for and what the client needs most.

SUGGESTED READINGS

Bloom, B. L. (1997). *Planned short-term psychotherapy: A clinical handbook.* Boston: Allyn and Bacon.

Book, H. E. (1998). *How to practice brief psychodynamic psychotherapy.* Washington, DC: American Psychological Association.

Borden, W. (Ed.). (1999). *Comparative approaches in brief dynamic psychotherapy.* New York: Haworth Press.

Chambliss, C. H. (2000). *Psychotherapy and managed care: Reconciling research and reality.* Boston: Allyn and Bacon.

De Jong, P. (1998). *Interviewing for solutions.* Pacific Grove, CA: Brooks/Cole.

Haley, J. (1984). *Ordeal therapy: Unusual ways to change behavior.* San Francisco: Jossey-Bass.

Hoyt, M. F., & Holt, M. (2000). *Some stories are better than others: Doing what works in brief therapy and managed care.* New York: Brunner/Mazel.

Littrel, J. M. (1998). *Brief counseling in action.* New York: W. W. Norton.

McNeilly, R. B., & O'Hanlon, W. H. (2000). *Healing the whole person: A solution-focused approach.* New York: Wiley.

O'Hanlon, B., & Beadle, S. (1999). *Guide to possibility land: Fifty-one methods for doing brief, respectful therapy.* New York: W. W. Norton.

Quick, E. K. (1996). *Doing what works in brief therapy.* New York: Academic Press.

Talmon, M. (1990). *Single session therapy: Maximizing the effect of the first (and often only) therapeutic encounter.* San Francisco: Jossey-Bass.

■ ■ ■ ■ ■ ▬▬▬▬▬▬▬▬▬▬▬▬▬▬▬▬▬▬▬▬▬▬▬▬▬▬

CHAPTER 10

THEORIES ON THE EDGE

One of the most delightful (and frustrating) aspects of our profession is the ever-changing nature of our theories. Every few years, there is another stage of evolution in which some models disappear and others arrive on the scene. Theories that once enjoyed prominence a decade ago are now relics of another era. New approaches continue to rise in popularity.

Remember that at one time every theory was on the edge of respectability. Freud was branded a charlatan and his psychoanalytic approach equated with a form of witchcraft. Likewise, every other new therapy that has emerged since then has had to fight major battles to be taken seriously.

■ ■ ■ ■ ■ ▬▬▬▬▬▬▬▬▬▬▬▬▬▬▬▬▬▬▬▬▬▬▬▬▬▬

FOR PERSONAL REFLECTION OR CLASS ACTIVITY

Working together in teams, talk about theories that once were held in great esteem in our culture but are now considered obsolete. For instance, when I was growing up as a child, there was a theory that if you went in the water immediately after eating, you would die of a stomach cramp. On hot summer days we would beg our parents to be allowed to go in the swimming pool, to which they would respond by assessing carefully what we had for lunch.

"Hamburger. Fries. Chocolate shake. That's forty minutes."

"But Ma," I would plead, "I didn't eat all the fries. And I left part of the bun."

"Okay, deduct five minutes, but then add them back because you had ketchup too."

Imagine my consternation when many years later I took a scuba-diving course and was ordered to eat a big breakfast before we went on our open-water dive. When I pointed out that this would result in stomach cramps, my instructor laughed and said that was an old wives' tale and that, in fact, food was needed to protect one from hypothermia.

Make a list of many other theories that are now no longer valued or taken seriously.

Many of the theories in this chapter are not often included in a theories text except in passing. Some theories are still so innovative, new, or radical that they have yet to receive wide acceptance. Others are growing in popularity and influence but have yet to find their way into mainstream practice. Nevertheless, they are still worthy of serious scrutiny. Approaches such as the following will be covered: chaos and complexity, feminist approaches, expressive approaches, bioenergetics, transpersonal theories, computer-assisted therapies, thought field therapy, hypnotherapy, eye movement and desensitization reprocessing, and theories from other parts of the world (Morita, Naikan, Buddhist, healers). Theories are also mentioned that are no longer as popular as they once were: transactional analysis, neuro linguistic programming, and others.

This review of cutting-edge approaches is not intended to be comprehensive or exhaustive but merely to give you a flavor of other theories that are being used in the field. Once you have learned the basic material in this text, it is likely you will have many other opportunities to study some of these models at a later time.

CHAOS THEORY

It is always interesting when ideas from other disciplines are borrowed and adapted for use in clinical applications. You have seen, for instance, the way that family therapy evolved as a result of work in mathematical systems theory. Chaos theory is another way of looking at the world that has its roots in physics, computer science, and pure mathematics. Meteorology and weather forecasting have been involved in its development as well since something called the butterfly effect has been used to describe how an insect in one part of the world could flutter its wings and create a series of events that results in a monsoon in another part of the world (Lorenz, 1996). Proponents of chaos theory have, thus, cautioned that predicting weather will always be severely limited in accuracy because of all the factors that can influence the ultimate outcomes. The same, of course, can be said of human behavior.

■ ■ ■ ■ ■ ▬▬▬▬▬▬▬▬▬▬▬▬▬▬▬▬▬▬▬▬▬▬▬▬▬▬▬

FOR PERSONAL EXPLORATION AND STUDY

I realize that you already have plenty of reading to do in your busy life so it is with a certain caution that I make this recommendation. Perhaps if you do not have sufficient time now, once you graduate you can complete this assignment then.

One of the problems with the theories in counseling and psychotherapy is that they have been so insular and parochial in their focus. Freud, of course, combined his knowledge of neurology, physics, philosophy, and archaeology to create psychoanalysis. The family systems theorists, as well, have been quite interdisciplinary in their approaches. Many of the other theories you have studied, however, do not make sufficient use of ideas in other fields—not only the social sciences but also the humanities and sciences. Chaos theory is intriguing precisely because it does transcend so many far-flung disciplines.

Use chaos theory as a portal to expand your base of knowledge and the way you look at change. Whether you ever apply its concepts to your work, you will find it challenging to familiarize yourself with the basic principles. Start by delving into a few sources that are particularly accessible (though by no means easy reading): Cohen and Stewart's (1994) *The Collapse of Chaos*, Coveny and Highfield's (1995) *Frontiers of Complexity*, Gleick's (1987) *Chaos*, and Lewin's (2000) *Complexity*. You might also wish to look through the journals, *Nonlinear Dynamics, Psychology, and the Life Sciences* published by the Society for Chaos Theory in Psychology and the Life Sciences.

While we are on the subject of expanding your base of knowledge about theory, you might find it interesting as well to look at a more general introduction to theories on the edge of science such as Horgan's (1996) *The End of Science* or Boorstein's important works on the history of human discovery (*The Discoverers*, 1983) and creativity (*The Creators*, 1992). Also related to the history of creative ideas is Gardner's fascinating study of the creative process (*Creating Minds*, 1993) through the lives of Albert Einstein, Pablo Picasso, Igor Stravinsky, T. S. Eliot, Martha Graham, and Mahatma Gandhi.

A number of writers (See Cohen & Stewart, 1994; Coveny & Highfield, 1995; Gleick, 1987; Lewin, 2000; Prigogine & Stengers, 1984) have described ways that this strange branch of mathematics can be used to understand a number of other complex phenomena, especially those that involve nonlinear relationships between factors. Its basic idea is to look for the underlying patterns of natural systems that keep things stable in the face of ever-changing circumstances. This is a science that focuses on behaviors or events that appear random and unpredictable but that, in fact, have some type of underlying order.

If this sounds a bit confusing and arcane it is because those who write in this area tend to use the complex terms of *fractals, turbulence, strange attractors*, and *iteration*. In other words, as in so many theories, you must first learn a new language before you can understand the concepts.

■ ■ ■ ■ ■

FOR PERSONAL REFLECTION

Think about several of the theories that have been most influential in the field. Compare their language systems and vocabulary with one another, noting the ways that their very structure can only be understood if you know the words that describe their components and processes.

Some Basic Ideas

This theory is still so relatively new and so recently applied to the practice of therapy that there have not yet been very well-developed ideas written in comprehensible prose (to those of us without a strong background in physics and mathematics). This is a very hot theory these days in a host of different fields from economics and finance to art, music, meteorology, computer modeling, and so forth. There is even a new branch of science called chaoplexity, which seeks to understand emergent phenomena (those that are fluid and cannot be grasped by examining discrete parts).

If this sounds a bit like Gestalt theory, that is because there are some similarities, just as there are with systems theory. In each of these models, strong emphasis is placed on understanding the whole rather than the parts. Traditionally, science has operated by breaking things up into pieces and then dissecting and analyzing them. Chaoplexologists, however, are after synthesis and grasping the big picture. "Where chaos begins," wrote James Gleick (1987) in his groundbreaking introduction to the subject, "classical science stops. For as long as the world has had physicists inquiring into the laws of nature, it has suffered a special ignorance about disorder in the atmosphere, in the turbulent sea, in the fluctuations of wildlife populations, in the oscillations of the heart and the brain" (p. 3). Chaos theory is, thus, the study of irregular, erratic, puzzling aspects of the world.

There are several general principles of chaos theory:

1. Complex phenomena (such as human behavior and problems) involve nonlinear trajectories. This means that precise predictions are not possible.
2. Little things can have a huge impact on big things. The most casual gesture or apparently inconsequential statement can influence others' behavior in dramatic ways.
3. Look at overall patterns and forms, as well as the underlying structure of things.
4. Rather than signifying random, meaningless motion, chaos in this context means that even things that appear to be without order actually have an underlying stability.

Chaos and Therapeutic Systems

Because human behavior in general and client behavior in particular are not known to follow rigid rules of logical, sequential, linear progression, chaos theory has been especially useful to a number of thinkers in the field in trying to make sense of complex phenomena related to the practice of therapy and the training of practitioners (Abraham & Gilgen, 1995; Brack, Brack, & Zucker, 1995; Hager, 1992; Iwakabe, 1999; Moran, 1991).

Followers of this theory seem particularly attracted to its respect for what is unknown as well as known. Because it is one variety of systems theory with its focus on larger processes, it has been embraced by quite a number of other theorists including those with strong psychoanalytic (Iwakabe, 1999), constructivist (Perna, 1995), feminist (Murphy & Abraham, 1995), and multicultural components (Wilbur, Kulikowich, Roberts-Wilbur, & Torres-Rivera, 1995).

FEMINIST THEORY

You are probably not surprised to learn that there is not only one feminist therapy but actually dozens of them. There is liberal feminism, radical feminism, feminist postmodernism, feminist family therapy, feminist standpoint theory, feminist psychoanalysis, socialist feminism, and so on. Obviously, a feminist slant can be taken on any therapeutic approach. What they all share in common are beliefs that (Enns, 1997):

- You can't look at personal problems without considering their political and contextual roots.
- Issues such as freedom, independence, power, and choice have very different meanings in women's lives than in those of men.
- Women's normative behavior has been pathologized in diagnostic manuals, offering labels such as *dependent, passive,* and *compliant.*
- Women's values of listening and nurturing have been undervalued.

You have certainly noticed that almost all of the theories that have had the greatest impact on the field were developed by older white men. (Some exceptions include Virginia Satir, Karen Horney, Anna Freud, and Melanie Klein.) It is, thus, a safe conclusion that patriarchy and sexism have had a huge impact on the way things have evolved. Until relatively recently, there were virtually no female or minority senior faculty or supervisors. The dominant language in the field was also influenced primarily by traditional male language that values power over collaboration.

The writings of feminist thinkers (Brodsky & Hare-Mustin, 1980; Chaplin, 1988; Gilligan, 1982; Rosewater & Walker, 1985; Unger & Crawford, 1996) point out the unique ways that women develop differently than men. In almost any arena in which you would care to observe, the norms are rigidly prescribed for how the genders are supposed to behave. Look, for instance, at the ways that emotion is accessed and expressed differently by men and women. Until about the age of puberty, both boys and girls cry about the same amount to time, yet once adolescence kicks in, boys learn to stop crying or they will be teased mercilessly (Kottler, 1996). It turns out that girls are far more emotionally sensitive and responsive than boys in most emotions except one (guess which one that is). If you picked anger, you're right on target. Except for anger, boys don't "do" feelings very well.

■ ■ ■ ■ ■ ▬▬▬▬▬▬▬▬▬▬▬▬▬▬▬▬▬▬▬▬▬▬▬▬▬▬

FOR PERSONAL REFLECTION

Figure out why it is more adaptive for males to be superior in reading anger accurately in others. Hint: Think in relation to struggles for power and dominance.

▬▬▬▬▬▬▬▬▬▬▬▬▬▬▬▬▬▬▬▬▬▬▬▬▬▬▬▬▬▬

Girls learn at an early age that the way to get their needs met is by using gender-based strategies that appeal to emotion, that involve being deferential, and that play on physical attractiveness (Belenky, Clinchy, & Goldberger, Tarull, 1986). Picture, for example, that you want to return a pair a shoes to a department store but you don't have a receipt. You try asking, then pleading, finally threatening, but with no visible effect. What is your next alternative? If you are a woman, crying *might* work (especially if the sales clerk is a male), but this is certainly *not* the case for a man. One person I talked to said that she loves the sort of man who *can* cry but *doesn't*. In other words, women like the idea of a sensitive man but actually feel more than a little uncomfortable when in the presence of one who is weeping uncontrollably. In the same ways that men are limited by their gender roles, so too has this been the case with women.

This has huge implications for the ways that you might work with clients. Imagine all the ways that diagnostic labels are gender-loaded. Women who are very emotionally expressive are called hysterical. If they do their assigned roles well, they are referred to as seductive, dependent, or passive. In one study, both female and male therapists were inclined to describe healthy psychological traits (logical, assertive, analytic) as typical of the male role whereas supposedly normal, healthy women are likely viewed as dysfunctional (Hyde, 1991).

Women are designated as the emotional caretakers in relationships, often the one who will come into sessions on behalf of others in the family. That is one reason such a disproportionate number of women will end up as your clients, not because they are more emotionally unstable than men but because they are used to being the ones who talk about things while their husbands, fathers, and sons sit at home.

■ ■ ■ ■ ■

FOR A CLASS ACTIVITY

On the board (or in your notebook), make two columns, one representing "Male," the other "Female." Include under each column all the words and descriptors that you can think of to describe boys and girls. Make the list as exhaustive as you can. To get you started, recall the rhyme of what boys ("puppy dogs' tails") and girls ("sugar and spice and everything nice") are made of.

 After you have completed the list, talk about how these cultural expectations shape the sorts of problems that males and females develop in later life.

Working from a Feminist Perspective

Feminist therapy is not just about women, for women, and by women. It is a liberating philosophy that frees men as much as women from their enculturated roles and assigned responsibilities. If the consequence of feminist action is that it results in women acting more like men in terms of power and opportunity, then they will start dying off with the same regularity as their male counterparts. At its best, feminism liberates both men and women from culturally predetermined jobs. More and more often you will see fathers staying home to take care of the kids while mothers choose the high-powered career path. But the important point here is that you don't impose your own values or political action on your clients. For every woman (or man) who feels trapped by gender and limited opportunities, there are others who feel quite comfortable with their positions.

■ ■ ■ ■ ■

FOR PERSONAL REFLECTION AND A FIELD STUDY

Imagine that a new client comes in to see you who has very different ideas about her assigned role in life than you do. Rather than valuing education and a career, she is a stay-at-home mom who is following in her own mother's footsteps. She is extremely deferential toward her husband and even her two teenage sons.

 Her presenting problem is that she's depressed. You suspect there is a relationship between her symptoms and her sense of helplessness.

Now here is the dilemma: How do you help her deal with her problems without imposing your own values about women's roles?

Find out how other therapists you know restrain their values when clients live very different lives from their own lifestyle choices.

Nevertheless, it is often profitable to spend some time in sessions exploring the influence of gender on one's life decisions and choices (see Hill & Rothblum, 1999; May, 2000). What is frequently discovered is that clients are thinking narrowly and with limited vision because of what they imagine is possible.

- "A strong man is supposed to take care of his family. That's what my grandfather and father always did, even though it killed them both prematurely."
- "I'd never thought about being a doctor. In school girls were told we had a choice of being a nurse, a teacher, or a housewife. Because I had no intention of staying home to raise babies, it seemed like being a nurse was the only way out."
- "I wish my wife would initiate sex more often instead of it always being left up to me. But I guess it's my job to do that. She's just not comfortable with that sort of thing. In fact, she tells me it's the wife's duty to take care of the man but not to enjoy sex herself."
- "I love kids. If I could have my way, I'd much rather stay home and take care of the house and children. But as the oldest daughter in my family, it was expected that I would lead the way career-wise, do something important with my life. I think the most important thing I can do would be to be a mother to my children, but if I tried that, my mother and sisters would feel so betrayed. They'd never forgive me."
- "I am usually the only male at staff meetings. Almost all the therapists are women where I work, and so are the clients. So I feel like an alien most of the time. I'm really not allowed to express the male part of me or I would be ridiculed. They are always making jokes about guys, and I have to go along with it. I actually prefer working with women, but not to the point where I have to feel ashamed for being a man."

So many clients have stories such as this in which their freedom and choices feel limited as a result of gender issues. Your job is not only to create a climate in which it is safe to talk about these things but also to invite such discussion when appropriate.

Whether you ever practice a form of feminist therapy, you would certainly be expected to operate in a nonsexist, nonbiased manner so you don't continue to contribute to the marginalization of women and minority groups. What this means, in particular, is that you *must* become aware of your own gender (and other) biases, regardless of your own background. Furthermore, you must be comfortable adapting the types of relationships you construct depending on your clients' backgrounds and needs.

EYE MOVEMENT AND DESENSITIZATION REPROCESSING (EMDR)

This theory could easily have been included in the chapter on cognitive therapies because it clearly capitalizes on internal thinking and imagery processes in its treatment. I have chosen to include it here mostly because it is considered cutting edge, meaning that it is not only rather new on the scene but also somewhat controversial. In spite of the best efforts by supporters to explain how this method works, research support is considerably lacking—not in demonstrating that it works (because it does) but in explaining adequately how and why it works.

How It Was Developed

Francine Shapiro (1989) first developed EMDR as a way to help people recover from posttraumatic stress. This disorder is commonly seen among victims of child abuse, combat fatigue, disasters, or other calamities that subject humans to high-stress situations from which they have difficulty recovering. Such individuals are typically plagued by haunting images, nightmares, and disturbing thoughts that limit their healthy functioning.

Interestingly, quite a number of other schools of therapy might legitimately claim this theory as one of their own. It is cognitive in that it works through thinking processes. It resembles the psychoanalytic approach in dealing with unconscious and unresolved issues of the past. It is behavioral in seeking to recondition people to respond differently to internal stimuli. And it has also been called a kind of hypnotic induction procedure in which clients are introduced into hypersuggestible states so they become more amenable to surrendering dysfunctional behaviors.

A Simple Explanation for a Complex Phenomenon

A person arrives at the therapist's door incapacitated by debilitating symptoms. She has suffered terrible physical and sexual abuse as a child that continues to impact her life. She has continual nightmares and exhibits extremely anxious reactions to any new situation she might confront. She is very mistrustful of others and has been unable to have a satisfying intimate relationship with a partner throughout her life.

■ ■ ■ ■ ■ ▬▬▬▬▬▬▬▬▬▬▬▬▬▬▬▬▬▬▬▬▬▬▬▬▬▬

FOR PERSONAL APPLICATION

What are some examples from your own life in which you are haunted by traumatic, disturbing images? When your guard is down, when you are tired or distracted, when you drift off to sleep, when you least expect it, your mind feels invaded by painful memories that you would prefer to forget.

Think about how your own unresolved, painful experiences from the past continue to plague you in the present and limit your functioning in several areas.

The therapist asks the client to bring to mind one of the most disturbing, recurring images. She is urged to focus on the absolutely worst part of the memory and to describe it in detail, all the while she identifies exactly when and where she feels the most debilitating symptoms. During this narrative, the client is asked to follow the therapist's finger with her eyes, back and forth, as it is moved in front of her face. The therapist continues this consistent movement, guiding the client's eyes from one side to the other.

The eye movements are introduced as "sets," during which time the client is asked to bring up the disturbing image again, but this time erasing it in the process. Again and again this process is repeated, and each time the client is asked to describe what is happening internally. Eventually, clients report that the image loses its power altogether and they no longer have such disturbing thoughts.

■ ■ ■ ■ ■ ▬▬▬▬▬▬▬▬▬▬▬▬▬▬▬▬▬▬▬▬▬▬▬▬▬▬

FOR PERSONAL REFLECTION

Based on the theories you already learned about, how would *you* explain the process by which EMDR helps people? As a hint, you might go back and look at behavior therapy and the concept of desensitization, or psychoanalysis and its notion of unresolved conflicts, or perhaps cognitive therapy and the process of restructuring.

Other explanations that have been offered include the neuropsychological changes that take place as a result of eye stimulation, the benefits of eye movements that simulate REM sleep, brain activation in certain cortical centers, counterconditioning, and something Shapiro (1995) calls accelerated information processing, which most closely relates to hypnotic methods. Shapiro concludes her review of possible theories by stating that it is all very complex. Indeed, it is.

Thousands of practitioners swear by this approach to therapy, claiming miraculous cures within a matter of weeks. Shapiro (1995, 1997) has since started publishing research reports on its effectiveness, although the results are less than impressive. It seems as if this is one of those treatment procedures that currently defy our ability to explain thoroughly how it works. If you really think about it, however, most theories in this book are based on a degree of faith.

One of the things that gave EMDR such a skeptical reception in the profession is that therapists had to pay large sums of money to buy their training from approved teachers and then sign contracts saying they wouldn't reveal what they learned. As more and more therapists have experimented with this method, there is considerable enthusiasm for its use even though many are at a loss to explain adequately how it works. Because it is still relatively new on the scene, further research and development of the theory are forthcoming (see Lovett, 1999; Shapiro & Forrest, 1998).

EXPRESSIVE THERAPIES

Although hardly new or even necessarily separate from other theories already covered (humanistic, existential, Gestalt, client centered), expressive therapies are somewhat innovative in their emphasis on different facets of the therapeutic experience. Unlike verbal and didactic therapies (those that use speech and instruction), expressive therapies access primary experience (the way this text tries to do in the reflective exercises).

In volumes devoted to such methods (Weiner, 1999) the use of drama, dance, music, art, ritual, and other expressive forms follow the earliest healing practices. Most expressive or transpersonal therapies hold beliefs that:

1. Talk is not enough.
2. Active methods involving a person's mind, heart, and soul will have a greater impact than those that use only the intellect.
3. Language as a secondary experience (a translation of inner states) is not always an accurate representation of experience.
4. Creativity and movement are critical to self-expression and growth.
5. The goal of therapy is to facilitate growth toward higher levels of personal development and enlightenment.

The theoretical base for expressive approaches is diverse, stemming from:

- the most ancient healing rituals
- experientially based family therapies

- Gestalt techniques
- psychodrama
- transpersonal/body therapies (Rolfing, bioenergetics)
- active therapy

All of these approaches hold that people change and grow when they are encouraged to express themselves more fully, but rather than talking about feelings, they seek to act them out in the form of art, dance, music, drama, or spiritual transcendence (Greenwald, 1973; Wilbur, 1981; Wittine, 1989). Instead of asking someone *what* he or she is experiencing, the person would be directed to *show* what he or she is experiencing.

FOR A CLASS ACTIVITY

It is perhaps hypocritical of me to tell you about expressive theories and then ask you to think about them. After all, this violates the major premise of this theory that stresses primary experience rather than the intellect.

People in general, and therapy/counseling students in particular, are often inhibited when it comes to using more creative forms of personal expression that involve acting out internal reactions rather than merely talking about them. Even if you will not practice these approaches in pure form, it is still useful to gain experience employing some of their methods.

In small groups, play with several different modalities together. Start off by drawing a picture that best represents the way you feel about therapeutic theories thus far. After you are done, talk about what came up for you.

Next, each of you should use some form of dance, movement, or sculpted posture to demonstrate the theory you favor most. After you have illustrated your preference, invite the other participants to guess what you were communicating.

Discuss ways that you might use various expressive therapies in your work.

Sculpting

When families begin talking about their struggles, they are invited to take on the physical poses and postures they are describing. This represents a three-dimensional picture of the family's (or person's) essential experience (McLendon, 1999). Derived from Satir's (1988) work in experientially based family therapy, sculpting serves both a diagnostic and treatment purpose: It dramatizes the nature of relationships.

Imagine, for instance, a mother describing her feelings of being overwhelmed by her dependent children and needy husband. She is instructed to stand in the middle of the room, with each of her two children hanging on one pant leg. Her posture is "sculpted" by the therapist so that she is bent over, extending her arm for help. Her husband is draped over her back, adding to the burden. After the sculpture is completed, participants are invited to talk about what it was like for them and what they became aware of or learned as a result.

This sculpture might not be the way things really are in this family (at least according to the perspective of the husband or children), but it is the way the mother experiences things. The sculpture could then be rearranged until everyone is satisfied.

FOR A CLASS ACTIVITY

Role-play or enact a sculpture. In small groups, one volunteer describes the configuration and dynamics of his or her family, including the strengths, weaknesses, and sources of pleasure and frustration. Present a picture of the relationships that exist between the members, providing enough information so that others can participate in the sculpture that the volunteer enacts.

The volunteer should direct everyone in position around him or her to best represent the family relationships.

Talk about the experience afterward, not only for the person who directed the sculpture but also for others who participated or identified with the situation.

Drama Therapy

At the beginning of the nineteenth century, at about the same time that Freud was refining his theories in Europe, J. L. Moreno (1946) spent his time watching children interacting on playgrounds. Although this might be the sort of thing that would get you arrested today, Moreno was discreet in his observations, operating like an anthropologist who is studying the behavior of a foreign culture. In his field notes, Moreno became aware of the natural, spontaneous ways that children dramatized their feelings, expressing their emotions through various roles they played and scenarios they acted out. He wondered what would happen if adults could regain some of the creativity, spontaneity, and drama of their childhoods. Would such activities help them to work through problems, express feelings, and resolve struggles?

From such musings, a number of other theoreticians and practitioners (Blatner, 1997; Johnson, 1995; Landy, 1993; Moreno, Blomkvist, & Rutzel, 2000) have developed a field of drama therapy in which whatever comes to mind is played out. Images, stories, and fantasies are portrayed in real time—focused on the work of an individual, family, or whole group. First, a scenario is enacted spontaneously and then it is connected to what has occurred in one's own life.

The goals are:

- to put feelings and thoughts into action, creating or recreating direct experience
- catharsis or release of tension
- self-reflection, awareness, and insight
- laboratory for experimentation
- rehearsal of alternative strategies
- vicarious learning

There are many variations in the structures and formats that are used, but generally the therapist serves as the director of the experience, helping to set the scene, choose the characters, and enact the scenario. The identified client is the protagonist, the hero of the story who faces some adversity that must be overcome. Another participant plays the antagonist who is the primary adversary in the story. This could mean an abusive spouse, a neglectful parent, a disrespectful boss, or a deceased ancestor. Other characters are chosen to play supporting roles in the story. Doubles and alter egos are also selected to give support to the protagonist or to reflect unexpressed or underlying feelings.

In the illustration to follow, the protagonist has been complaining about her timidity and passivity in various situations in her life. She rarely asserts herself at work, at school, or at home, preferring to play it safe. When asked to pick one scenario she'd like to enact, the client decided to pick the one that is most immediate: the classroom environment. Although she often has things she'd like to say in class, she holds herself back because of fears of being judged as stupid or inadequate.

After choosing one person to play the instructor, the authority figure whose approval she craves the most, she also picked individuals to play various consulting roles. One auxiliary ego would sit behind her and express the assertive part of her, while the other would speak out loud her fears. In the following dialogue, the following characters are identified:

Protagonist—the woman who struggles with being assertive

Instructor—the authority figure whose approval she wants

Ghost—an amalgamation of her father, older sister, and fourth grade teacher, none of whom approved of her the way she wanted

Approval Seeker—the "perfect" classmate whom the instructor seems to like best. This woman always seems to say the right thing and earn smiles from the instructor.

Teaser—another classmate who ridicules her and makes her feel self-conscious about her passivity

Assertive Self—the auxiliary ego who will say out loud what the protagonist really wants to say but holds back

Fearful Self—the auxiliary ego that expresses out loud the unexpressed fears

This seems complicated and chaotic but when you actually see and experience such a dramatic enactment, it all comes together as shown next.

Instructor: Does anyone have anything to say about this?

Protagonist: Um, well, I was thinking . . . I mean . . .

Fearful Self: See, there I go again. I'm making a complete fool of myself.

Teaser: Well, if you're done with your articulate statement, I have something to say.

Protagonist: Well, okay, if you have . . .

Assertive Self: (To teaser) Excuse me. But I am absolutely not done. And I'd appreciate it if you'd wait your turn.

Ghost: You might as well just give up. You don't belong in school anyway. You know you're not smart enough. I've been telling you that for years.

Well, you get the picture. They all have their say, expressing out loud the voices the protagonist hears inside her head every day. After the drama unfolds for awhile, time will be taken to process what has occurred and to give others a chance to share how they are identifying with various roles.

■ ■ ■ ■ ■ ▬▬▬▬▬▬▬▬▬▬▬▬▬▬▬▬▬▬▬▬▬▬▬▬▬▬▬▬

FOR A CLASS ACTIVITY

In a fishbowl in the center of the room, your instructor, a visiting expert, or an experienced drama therapist will demonstrate a psychodrama. Another alternative is to meet in small groups and use the foregoing example as a guide for structuring your own dramatic experiment. One of you will volunteer to be the director to lead the scenario while each of the others will take on a particular role as a character in the story or as an auxiliary ego. You can include not only those mentioned previously but also consultants who are feeling communicators (saying out loud feelings that are sensed), doubters (who express self-doubts), or confidence boosters (who offer support and encouragement as needed).

As beginners, your job is not to be very skilled or adept at this modality but rather simply to gain some basic experience in what it's like. Be patient with yourself because most therapists require years of training and supervised practice in order to become proficient in these therapies.

Bioenergetics

Based on the work of Wilhem Reich (1945), a psychoanalyst who used breathing work in his therapy, Alexander Lowen (1958) created a therapy to heal the split between mind and body. "The body will heal itself," writes Lowen (1997), "if one surrenders to it" (p. 144). This means trusting not only what one thinks and feels but also what one senses and experiences in the body.

Because the goal of this approach is the integration of body and mind, rather than talking about problems participants in the process are instructed in the use of physical exercises, deep-breathing techniques, and massage. Although the intent of cathartic expression parallels what psychoanalysts had in mind, bioenergetics definitely takes the idea to the edge. Clients are helped to work through blocks that get in the way of expressing themselves. Because core energy flows not only at the level of mind and emotion but also through the body, spirit, and will, the work seeks to bypass the intellect into a more direct form of experience (Gendlin, 1981; Pierrakos, 1987).

In describing his form of body therapy, Gendlin (1997) offers his first and most important principle: to remain present with the client and keep a close connection. Like a meditative process in which your attention may temporarily wander, it is important to remain focused. "I may think a thousand things," he says, "but I do not pursue them for a long time. I return after moments, and stay here with attention and presence, so that I am really here" (Gendlin, 1997, p. 206). You would recognize this advice as part of most other humanistic/existential theories.

Art Therapy

Representative of another form of expressive therapy on the edge, art therapy encourages clients to express themselves through the media of drawing, painting, sculpture, clay, and collage. Although this approach is often used with children, the intellectually impaired, and older adults because it doesn't require verbal fluency, it can be adapted for a host of other populations.

Art therapy was originally designed as a diagnostic aid (Kwiat-kowska, 1978), then later to promote insight (Rubin, 1999), and eventually as a more action-oriented method (Linesch, 1993; Riley, 1994).

■ ■ ■ ■ ■

FOR PERSONAL REFLECTION OR A CLASS ACTIVITY

Draw a picture of your family. This could be a representation of your family of origin or your current family. (If you have time, do both.)

Draw your family doing something or involved in an activity that best captures the spirit of what you are trying to portray. Don't worry about your artistic accuracy. Use stick figures if you want.

When you are done, write down a few of the things that family members might be saying to one another or to you.

Talk to someone about what this exercise revealed to you.

Dance Therapy

Same idea, different domain of expression. This time, rather than expressing themselves through art, people are encouraged to do so through movement.

Almost all human cultures from the beginning of time have used dance to mark rituals, celebrate ceremonies, prepare for war, or entertain citizens. It has also been used to produce altered states of consciousness similar to hypnotic trance states (Levy, 1988).

Like any of the other expressive therapies, this modality is linked to a variety of other theories you have studied such as psychoanalytic, humanistic, and Gestalt (Dosamantes, 1990). Clients, whether in individual, group, or family settings, are helped to express their inner states through body movement.

THERAPIES FROM THE EAST

Most of contemporary psychology, counseling, family therapy, social work, and medicine are shaped by Western ideas. In fact, the whole concept of therapy is an outgrowth of our affluent culture that prizes growth experiences. There have always been philosophers, clergy, and teachers available to provide guidance to the lost and lonely, but psychotherapy and counseling were invented and practiced exclusively in Europe and North America.

There is, however, a long tradition of practicing psychological healing in Asia, Africa, and elsewhere, although the orientation is considerably different than what we are used to. Placing these approaches in a chapter on cutting-edge approaches makes them appear as if they are innovative, but that is only because they seem novel to us. Actually, the practice of yoga, meditation, acupuncture, martial arts, and Zen have been around a very long time for the relief of symptoms that we would ordinarily treat with therapy (Rosenbaum, 1999).

A Different Way of Thinking about Change

Certainly you are familiar with some aspects of Eastern religions and philosophy. You must know, for instance, about the concept of reincarnation, which states that our existence in this lifetime is but one of many lives that we will experience. Or that in the teachings of Zen, true enlightenment comes with clarity of mind and complete awareness of one's self in relation to the world. Or that in Buddhism, pain comes from desire, so that by reducing one's desire for things, one also eliminates suffering. Or in Hatha-yoga, greater serenity and peace are possible through the discipline of one's mind and body.

Every Asian country, as well as those in Africa and other non-Western places, has its own brand of "therapy" that is intended to reduce personal problems and address psychological issues. One thing to keep in mind when looking at these approaches is that change is viewed as part of a much larger process that involves one's body and spirit as well as mind.

Eastern Therapies

There are several kinds of therapy that have emerged from the East, especially from Japan. In both Morita therapy (Fujita, 1986) and Naikan therapy (Reynolds, 1980) principles of Zen Buddhism are structured into a treatment program that has as its goal to reduce a person's obsession with self.

The person is isolated in a small room and allowed no visitors except daily sessions with the therapist. Complete bed rest is often prescribed during the initial period as a way to slow down the client's mental activity. In a later stage, clients may be required to complete tasks that keep them busy, such as working in a garden or tending a stove.

The therapist's role is to act as a coach and confessor, encouraging the client to examine his or her life. It is, thus, an Eastern version of what we might call existential therapy. Attempts are made to refocus the mind toward more socially and morally responsible directions rather than the sort of egocentric self-involvement that is typical of contemporary neuroses (Burlew & Roland, 1999).

The time alone is spent in meditation and working through specific assignments in a journal. Often clients are given physical labor to do that occupies the body as well as the mind and spirit. The goal of all this is to help the person to become more objective, as well as less overly focused on his or her problems.

What makes these approaches cutting edge is that they do the opposite of most Western therapies that ask the client to talk about problems. Instead, the intention of this approach is to move the person away from such a narrow view of life, to appreciate better the natural world, and to feel grateful for the gifts that life has to offer. Meditation is at the core of such a transformation.

COMPUTER-ASSISTED THERAPY

Therapists who employ the computer to deliver their services are not necessarily following a coherent theory as much as they have adapted their current model to a different means of communication. As this technology develops and becomes more popular, this will assuredly change as the unique nature of this kind of communication demands its own methodologies.

Models and Colors of This Modality

We are not just talking about one form of therapy but many kinds that are used in different ways, depending on the technology available and the sorts of problems that are being dealt with. Computer-based counseling comes in a variety of delivery systems:

1. Computer simulations in which programs are developed to respond to client written or verbal statements.
2. Internet-based conversations in real time in which clients and therapists conduct a session in writing.
3. Internet-based dialogue in which e-mail messages are sent and responded to.
4. Web-based interactions in which programmed instructions are followed to gain information or guidance in a specific area.
5. Videoconferencing via the computer in which sessions are conducted almost as they would be in person.

In each of these types of computer therapy, whichever theory of intervention is being applied must be altered considerably to fit the unique kind of communication taking place. Imagine getting an e-mail communication from a client, for instance, that says the following:

> I am not sure about what to do about this situation. Sometimes it seems so pointless and I wonder if I should even pursue it further.

Understandably, there is no context to this message for you to figure out what is going on, but there are also no nonverbal cues or voice tone that lets you "read" what this person is really experiencing. Is he or she feeling just a little disappointed, suicidally depressed, or just confused and musing aloud about where to go next? Of course, you can check that out, but you would have to do so in a way that is quite different from how you would proceed in face-to-face therapy.

Some Unique Advantages and Disadvantages

It is easy to predict that the computer will only become more important in our lives, including the ways that therapists and clients might communicate with one another. Critics of this technology would say that people are already estranged enough in their lives from authentic connections to others and that the computer only inserts another layer of insulation. Instead of venturing out of their homes, people will be spending more and more time in front of their computer screens. They will shop on the Web instead of visiting stores, send e-mail instead of visiting friends in person, work at home instead of commuting to a workplace with other people around, and play video games and use interactive computer media instead of being with real live people in daily interactions. And there is no reason to think that more and more people won't want their therapy on the computer as well.

After all, many people report that computer-based communication is more anonymous, confidential, and private than face-to-face therapy, as well as being far more accessible (Haas, 2000). Of course, it is also much easier to be deceptive and hide. How do you know, for example, that the woman who writes to you about her eating disorder and sexual dysfunction is really who she says she is? There are no nonverbal cues to even confirm her identity (perhaps she is really a boy who is a child playing games). There are fewer data available to make sense of what a person is really saying.

Another consideration is the way more and more people are insulating themselves from the world outside computers. One of the fastest-growing psychological problems is "Internet addiction disorder," in which people are spending the majority of their waking hours in front of a computer screen. It has even been estimated that up to 10% of all Web users have a serious problem of addiction to their computers (Yang, 2000). Offering therapy via this medium may then only contribute to further isolation.

Some consumers of computer-based therapy say that it is the only way to go. They feel safer in ways that would never have been possible before. It is certainly more convenient, although that could be a disadvantage as well because change efforts aren't normally associated with comfort. Finally, there is a different pace to the communications, a whole different texture to the interaction, that facilitates thoughtful reflection in between messages. With limited cues, the modality focuses attention on the content of what is communicated in ways that would not ordinarily be practical.

Therapists who do this type of work say that they appreciate all the ways the computer saves time in taking a history, collecting background information, administering assessment instruments, and formulating a diagnosis (Gilliland & James, 1998). It also does better at routine, regimented therapeutic tasks, especially those that are didactically based such as teaching assertiveness training, relaxation training, or cognitive restructuring.

Certain ethical problems will continue to make this therapeutic modality challenging for practitioners. Several problems include the possibility that communications may be less private, the lack of regulation among people who claim to be experts on the Web, and the lack of systematic research to date on the validity of these methods.

In Summary

This concludes our treatment of major therapeutic approaches. In this chapter, we have examined those theories that are not yet part of mainstream practice but still have wide application to a variety of settings, client populations, and clinical styles. The previous chapters have covered most of the major therapeutic systems, although the coverage was hardly exhaustive.

At this point, you are probably feeling more than a little bewildered and overwhelmed by all the new concepts, terms, and different ways of looking at human difficulties and their resolution. In the last two chapters of the text, I will help you to pull everything together, look at common elements, and integrate what you have learned into a framework for guiding your practice.

SUGGESTED READINGS

Abraham, D. F., & Gilgen, A. R. (Eds.). (1995). *Chaos theory in psychology.* Westport, CT: Praeger.

Bankurt, C. P. (1997). *Talking cures: A history of Eastern and Western psychotherapies.* Pacific Grove, CA: Brooks/Cole.

Blatner, A. (1997). *The art of play therapy.* New York: Brunner/Mazel.

Boorstein, D. J. (1992). *The creators: A history of heroes of the imagination.* New York: Random House.

Burlew, L. D., & Roland, C. B. (1999). Eastern theories. In D. Capuzzi & D. R. Gross (Eds.), *Counseling and psychotherapy: Theories and interventions* (2nd ed.). Upper Saddle River, NJ: Merrill.

Enns, C. Z. (1997). *Feminist theories and feminist psychotherapies.* New York: Harrington Park Press.

Gardner, H. (1993). *Creating minds.* New York: Basic Books.

Gendlin, E. (1995). *The focusing approach: Experiential psychotherapy.* New York: Guilford.

Hill, M., & Rothblum, E. (Eds.). (1999). *Learning from our mistakes: Difficulties and failures in feminist therapy.* New York: Haworth.

Landreth, G. L. (2000). *Innovations in play therapy.* Philadelphia: Brunner/Routledge.

Lovett, J. (1999). *Small wonders: Healing childhood trauma with EMDR.* New York: Free Press.

Rubin, J. (1999). *Art therapy: An introduction.* New York: Brunner/Mazel.

Shapiro, F. (1995). *Eye movement desensitization and reprocessing: Basic principles, protocols, and procedures.* New York: Guilford.

Wiener, D. J. (Ed.). (1999). *Beyond talk therapy: Using movement and expressive techniques in clinical practice.* Washington, DC: American Psychological Association.

■ ■ ■ ■ ■

CHAPTER 11

INTEGRATIVE APPROACHES TO DOING THERAPY

Many of the theories reviewed in this text have been criticized as being irrelevant, limited in scope, and biased because they were developed mostly by "old white guys." Except for the notable exception of feminist approaches, members of the dominant culture—upper-middle-class white males—have authored (or at least published) the most popular theories. There are other exceptions as well—Anna Freud, Virginia Satir, and others—but persons of color are significantly absent in the recognition of their ideas.

Given that the majority of clients are women (often over three-quarters in some settings) and many are from oppressed minority groups, it is a legitimate concern about the applicability of theories that were generally developed for use with the majority culture. Many of the models are, thus, infused with the values that are typical for those in a relatively affluent society. Issues such as freedom, autonomy, and independence that ring so loudly in the theories of Americans are not necessarily appropriate for immigrants from Asia, Latin America, Africa, and other cultures that stress interdependence, cooperation, and collective needs.

PUTTING IT ALL TOGETHER

Most clinicians use four or five different theories in their practice during usual operation (Garfield & Bergin, 1994). Just think about the challenges this presents! It is hard enough to come to terms with only one of these complex models, much less try to employ several of them at different times in the same session. It is for this reason that you must not only develop mastery of a theory's content but also of its essence. This allows you to combine the best features with other models you find most appealing.

Attempts to synthesize the theories of counseling and therapy have taken several different directions—those who seek to find common elements, those who combine theories into a single approach, those who practice what is called technical eclecticism or the integration of several techniques into one framework, and those who compile manuals of symptom-specific treatments (Kottler, 1991). Each of these approaches has certain advantages as well as limitations.

Almost from the very beginning of the profession, when there were only two main approaches—psychoanalysis and behaviorism—practitioners such as French (1933), Kubie (1934), and Rosenzweig (1936) tried to combine the theories into a single, comprehensive approach. Many years later, theorists (Dollard & Miller, 1950; Wachtel, 1977, 1997) are still working furiously to merge these two radically different perspectives into one model.

Are There Real Differences?

Some approaches you have studied do work better for specific kinds of problems. The American Psychological Association (APA, 1995), for instance, has set up a task force to validate which methods are best for particular complaints, such as using behavioral strategies for phobic disorders. More generally, however, comprehensive reviews of various approaches to therapy have generated consistent findings that there is little difference in their effectiveness (Asay & Lambert, 1999; Robinson, Berman, & Neimayer, 1990; Seligman, 1995). Even when differences do appear, it seems just as likely that the perceived superiority of one approach over others is more due to the research methodology rather than the actual treatment (Lambert & Bergin, 1994).

There are several ways to account for the similar effectiveness of approaches that seem to be so different:

1. The approaches aren't that different after all. They are really just doing the same essential things.
2. What practitioners actually *do* in their sessions is more generic than their espoused beliefs would appear.
3. There are many different paths to achieve the same outcome.
4. There really are major differences but the research measurements aren't sensitive enough to pick them up.

The most logical explanation (read: the one I like best) is that various theories are really far more alike than it would seem. In spite of their radical divergences in therapist role, underlying philosophy, identified goals, and preferred techniques, there are indeed elements they share in common.

IT ALL LOOKS THE SAME TO ME: COMPARISONS AND DIFFERENCES

One of the most important tasks in your effort to learn theories of counseling and therapy is to be able to see ways that each approach is related to several others, as well as to understand ways they are different. This is not an easy assignment, especially considering that the inventors of each system go out of their way to emphasize the uniqueness of their approach, often masking the ways they say the same things as others in slightly different language.

There are a number of ways that you can work to integrate what you have learned so far. You can spend considerable time studying each of several favorite models, reading the original sources and secondary sources. You can also make an effort to put theories into practice, either by applying them to your work with clients or your own personal struggles. As preparation for both of those strategies, I would first suggest that you pull things together by trying to group the major theories according to their most significant features.

Before we get more deeply into the universal features of the theories you have studied, let's first examine some of their differences. In Table 11.1 you can see highlighted the ways that each approach differs from others in terms of (1) treatment goals, (2) underlying philosophy, and (3) favorite techniques.

■ ■ ■ ■ ■ ▬▬▬▬▬▬▬▬▬▬▬▬▬▬▬▬▬▬▬▬▬▬▬▬

FOR PERSONAL REFLECTION OR A CLASS ACTIVITY

Review the theories summarized in Table 11.1. Instead of concentrating on how each model is different from the others, look at their common features.

After you have studied the convergences rather than divergences, take all the theories in the Table 11.1 and group them into three main categories that make sense to you.

After you have placed each theory in one of three categories, give each of the groups a name that describes the principal feature they share in common.

Consider other ways that you could group the theories according to dominant characteristics and shared beliefs.

Discuss your factor analysis with classmates to compare your different conceptions.

TABLE 11.1   **Summary of Therapeutic Approaches**

THEORY	GOALS
Psychodynamic Sigmund Freud Carl Jung Heinz Kohut Otto Kernberg	Resolve conflicts from the past; change character; promote insight; strengthen ego
Client-Centered Carl Rogers Natalie Rogers Gerald Pine Eugene Gendlin	Create authentic relationship; increase awareness; express feelings; development of self
Gestalt Fritz Perls Laura Perls Miriam Polster Erving Polster	Increase self-awareness in present; integrate split between conflicting selves
Behavioral B. F. Skinner Joseph Wolpe Albert Bandura John Gottman	Identify target behaviors; modify dysfunctional behaviors; learn adaptive responses
Cognitive Aaron Beck Albert Ellis Donald Meichenbaum Arnold Lazarus	Increase awareness of cognitive activity; identify and challenge irrational beliefs; teach adaptive behavior
Reality William Glasser Robert Wubbolding	Assume greater responsibility; become more skilled at meeting needs
Existential Rollo May Irvin Yalom Victor Frankl Jim Bugental	Explore core issues that give life meaning; address barriers to increased freedom and responsibility
Adlerian Alfred Adler Rudolph Dreikurs Jon Carlson Don Dinkmeyer	Provide support and increase motivation; challenge dysfunctional beliefs; work through feelings of inferiority

PHILOSOPHY	TECHNIQUES
Past determines the present; basic drives; role of the unconscious; developmental history	Transference; catharsis; uncover defenses; analyze resistance; interpretation
Humans as growth oriented; increased awareness of self and others to improve self-esteem and personal functioning	Empathic resonance; active listening; deep reflection of feelings; search for meaning; group interactions
Explore unfinished business through direct experience; people as fragmented and cut off from core selves	Confrontation; role-playing and psychodrama; enactments; group interactions; risk taking
People shaped by environment and experience; all behavior is learned and reinforced	Goal setting; contingency contracting; skills training; reinforcement; relaxation training
People learn maladaptive patterns; thinking precedes feeling and action; problems stem from core beliefs	Dispute irrational beliefs; confront distortions and exaggerations; introduce alternative thinking
People motivated to meet needs; greater self-control is possible; focus on success	Examine consequences of choices; challenge people to be accountable; develop action plans
Search for underlying meaning; struggles with personal responsibility, isolation, angst, death, and freedom	Collaborative, authentic relationship; being in the moment; focusing; confrontation; eclectic methods
Birth order and early family experiences shape personality and social behavior; lifestyle a function of social interest	Conduct lifestyle assessment; interpret early recollections; explore mistakes and core fears; develop action plan

(continued)

TABLE 11.1 Continued

THEORY	GOALS
Systemic Murray Bowen Salvador Minuchin Carl Whitaker Virginia Satir	Identify underlying structures and patterns; realign system so that it is more healthy for members
Constructivist Kenneth Gergen Michael White Tom Andersen Michael Mahoney	Identify societal influences and personal narratives; re-story life circumstances in more helpful ways
Brief Milton Erickson Jay Haley Steve de Shazer William O'Hanlon	Produce symptomatic relief; limited, specific, and focused goals; discover patterns and change them
Feminist Carol Gilligan Rachel Hare-Mustin Annette Brodsky Lenore Walker	Examine issues of power and gender roles; explore themes of marginalization and oppression; work to change systems

Insight versus Action

One obvious way to think about the theories of intervention is in terms of the relative importance they place on the value of promoting some degree of understanding as opposed to stressing action. You will recall, for example, that strategic, behavioral, problem-solving, and other brief therapies tend to minimize the role of insight in the change process, preferring instead to work solely on a level of constructive behavior: It isn't what you say or understand that matters but what you *do*.

In direct contrast to this emphasis on doing, you have read about other approaches that work at a level of promoting greater self-awareness and understanding. It is believed that such personal revelations become transformative when clients are helped to apply their insights to their daily lives. Psychoanalytic, existential, and client-centered theories most closely fit this style. They might approach matters with clients in a very different way, but they all share the conviction that "truth" will set you free.

PHILOSOPHY	TECHNIQUES
Individual behavior and problems a function of larger context; families are living systems that seek stability	Reconceptualize problems; set boundaries; restructure power and control; improve communication
Cultural influences shape individual perceptions; subjective nature of reality; problems exist in language	Collaborative conversations; externalizing problems; examine cultural influences
Problems result from repetitive, maladaptive patterns; forget about how they developed and work to change them	Reframe problems; use directives; action plans and homework; focus on what works; flexible, pragmatic methods
Personal problems have political and contextual roots; freedom and power have different meanings for women than men	Support cultural and gender differences in relationship; challenge and confront stereotypes; use of empowerment

FOR PERSONAL REFLECTION

Like any of the polarities mentioned in this context, dividing theories based on insight or action is a gross simplification. After all, some theories fit right about in the middle. If you could imagine that any theory can be located on a continuum of insight versus action, which ones would you nominate to place approximately in the center?

INSIGHT ——————————————————— ACTION
Psychoanalytic   Brief

You could easily make a case that theories such as cognitive, narrative, Adlerian, Gestalt, and multimodal include features that promote both insight and action. Which others do you think belong in the middle of the line?

In addition, which theories that you read about could you legitimately place on either end of the continuum, depending on the way the approach is interpreted and practiced?

Cognitive versus Affective

Another obvious way to compare therapeutic approaches is to look at the relative emphasis they place on thoughts or feelings. Cognitive, existential, constructivist, and psychoanalytic approaches tend to be fairly intellectual, uncovering internal thought processes that may be dysfunctional or counterproductive. They might have very different names for the problems and choose to focus on different facets of cognitive processes, but they all agree that changing the way you conceptualize your world will dictate the ways you respond.

In marked contrast to this cognitive, intellectual, rational, logical, traditionally male way of seeing the world, other theories stand at the opposite end of the continuum. According to client-centered, Gestalt, and expressive therapies, therapists should be spending their time helping people to access their unacknowledged feelings, to understand their origins, and then to express them fluently and constructively. You can visualize, therefore, that the first set of theories claims that controlling thoughts alters feelings, whereas the second group believes that dealing with feelings changes underlying cognitive structures. Of course, one obvious conclusion is that both models might apply to people depending on their characteristic style and needs, but that is far too sensible to be adopted by battling parties.

FOR HOMEWORK AND A GROUP PROJECT

Your university library or department most likely has a collection of demonstration videos in which noted theorists and practitioners show how they apply their ideas with clients. You have probably seen a few of these in class, although there are hundreds of others that you could watch in your spare time.

There is no better way to learn about the various therapeutic approaches, comparing their differences, and integrating their commonalities, than to watch as many videos as you can. It is for this reason that I'd strongly suggest that you organize a video club in which you invite a few classmates to watch various therapy films together and then talk about your reactions.

The publisher of this text, for example, has one series called *Psychotherapy with the Experts* in which several different theories are demonstrated (existential, solution focused, reality, mind-body, multimodal, feminist, systemic, integrative, object relations, cognitive, Adlerian, and person centered). A dozen other publishers also produce their own video series that covers similar ground. It doesn't even matter so much which videos you see because each one will highlight things that you like and dislike about that particular approach. The most important part of this exercise is what takes place afterward—how you process what you observed and what you learn from it. That is one reason it is preferable to see the sessions with others so that you can make sense of what you witnessed.

Present versus Past

Again you have heard considerable debate between combatants about whether the better approach is to deal with unresolved issues in the past or to concentrate primarily on what is going on in the present. In one corner, weighing in with the psychoanalytic schools of thought, there is the very strong conviction that real change isn't possible unless you deal with the underlying origins of the presenting problem. This approach is also shared by some family systems theorists, such as Murray Bowen, who believe that present family interaction patterns are often influenced or perhaps even inherited from previous generations.

In the other corner, shaking their heads in amusement at how misguided the past-oriented theorists are, sit those who believe that the only valid focus of treatment is to remain in the present. Anything else is, at best, a waste of time. Theories that must immediately come to mind in this regard form an improbable alliance. Just imagine, for instance, that behavioral, reality, and strategic approaches share this corner with Gestalt and client-centered models. All of them essentially ignore what has happened previously and keep pushing the client to stay in the here and now.

Flexible versus Rigid Roles

Although there are several other ways to categorize the theories, the last one examined here looks at the degree of freedom the therapist has to improvise and operate pragmatically. In other words, how carefully prescribed is the clinician's therapeutic options? How much flexibility and pragmatism are permitted in practicing this system without abandoning the core ideas?

Again, there are some strange bedfellows. It may be apparent that a theory such as psychoanalysis has a very rigid set of rules for how the practitioner may behave, but so does the client-centered, behavioral, and rational-emotive therapist. In each case, the clinician is expected to apply the theory by following the established procedures.

Contrast these theories with others in which the therapist is allowed, even encouraged, to be as flexible, pragmatic, and eclectic as possible; any intervention is permitted as long as it gets desired results. Reliability of methods is far less important than creativity and flexibility. You will remember, for example, that the existential theory really has no techniques at all: Its practitioners follow a consistent philosophy but in any way they want. Then there are models such as Gestalt and strategic that are absolutely loaded with practical strategies borrowed from every conceivable source. Finally, there are eclectic and integrative approaches such as multimodal therapy that encourage clinicians to borrow methods from all other theories.

Making Further Comparisons

These four ways of organizing the theories get you started thinking in both convergent and divergent ways. First, with each approach, you ask yourself:

- What else does this remind me of?
- How does this resemble other ideas with which I am already familiar?
- What are some common threads that appear to be running throughout each approach?

Second, you can sort the theories by emphasizing the ways they differ from one another. In some ways, this might be harder to do because it requires you to understand enough about all the approaches so that you can begin to recognize their unique contributions. When you combine both sorting strategies, you are well on your way toward completing the difficult task of integrating what you have learned this semester. Before we move on to how you might customize what you have learned, it would be helpful to summarize once again how the various models might be classified.

Cheston (2000) offers one paradigm that organizes the theories into four main groups according to the practitioner's role and presence (way of being), chosen knowledge base (ways of understanding), and clinical methods (ways of intervening).

	WAY OF BEING	WAY OF UNDERSTANDING	WAY OF INTERVENING
Psychodynamic	Neutral, detached, objective posture to facilitate transference; quietly supportive	Search for unconscious motives and unresolved core issues	Increasing awareness of hidden, repressed material; work through transference

	WAY OF BEING	WAY OF UNDERSTANDING	WAY OF INTERVENING
Humanistic	Warm, caring, authentic relationship focused in the present	Understand client's world; greater self-awareness and self-expression	Promote insight and awareness of underlying feelings
Cognitive-Behavioral	Assertive, active, challenging stance	Look at reinforcers and underlying thinking patterns	Dispute irrational beliefs; use behavioral homework
Systemic	Joins the family to influence from within; functions as mediator and referee	Examine the structure and dynamics of interactions	Alter family structure; specific therapeutic tasks

HOW DO YOU KNOW IF YOU'RE AN INTEGRATIVE THERAPIST?

I am frequently asked what kind of therapist or counselor I might be. When someone puts me on the spot like this, I am never quite sure what to say. In some ways, I'm proud of not knowing what I am and just as pleased that critics can't guess either. In some reviews of my books, I have read that I am everything from a psychoanalyst or humanist to a cognitive theorist. I plead guilty to all three plus a dozen others that strike my fancy.

When Clients Compare Notes

I have this fantasy of a bunch of my clients, or ex-clients, sitting around comparing notes about what I'm like as a therapist. Some would insist that I am a brief, problem-solving therapist—I saw them for only a few sessions and immediately cured them of their symptoms. They're not sure what I did, but whatever it was, it was powerful.

Another contingent of clients would shake their heads in disbelief. I have been working with them for years in long-term, relationship-oriented therapy in which we have been examining lifelong patterns and themes that resonate with issues of personal freedom and responsibility. These clients experience me as warm, affectionate, engaging, funny, and playful. They feel that I am part of their family and I feel that I am, too.

Still another group of clients, composed mostly of affluent business folks, successful professionals, and male blue-collar workers, would think the others were talking about someone else other than me. With them, I come across as straightforward, direct, and no-nonsense. We have been engaged in work that will last between several weeks and several months. The sessions are heavily steeped in action-oriented and cognitive methods, which are in marked contrast to work with other clients.

Last but not least are the people I see in family or group sessions. My style is again quite different from what I do during individual consultations because I am really using other theories as a base. I still retain some of my core beliefs about what is good for people and how change takes place, but the multiple interactions and complexity of these formats require me to apply another therapeutic style.

I suppose what this means is that, like the majority of practicing therapists, I am integrative, combining what I believe are the best features of each approach depending on the situation and the client's needs (perhaps also my own whims).

Sending Recall Notices

Every so often, a client I haven't seen in awhile returns for a booster session or perhaps because of another set of problems. It would be perfectly reasonable for this person to expect that we would proceed according to a plan similar to the one that worked well last time. After all, I appear to be the same person and professional I used to be. The office looks basically the same. And the client has fond memories of our previous visits, proud of the struggles we endured together and the terms we negotiated. The only problem is that in the intervening years, or even months, I have continued to evolve as a therapist, abandoning old methods in favor of new ones I have since learned or invented.

"So," the client begins, beginning where he remembers we left off last time, "I suppose you'll want me to tell you about some of the disturbing thoughts I've had lately that have been interfering with my intimate relationships."

I cringe at the language he is using. Did I once talk that way? I have since moved on in my theory development. I might look the same, a little older perhaps, but I don't do therapy the way I used to. I sigh to myself, thinking that this would be a whole lot easier with someone brand new who doesn't come with expectations for what we will be doing together.

Sometimes I feel exhausted by all the changes that take place in the field. It reminds me of software upgrades. My computer word-processing program works perfectly, doing just what I want it to do. Of course, I only use about 5% of its complicated features, but that's plenty to get the job done. Then every year, I am badgered into upgrading my version of Microsoft Word; sometimes I don't even have a choice in the matter—my employer or publisher will insist on the latest version. Then there are the inevitable glitches, crashes, and annoyances that come with a new operating system, and I find myself longing for the good old days of my manual typewriter that only required a ribbon change a few times per year.

I think of the developments in therapy the same way. I have been perfectly content working with clients in my usual way; they seem like satisfied customers as well. Then just about every year, I get some notice in professional journals, or a flyer in the mail, announcing that some new therapy has been invented and I had better get with the program, learn this new stuff, or I'll get left behind. So I dutifully order the latest books, attend the obligatory workshops, and discover that whatever I have been doing up to this point is obsolete, old-fashioned, downright wrong, and probably dangerous. I am told that instead of doing one thing, I should be doing another (often the exact opposite of my current strategy).

This reminds me of car manufacturers that send out recall notices to their customers, informing them that there has been some defect and that they had better bring their vehicle in, forthwith, or it might catch fire or blow up or fall apart. I wonder if I should send such notices to all my ex-clients letting them know that whatever we once did is no longer considered the optimal treatment. And whatever gains they thought they had made were really just illusionary. They'd better come back immediately so I can fix whatever I now understand was wrong and apply the newest treatment strategy.

Forget What People Say, Pay Attention to What They Do

Therapists are fond of claiming that talk is cheap. Clients go on and on about the changes they intend to make, the things they want to do, the plans they have, but all this means little if they don't act on their intentions. Furthermore, people often present themselves in one way that may have little to do with their actual conduct in the world.

If you are nodding your head in agreement, remember that this same pattern occurs with therapists as well. What practitioners say they do in their sessions isn't necessarily what they are really doing behind closed doors. I can tell you my favored theory, the one that demands my loyalty. I can read all the appropriate literature in that specialty, attend the conferences and workshops devoted to it, hang out only with those professionals who share my theoretical beliefs, and tell anyone who will listen how much better my theory is than all others. Nevertheless, when I am with my clients, I might behave far more flexibly than I would lead anyone (including myself) to believe. I might call myself a true believer of one theory but actually practice far more intregratively and eclectically than advertised.

You Have to Do What the Situation Calls For

One of the reasons that most therapists adopt an integrative framework is because their clients demand it. In one sense, the job of a therapist is not to change people but to create an atmosphere that is conducive for them to change themselves. Clients are active self-healers (Bohart & Tallman, 1999).

Clients present a whole variety of problems in need of attention, everything from relationship difficulties (with family, friends, or coworkers), debilitating emotions (depression, anxiety, loneliness), and learning disabilities, disturbing thoughts or images (illusions, delusions, hallucinations, irrational thoughts), to disillusionment (emptiness, meaninglessness) or dysfunctional behaviors (compulsions, addictions, self-defeating actions). Would you really expect to treat someone with career indecision the same way as you would someone who is severely depressed and actively suicidal? Would you adopt the same approach with an 80-year-old Chinese woman who complains of disappointment in her grandchildren as you would a Mexican American teenager who wants to extricate himself from a gang?

There is one movement in the field called the manualization of therapy, which describes the process of developing specific, standardized treatment practices (only those that have been empirically validated) for each of several diagnoses (Task Force on Promotion and Dissemination of Psychological Procedures, 1995). You might, for example, use a cognitive-behavioral approach with reactive depression and a form of structural family therapy with a case of oppositional disorder. There is, thus, a vision that some day, just like doctors, therapists would simply type in the particular problem that is presented, add a client profile, and the computer will spit out the preferred treatment procedure.

You will recall that this type of technical eclecticism is essentially atheoretical. Perhaps the computer is operating under an overall software framework programmed into its system, but the therapist just follows directions. An alternative to this rather mechanical approach to helping is one in which you are the one responsible for developing your own theoretical approach that is elastic enough to embrace a variety of interventions and styles depending on the client, situation, problem, and stage of treatment. This framework could be based on any one of a dozen different philosophies. It could be existential, Adlerian, psychoanalytic, client centered in nature, as well as many others.

■ ■ ■ ■ ■

FOR PERSONAL REFLECTION

Think about the stages in the therapeutic process. Come up with between four and six different stages that essentially include a beginning in which the relationship is first formed, problems and background are explored, and a diagnosis is agreed upon; a middle stage in which the work is done; and an ending stage in which the client is launched back into the world with suitable closure and preparation to deal with setbacks.

Given the specific objectives, challenges, and tasks of each stage in the therapeutic process that you have identified, would you really think that you would maintain the same sort of relationship and adopt the same strategy throughout the entire process? Would you not want to employ one kind of style in the beginning that might be different from the middle and end? Would you likely use procedures in the working stage that you wouldn't be inclined to rely on in the others?

Just as you might be inclined to customize a therapeutic approach for each individual client that takes into consideration the problem presented, cultural background, the time allotted, and so on, wouldn't you also individualize the treatment according to which stage you were in? Perhaps you would be more client centered in the beginning when you are first establishing a supportive relationship and then far more directive later. Or maybe you would deal with affective material in the first stages when catharsis is important and then move on to cognitive and behavioral material later.

Depending on which stages you have settled on, how would you alter your style over the length of your relationship?

I'm Fickle

I don't know about you, but I get bored easily. After I've been doing something a particular way for quite awhile, my interest and attention start to drift. If I don't change what I'm doing or the way I'm doing it, my efficiency and proficiency dwindle. I once used to work in a factory in which my job was to stand at a table all day and collate pieces of paper together, stuffing them into an envelope. Except for brief fifteen-minute breaks in the morning and afternoon, and half an hour for lunch, I did this all summer. Surprisingly, however, I never felt bored with my job. I found an endless number of ways that I could stay engaged with the work—going clockwise or counterclockwise, using my left hand or right hand to gather, talking to my coworkers, and enjoying amazingly elaborate fantasies.

I don't mean to imply that seeing clients is like working on an assembly line—although to burned-out professionals it often seems that way. Every person is completely unique. Even when multiple clients present what appears to be the identical problem—vocational dissatisfaction, grief, or loneliness—each story is different. When our work is at its absolute best, we see each individual with a fresh eye and clear spirit.

You probably don't want to hear this so early in your career, but like the worker in a factory, therapists also struggle with staying engaged in their jobs. I have done surveys over the years at therapist workshops I lead in which I ask these experienced professionals to estimate the percentage of time they remain in the session, completely engaged with the client. Much of the time, you see, therapist attention wanders. We drift away in our own fantasies. Whenever we are bored, or perhaps threatened, by what is going on, we go off into our own worlds. We sit there politely and pretend to listen. We teach ourselves to nod our heads at appropriate intervals, but only a small part of us is really in the room; the rest of us is thinking about what we will do later, or reliving favorite events from the past. We work out problems in our heads or struggle with our own issues that are sparked by something the client said. Sometimes we just turn our brains off altogether and go into sleep mode like a resting computer.

Throughout my career, there have been times when it feels like I am actively engaged with my clients an incredible amount of the time. But even when I am optimally effective, extremely interested in the client, and as completely focused on the conversation as I can be, I would estimate that I still leave the room at least a quarter of the time. The client says something that reminds me of another client, so for just a moment I try to remember who that might be. My stomach grumbles—for a moment I think about lunch and where I'll go until I bring my attention back. I am continuously reminded of unresolved issues that I have not yet fully resolved. There are problems in my life that are just there, underneath the surface, popping up at inopportune times. There are errands I have to do later, things I want to remember, ideas for a new book or article, and all of these thoughts intrude on my attention—that is, until I catch myself and bring my concentration back to the task at hand. As I've said, during the best of times I can stay present about 75 percent of the time.

Back to my survey. When I ask large groups of therapists to estimate the percentage of time that they are fully focused on what clients are saying, I hear numbers that range from 20% to 80%. That fits perfectly with my experience because there have also been times when I am not so interested in a client, or otherwise distracted, when I am barely present at all. I just sit there like a puppet, letting the client drone on and on. Every few minutes, I will leave my fantasy, come back into the room, and ask the client: "Excuse me, you've been talking at some length about this issue. I wonder if you might summarize what you've been saying."

Because I haven't been listening, this allows me to pick up the thread of the conversation long enough to drift off again.

I am not proud of this admission and certainly hesitate to share with you the reality of doing therapy or counseling for very long. I know many, many therapists who don't struggle with this challenge at all. They have been in practice for many decades, using the same theoretical approach, working in the same office, and seeing essentially the same kinds of clients. Yet they feel energized and thoroughly engaged in their work and report that they have little trouble paying full attention to their clients.

I sincerely admire, even envy, those who say they can remain so engaged. I knew people who worked with me around the collating table at the factory who had been doing this job for years, and although they didn't particularly like it, they had little problem sticking with the task. I suppose there is also great variety in the ways that therapists deal with their need for simulation and novelty.

One of the ways that I have tried to stay excited by my work is by constantly experimenting with new approaches and evolving my own theoretical orientation. I mentioned in the introduction to this text that I was at one time an avid, passionate, true believer of rational-emotive therapy. I took a doctoral practicum applying this method. I read every book I could get my hands on and subscribed to specialist journals in REBT. I associated myself with other like-minded therapists and practiced this approach exclusively for several years. I found it incredibly helpful and effective with a wide range of clients. Furthermore, I loved the ways I could be provocative, challenging, and dramatic in sessions disputing irrational beliefs and imitating my mentors. The only problem is that, after awhile, I grew tired of identifying the same irrational beliefs, following the same routines, and applying essentially the same interventions.

The next time I saw Ellis in action, he looked bored, too, as if he had been through this a thousand times before (which he had). Members of the audience must ask him the same questions in every city. He follows the same routines with every workshop. I had even heard him use the same examples before. During a break, I told him that he looked bored much of the time and asked him if that was the case. He looked at me with a smile, shrugged, and then said this was all about converting people to his way of thinking. He believed so strongly that what he was doing was important and valuable to learn that his own boredom didn't matter.

Well, Ellis might not have a choice because of his commitment to sell REBT around the world, but I assuredly do. Since that time of being an exclusive practitioner of the cognitive approach, I have tried a dozen others. And I like them all. Throughout my career, I have changed theories the way someone else might add to their wardrobe every few years. Even though the clothes you already have are perfectly serviceable, sometimes it just feels good to wear something new.

There's Too Much Good Stuff Out There

It's true. Almost every year, there is some new innovation in our profession that adds greater options to our work. When you limit yourself to only one theory, you make a decision to focus your attention on the contributions and improvements in that particular system. For busy professionals, that is often the only reasonable choice to make. You may end up working in a setting that has adopted a particular therapeutic approach, or you may work with colleagues who all share an interest in the same model. Or you may just simply find yourself enamored with one theory that seems to fit you like a glove. It feels good to master one system well and to be able to apply it in a variety of situations. It is kind of like the best in a monogamous relationship: Why wonder what it would be like to have multiple partners when you are already satisfied?

If that is the situation in which you currently find yourself, read no further. You are indeed fortunate to select a compatible theory that fits with your values and style. You will find lots of support from other professionals who feel the same way.

If, on the other hand, you are always wondering what else is out there, if you continue searching for more and better strategies to help your clients, then you are probably going to have to look way beyond a single model. My experience of doing therapy is often feeling like I never know enough, that if only I read just one more book, attend one more workshop, get one more degree, I would finally be thoroughly competent enough to provide the sort of help my clients deserve.

It is not usual but also not uncommon that a client will leave your office dissatisfied with what you offered. There may be a number of reasons for this, many of which have little to do with you. The client may enjoy some benefits to remaining stuck. In some cases, there may actually have been substantial changes, but for one reason or another the client won't admit it. Another possibility is that it sometimes takes a period of time to gather a clear and objective assessment of how therapy works, a kind of delayed reaction.

As much as therapists might prefer one of these preceding reasons to explain why a client left unhappy, there are also times when the reason is due to our own ineptitude, mistakes, misjudgments, or poor training. Sometimes we fail our clients because we don't know enough, or we couldn't do enough. (Sometimes we also try to do too much.) I actually prefer to think this way because it gives me an excuse to learn more. One of the very best things about this profession is that we will never know enough, never become as thoroughly competent as we would prefer. You can't possibly keep up on all the innovations and developments each year, much less catch up to what has already been done. I really love this and it's why I can't imagine ever getting tired of this work. Just when you think you understand what is going on, some new idea comes on the scene that turns everything upside down. Or even more powerful, a client teaches you something about yourself that you never knew was possible.

■ ■ ■ ■ ■

FOR A CLASS ACTIVITY

One good reason to be integrative in your therapeutic approach is to look at your own experiences of transformation. In small groups, talk to one another about the most dramatic changes that you have undergone in your life and how they came about. After each person has had a chance to tell one brief life-changing story that happened as a result of an encounter with a teacher, therapist, serendipitous event, tragedy, or other life experience, look at some of the underlying mechanisms that were most responsible for acting as catalysts.

Classify your experiences according to the therapeutic ingredients that seemed to be most influential.

Talk to one another about the possibility of any single theory being useful to explain how your changes transpired.

■ ■ ■ ■ ■

FOR PERSONAL REFLECTION OR A CLASS ACTIVITY

It should by now be readily apparent that each of the theories presented offers something of use to most practitioners, regardless of specialty area. Identify each of the following contributions with the theory (or theories) most often associated with this idea.

- Only by coming to terms with the past can you hope to understand problems in the present.
- Each individual's perception of reality is shaped by his or her unique experience.
- People suffer most from a lack of personal meaning in their lives.
- You must uncover dysfunctional thinking and beliefs in order to restore healthy emotional functioning.
- It is the therapeutic relationship that heals most, especially one that is open, honest, and trusting.
- You must look at any behavior within a larger context that takes into consideration relationship patterns.
- It is not what you understand that matters most but what you put into action.
- If you try something and it doesn't work, try something else.
- People must be held responsible for their behavior and accountable for the consequences of their actions.

■ ■ ■ ■ ■ ▬▬▬▬▬▬▬▬▬▬▬▬▬▬▬▬

FOR A FIELD STUDY

Interview a few experienced therapists who have been practicing for at least ten years and preferably longer. Ask them to tell you about the development of their beliefs regarding therapy, including the models they have used, the practices they have evolved over time, and the ways their theoretical allegiances may have changed over time.

During your conversations, ask them to begin with their earliest experiences as students, when they first encountered the diverse viewpoints in the field. Then trace the progressive stages they have since gone through—internship, their first job, the mentors and supervisors that pushed them in particular directions, up until the present.

Based on what you learn from these interviews, think about what might lie ahead for you in your own professional development.

HOW TO BE INTEGRATIVE

Assuming that you decide to adopt an integrative framework (if not now, then sometime later in your career), there is some advice that might be useful to you in your journey. I warn you that such a road taken is not an easy one. It feels good to be part of an exclusive club of people who all share similar beliefs. Nevertheless, in today's climate of practice, even those who choose one theory as a home base still must become skilled at using an assortment of strategies that are borrowed from other approaches.

Believe There Is Value in All Approaches

First you must believe that it is a good idea to be integrative, but not all your instructors and supervisors will share this philosophy. They may quite legitimately suggest that as a beginner it is far more appropriate for you to stick with just one model until you become comfortable with it. Then perhaps later in your career you can add on additional layers.

Whether you begin your integrative efforts now, or at some later time, you still must see merit in all approaches to helping. This means being respectful of those who have perspectives that are different from your own. It means being a critical consumer of research. It means trying out as many different methods as you can get your hands on. And it means resisting the impulse to remain safe and secure in your comfortable world, reluctant to venture out to discover what others are doing. This is much more difficult than it sounds.

Imagine that you settle on an excellent way to do therapy. You feel confident in your approach, get lots of good support for your efforts, and most important, see clear and compelling evidence that your clients are improving. Moreover, when you read research studies in the literature, you find solid support demonstrating the effectiveness of your methods.

Now, picture further that you come across someone at a conference or professional gathering who does therapy in seemingly the diametrically opposite way that you do; however you choose to work, this therapist appears to do something completely different. Furthermore, there seems to be research support for the effectiveness of this approach as well.

You may react critically and defensively to this encounter; after all, this alternative reality could very well threaten the validity of your own perceptions. On the other hand, you could also embrace such differences, intrigued with the possibility that there are many alternative paths to arrive at the same destination.

Be Skeptical of Truth

A lot of other folks are going to try and sell you their ideology. All may very well be convinced that they have discovered the "true" way to seek enlightenment, and they believe with all their hearts that the world would be a much better place if only others would adopt their beliefs. Of course, the Crusades was begun for just such a reason in which members of one religious system set out to convert or kill all those who didn't share their vision.

Hopefully, nobody will try to harm you because you don't adopt their preferred theory, but be forewarned that some people become mighty upset if you practice in a way that contradicts what they value most. In some cases, as low person in the staff hierarchy, you might very well have to use the methods favored by the institution or those in power.

There are some professionals who are utterly convinced that they have discovered the truth and that others are flat-out wrong for operating in different ways. I will tell you a little secret: As of yet, *nobody* really understands the complexity of how and why therapy works. Some professionals may *think* they know what's going on, but rest assured they are as confused as everyone else.

Get Outside Your Discipline

In order to be truly integrative, you have got to look far beyond your own field of psychology, psychiatry, nursing, family therapy, social work, counseling, or human services. When you read the biographies of the most prominent theoreticians, you will notice that they studied widely in fields outside their own. Sigmund Freud was a voracious reader of archaeology, anthropology, and literature. Albert Ellis and Rollo May were avid students of philosophy. Many of the other influential therapists read widely in the sciences, humanities, and fiction to broaden their education and widen their visions. You would do well to follow their lead.

Don't Think in Boxes

Look at the big picture beyond your individual cases. As part of your training, you will be taught the skills of differential diagnosis and systematic clinical assessment. That is one way to think about things, but there are others as well. You may be drilled in the methods of collecting data, formulating hypotheses, settling on diagnoses, and writing out treatment plans, but there are alternative ways to think about your cases. You can use intuition as well as logic, your heart as well as your head. You can ask yourself not only where this client fits in the *DSM-IV*, but also whom he or she reminds you of, and what part of yourself you can recognize in his or her experience. Take a step outside the usual parameters from which you make sense of things. Find alternative viewpoints to scan the territory. Look at cases from multiple angles. See every one of your clients as unique.

■ ■ ■ ■ ■

FOR PERSONAL REFLECTION

Hold onto this exercise for a time after you see a client, or after you have practiced therapy in a role-played situation. Teach yourself to be reflective after every session you conduct. Once you are done with the required paperwork—writing progress notes and case summaries, filling in logbooks, filing folders—take a few minutes before your next appointment or meeting and ask yourself the following questions:

- What really happened in this session? If I go beyond what my notes say, what was the core of the experience?
- What worked best with this client? What did I do that seemed least helpful?
- If I could have approached this session differently, what might I have done instead?
- What did I learn about this client today? What did I learn about myself? What did I learn about the way that therapy works?

It is probable you will address many of these questions in supervision, but even so it is always profitable to consider them within the privacy of your own mind.

Look at Links and Connections

Being integrative often means making connections between what you are doing now and what you have done previously. Try to make links between what transpires in your sessions using one approach and what happens when you have tried something else. Search for the essence of any strategy to discover the source of its power.

Yesterday I was teaching a class here in Iceland where I am working as I write these words. As is usually the case, I spoke to the students for a little while about some facet of counseling and then put them in groups to personalize what they learned and relate it to their lives. Because I understand very little of the Icelandic language and have not yet learned to read nonverbal cues very well here, I can't tell how I'm doing. I don't know if the students are satisfied with the way things are going. When I ask them, of course, they are polite and reassure me, but I can't be certain if they are just being nice. I feel lost, unable to rely on the usual ways I gather feedback, monitor progress, and measure outcomes.

Once I strip away the content of what I'm doing, and how they are responding, I am left with the barest structure of communication. I stand back and watch the students in their groups and find them engaged intently with one another. I can't understand their words but it is clear to me that each person is sharing something, taking turns, and responding in soft voices. Occasionally, I hear laughs and see other overt signs of affection. I'm not sure what they're talking about, or even if they are doing what I assigned, but it's clear they are neither bored nor disengaged. Of course, I will soon hear their reports, but I don't like to rely on that alone; I prefer to make my own observations as well.

I am stretching in new ways, learning alternative ways to teach counseling, understanding different facets of what promotes growth, because I can't rely on strategies that worked for me in my own culture. That is one of the absolutely marvelous things about this type of work we do: Every client we see (or class we teach) requires us to enter a culture that is often alien to us. If we hope to make contact with people, we have to get outside of ourselves and what is familiar. We have to make connections between what is going on and what we have witnessed before. We have to tie together the process that is unfolding with the maps we use to guide us, making corrections when certain landmarks don't correspond with what the guidebook says is supposed to be there.

Doing therapy is one of the most exciting adventures you can undertake, whether you are doing it in the neighborhood where you grew up or in a very foreign country. It isn't really an option to be integrative in your work; it is a necessity if you ever hope to make sense of what you're doing.

Resist the Urge to Label Yourself

I have already warned you that you will be asked often what sort of therapist you are. You could say, "A good one!" but that will only buy you a little time.

"No," the person will say with a nervous laugh, "you know what I mean. What kind of therapy do you do?"

Again you can try to sidestep the query with a clever riposte: "I do whatever the client needs most at the time," but that won't work either.

"Oh," the person will say with recognition, "you're one of those eclectic types."

You almost can't avoid being labeled by others. Both colleagues and clients alike will try to typecast you by putting you in one of their established categories. You have little choice except to play along with the routine and tell the person something that fits expectations. But that doesn't mean you have to really believe what you are saying. You can tell others that you are a brief therapist, or a Gestalt therapist, or an addictions counselor, or a neopsychoanalytic postmodern feminist grief specialist.

The consequences of such a label is that people then have certain expectations for how you are supposed to behave. I once worked in a psychiatric unit in which the three male, psychoanalytic psychiatrists all wore vested suits and two of them actually smoked pipes during meetings. The female social workers, also trained in psychoanalytic theory, provided a chorus for the psychiatrists. There was one psychologist in the room, a behaviorist, and he, naturally, wore a white lab coat with his name stenciled on the pocket. Then we interns, mostly trained in cognitive therapy, kept our mouths shut and acted as though we knew what everyone else was talking about. Our job was to present cases that all the other staff members would then fight over. Everyone had a designated role in this ritualized interaction, as well as a uniform that was consistent with each one's identified profession and theoretical allegiance.

You may, therefore, have to take on the designated label that others assign to you, but that doesn't mean you have to apply it to yourself. When you think of yourself as integrative, you don't fit in any category—except your own.

IDENTIFYING THE COMMON FACTORS

An integrative framework involves making connections between diverse theories and especially looking at what they all have in common. You must be asking yourself as you are reading this book how it's possible that all these theories could really work as well as their authors and advocates say they do. Is it really possible that you can help someone by reflecting their feelings *or* disputing their beliefs *or* uncovering their unconscious fears *or* helping them set goals *or* . . . ? You get the point.

What has got to be at work here are some universal therapeutic ingredients that are present in all these different theories. Aren't you just a little curious what those might be?

What Research Has Uncovered

Quite a number of studies have been undertaken to identify the factors common to all forms of therapy. Beginning with the early effort of Rosenzweig (1936), continuing with Frank's (1973) seminal work to present-day efforts (Hubble, Duncan, & Miller, 1999; Kottler, 1991; Norcross & Goldstein, 1992; Prochaska & DiClemente, 1982), there have been several universal variables that have been identified. These are the ingredients that you would find present in almost all the theories you have studied. They include:

1. *Hope and expectations.* Clients bring with them certain attitudes and beliefs that influence the potential outcome.
2. *Relationship.* The particular kind of alliance may vary among approaches, but all are in agreement that some type of relationship is needed in order to offer support and use as leverage to get compliance to treatment.
3. *Therapeutic techniques.* All the approaches *do* something, and certainly what they do has some impact on the proceedings (although probably not as much as practitioners think).
4. *Outside factors.* The client's motivation, personality style, presenting complaints, family influences, job situation, and other variables also play an important role.

These main ingredients can be supplemented with several other factors that can be recognized in most other theories currently in use.

Therapist Presence

What clients say is important in therapy is often quite different than what their therapists say is important. We, of course, believe it is our masterful interventions that make all the difference. Clients, on the other hand, most frequently mention the following (Llewelyn, Elliott, Shapiro, & Hardy, 1988; Phillips, 1984; Tallman & Bohart, 1999):

1. Having a private place to talk and the structured time to share one's concerns.
2. The therapist's personality, especially someone who is understanding, caring, and supportive.
3. Having someone help to understand oneself and one's situation.

There isn't much of a surprise in these findings. But it's important to remember that who you are is as important as what you do.

Use of Self

All of your techniques, skills, interventions, and strategies are filtered through your personality and interpersonal style. The unique ways that you see the world and communicate to others are what give power and life to your therapeutic work.

I have long believed that one way to explain how professionals as diverse as Sigmund Freud, Fritz Perls, William Glasser, Albert Ellis, Alfred Adler, and Carl Rogers could all be so potent in their work, even though they seem to be doing such different things, is because they are really all capitalizing on the same factor. Think about it: What do they all have in common?

It certainly isn't the sort of relationship they developed with clients, or the methods they employed, or even the types of things that they would talk about. What each of these professionals had in common was their charisma—the power of their selves. There is no way that you could spend time with any of them in a room for very long that you wouldn't come out of there different from when you first walked in. This isn't because they reflected your feelings, disputed your beliefs, or interpreted your dreams, but because they all possessed a self that was persuasive and influential.

The Placebo Effect

In introductory psychology classes you first learned about the power of expectations to promote cures. Patients who were given sugar pills (especially tiny green ones) often improved just as rapidly as those who received actual medication—if their physician programmed their reactions by telling them that they would be helped.

In therapy, as well, the professional's positive expectations for a cure operate as very powerful medicine indeed. If you believe strongly that what you are doing is going to help your clients, and you are persuasive in convincing them that this is the case, then almost whatever you do within reason may be useful.

Both Jerome Frank (1973) and Jefferson Fish (1973) have written extensively about this effect in therapy, noting how critical it is that you communicate your enthusiasm about the methods you are using. Imagine, for instance, that you visit a therapist for the first time. You are wracked with guilt, loneliness, and despair after the breakup of your marriage. You have little hope that you will ever find happiness again. Your life seems over.

The therapist listens to your sad story, nods her head in sympathy, and then says to you:

"I want you to know that your experience is familiar to me. I have literally seen hundreds of people in your situation, and I have been able to help all of them in some way. How quickly we make progress and how far you go are up to you, but I can reassure you that what you are presenting lends itself to improvement rather quickly. In fact, you will notice that you are already feeling some relief. For the first time in awhile you are feeling the barest glimmer of hope.

"I am very good at what I do and I know just how to help you. With your cooperation and commitment, we should make progress very rapidly."

Obviously, your spirit would be lifted by such an introduction to therapy and you would be set up with expectations that are intended to maximize hope and optimism. If you believe that what the therapist is offering to you will be useful, you are much more likely to respond favorably to the intervention (Snyder, Michael, & Cheavens, 1999).

Altered States

Another universal feature of most therapeutic systems is that they place clients in an altered state of consciousness in which they are more amenable to being influenced. It is like a hypnotic state in which people become hypersuggestible; they won't do anything they wouldn't do otherwise, but they have much less resistance.

You can easily test this out for yourself. Notice when your instructor (or author) says something to you in class, you pay very close attention. You listen carefully, take notes, and (hopefully) put great confidence in your instructor's (and author's) expertise. Now, what do you think happens when we go home or hang out with our friends? Do you really believe that anyone listens to us, or does what we say, any more than they would for you?

I got advanced degrees specifically because I wanted to be taken more seriously in my life, especially by my family (and get good restaurant reservations with the title "Doctor"). It didn't happen. When I talk at work, with my clients or students, I am like a godling: Everyone pays attention or at least pretends to do so. Yet as soon as I leave my classroom or office, I am ignored just as often as everyone else. So, what's the difference?

One explanation is that when we are in our professional mode, in our own domain, we can control the environment and atmosphere as carefully as any faith healer. The books on the wall and framed diplomas all attest that we know stuff. Our manner and style communicate a kind of smug confidence, as if we have the secrets to life that are there for the asking. Then we use our voices and manner to soothe clients, to reassure them, to lead them along in such a way that they will follow. We actually place them in a kind of hypnotic state in which they are far more likely to receive what we have to offer.

Helping Relationship

It is worth mentioning this universal ingredient again because it is so important. You have learned about several distinctly different models for how the therapeutic relationship should best be constructed so as to optimize benefits. In the psychoanalytic approach, you have an arrangement in which the therapist appears neutral, detached, and objective so as to maximize the projections of the client. The transference can be worked through precisely because the therapist tries so hard to be disengaged; whatever the client experiences in the relationship must be the result of his or her own perceptions based on resolved relationship issues.

Carl Rogers presented a very different sort of relationship, one in which warmth, genuineness, and empathy prevailed. Rather than appearing as an aloof, disengaged parental figure, a new model was built on an egalitarian exchange of mutual respect and trust.

Other models of the helping relationship conceive of the encounter as one that is essentially a teacher-student arrangement, or that of a coach or consultant working with someone one-on-one. To some this relationship is not so much a projected fantasy as it is a very real encounter between two or more people. More accurately, the working alliance is composed of both a real relationship and a projection (Gelso & Carter, 1994).

In whatever form it takes, the helping relationship provides support and encouragement to people during a time of need. They have a private place to unload their troubles and a regular structure in which to speak of their concerns. In this relationship, they feel heard and understood, a marvelously restorative experience.

In a relatively universal model of the helping relationship that would be employed by most practitioners, Capuzzi and Gross (1999) present a series of developmental stages. In the first part of the process, boundaries are negotiated and trust is built by discussing confidentiality and gathering basic information. The partners in the process get to know one another. Stage 2 involves more extended exploration in which goals are established, extensive assessment is conducted, and preparations are undertaken to begin change efforts. The third stage is characterized by collaboration and problem solving, experimenting with alternative behaviors within the safety of the supportive relationship. In the last stage, plans are made to separate from one another in a way designed to maintain the momentum.

Feedback

Where else can someone go to hear the truth? In almost all the systems you have reviewed, the therapist attempts to be as honest, sincere, and straightforward as possible. Clients report on the things they are doing and act in the sessions just as they would in the outside world. It is our job to provide them with accurate, clear, and nonthreatening reactions to what we observe.

According to each theory, the therapist might comment on a different aspect of the interaction. The reality therapist points out the ways someone is avoiding responsibility for a poor choice that was made. The existential therapist might do the same thing but in a very different way. The cognitive therapist would give the person feedback on the dysfunctional thoughts that are keeping him stuck. A client-centered therapist might talk to him about how he comes across in their own relationship, a Gestalt therapist might point out the inauthenticity in the way the feelings have been expressed, and a narrative therapist would offer observations on how he has internalized messages from his culture that might not be his own. In all of these instances, the theory suggests that clients should be confronted with certain aspects of their behavior that are less than fully functioning. Then they are offered alternative ways of responding instead.

Finding Meaning

Existential, cognitive, and constructivist therapies aren't the only ones that help clients find meaning in their lives. Even the most action-oriented brief therapist might concentrate mostly on presenting symptoms but still can't help but address the inevitable questions clients ask: "Why me? And why now?"

Human beings are extremely curious creatures. We can't help searching for answers to questions that plague us. Even when the therapist does not make this exploration an explicit part of the treatment, the client may be doing this sort of work on his or her own.

There are so many ways that therapists facilitate this search for meaning. It can be called consciousness raising, facilitating insight, or meaning making, but in all these forms the client makes a cognitive shift in the way things are viewed. In the following chart, some specific examples are provided for each of a few sample theories:

THEORY	TYPE OF MEANING MAKING	EXAMPLE
Psychoanalytic	Search for underlying and unconscious reasons for present problems	"The reason that I keep picking losers in my love relationships is that I am following the template established by my own parents."
Constructivist	How reality and personal narratives are constructed from cultural indoctrination	"It is not true that I am really a worthless alcoholic; that is the image I inherited from what the media, my family, and the dominant culture have told me."
Cognitive	Negative emotions stem from irrational thoughts	"I am so upset about this relationship ending, not because of what he said to me, but due to what I've been telling myself about that."
Reality	Look at what the person is doing and what impact it has	"The reason I keep getting in trouble at school is because I keep doing the same thing over and over even though it isn't getting me what I say that I want."
Client Centered	Access, understand, and communicate unexpressed feelings	"I walk around with so much anger inside me because I have never really told others how I feel."
Strategic	Reframe presenting problems in another way that makes them more amenable to change	"It's not that I am basically a shy person, just that I sometimes hide behind a safe persona when the situation calls for it."

In all its present forms, the act of helping clients create or find meaning in their experiences is an enterprise that is quite universal.

Rehearsal

Most therapies also share a strong belief that clients need opportunities to practice new ways of behaving and being. Sometimes this rehearsal is structured in sessions under the guise of role-playing; other times it is part of explicit or implicit homework assignments. Some approaches (behavioral, cognitive, strategic, problem solving) are far more deliberate about including rehearsal and practice as part of their methods. Yet even those models that don't give a lot of overt attention to actions strategies (existential, psychoanalytic, client centered) still encourage clients to take what is being done in sessions and apply it in their lives.

There would be considerable disagreement about what exactly should be done and how it should best be practiced. A Gestalt therapist or Satir family therapist would structure enactments right in session, whereas an Ericksonian or strategic therapist is much more concerned with what the client does outside of the sessions. Thus, task facilitation is also an important part of many (but not all) therapeutic systems in which clients are expected and encouraged to complete assignments that are considered good for them. This could be as simple as writing in a journal or reading an assigned book (bibliotherapy) or could be as complicated as involving prescriptive tasks that even include paradoxical tasks (those that are designed to be disobeyed).

The Process

One final way that all therapeutic systems are alike is in their organizing process. Regardless of the specific ways they go about their work, most models follow a sequential process that consists of the following stages:

1. Listen to the client. Engage him or her in the process. Assess what is going on. Construct a diagnosis and treatment plan. Negotiate goals. Decide who would be best to work with and what sort of relationship is indicated. Plant favorable expectations. This all takes place in the first few sessions.

2. Build and deepen the relationship. Work on trust issues. Explore presenting complaints in the context of the client's life. Gather relevant history. This stage can last anywhere from two sessions to two years, depending on the time available, the style of treatment, and client needs.

3. Promote insight. There are lots of ways to do this—explore secondary gains of the symptoms, uncover unconscious motives, construct personal meaning, dispute irrational beliefs, and a dozen other options. This stage can also last anywhere from a few sessions to a very long time. Much depends on the client's readiness, motivation, and openness, the therapist's preferred model, and the circumstances that led the person to seek help.

4. Modeling is not so much a discrete stage in the process as it is a consistent presence throughout the experience. Be who you want your clients to be.

5. Interventions are planned and implemented in sessions. Depending on the type of concern, the situation, and the time available, you might use any one of the models presented in this text. Such interventions can last a few minutes or many sessions. In each case, you would monitor very carefully how the client responds and what sort of outcome is produced.

6. Most approaches employ some sort of therapeutic tasks that take place outside of sessions. This can involve formal homework, therapeutic tasks, or reflective activities. Basically, the idea is that people don't really change unless they can apply what they are learning in therapy to their lives in the real world.

7. Finally, there is some sort of follow-up that addresses transfer of learning to other situations. You must assess the relative effectiveness of your interventions.

APPROACHES TO INTEGRATION

There are so many different ways that you might undertake the task of integrating the various theories into a workable system.

Blended Families

The first approach involves combining together the ideas and methods of two or more different systems and reconciling their differences. This is like mediating a dispute between opposing factions in which you help the parties focus on what they have to offer one another instead of dwelling on their differences.

There have been a number of successful attempts to blend theoretical families including marriages between psychoanalysis and behavior therapy (Wachtel, 1997), cognitive and behavior therapy (Lazarus, 1971), cognitive and humanistic therapies (Greenberg & Safran, 1987), cognitive and constructivist therapies (Mahoney, 1995), client-centered and Gestalt therapies (Prouty, 1994), and many others. You could almost take any two theories you wish and figure out a way to combine their best features into a combined model.

■ ■ ■ ■ ■ ▬▬▬▬▬▬▬▬▬▬▬▬▬▬▬▬▬▬▬▬▬▬▬▬▬▬▬

FOR A CLASS ACTIVITY

Each student will select the three theories that he or she likes the most. Rank order them according to your preference from 1 to 3.

Divide the class into partnerships (or small teams) in which people with the same choices work together in work groups.

Decide between you which two theories you will integrate and work together to combine their best features into a system that emphasizes their strengths but also overcomes their perceived weaknesses.

Give your new theory a name. Present it to the class.

Empirically Supported Methods

One of the consequences of the managed care movement in North America has been the emphasis on using integrative, case-specific treatments that have empirical research support for their effectiveness. The idea that has evolved is one in which a host of presenting problems would be cross-listed with those therapies that have been demonstrated to be most useful (Chambliss & Hollon, 1998; Task Force on the Promotion and Dissemination of Psychological Procedures, 1995). This means that practitioners are expected to select their treatments for a given client depending on what is recognized as a best practice by relatively universal standards in the profession. Assuming this is feasible (and there is by no means a consensus that it is possible), the future of our work would begin to resemble contemporary medicine in which clinicians select specific procedures according to what symptoms are presented.

If, for example, someone comes into an emergency room complaining of abdominal pain, the physician will ask a series of questions to determine where it is located and whether it is merely indigestion or perhaps something more serious such as pancreatitis, colitis, or appendicitis. After an examination, medical history, and series of tests are administered, a diagnosis would be arrived at, presumably the same conclusion that almost any other doctor present would arrive at and would recommend the same treatment. Of course, there would be some debate and disagreement among practitioners, but eventually they could settle on a prescribed course of action.

Using this same model, our field is moving in a direction of developing similar therapeutic regimens for specific emotional ailments that include particular medications, therapeutic strategies, or a combination of both. As one example, if someone comes in presenting symptoms of panic disorder, as opposed to generalized anxiety or phobic disorder, the therapist might proceed with basic education about the course of the disorder. Support and reassurance would be offered. The therapist might use cognitive interventions to reduce disasterizing and exaggerations of symptoms. Relaxation training might also prove helpful to teach control. In more severe cases, medication (imipramine, fluvoxamine) might be indicated.

A similar treatment protocol can be described for any of the most common complaints from acute reactive depression to posttraumatic stress disorder. In each case, there have been found to be some procedures and methods that are considered more useful than others.

■ ■ ■ ■ ■

FOR A FIELD STUDY

Ask three experienced practitioners how they treat acute anxiety differently from prolonged depression. Find out as much detail as possible about how they adjust their relationship, methods, and treatment procedures.

One Additional Thought

Earlier in the chapter I mentioned how there were several different explanations to account for why no single theory is superior to the others, and why they all seem to work. If you recall, one favored reason was that regardless of their espoused beliefs, most good therapists do essentially the same things with their clients. One other interesting hypothesis, offered by Tallman and Bohart (1999), contends that the reason various theories work equally well, even though they approach things so differently, is that they each provide opportunities for clients to do what they need to do in order to solve their own problems. As long as therapists don't get in the way too much by insisting that clients comply with their rigid agendas, the results are usually satisfactory.

To support this idea, they use the example of exercise methods. It doesn't matter so much whether you run or swim or bicycle or ski cross-country or take an aerobics class as long as you get your cardiovascular system in shape and do it on a regular basis. Of course, there are certain conditions that must be met—getting your heart rate into a certain range, sustaining the exercise for a minimum of twenty minutes, and repeating the process a minimum of several times per week, but other than that, what you do is less important.

Although it may be a bit early in your career to think about integrating theories that you have just learned, it is helpful to think of these frameworks as working models that must be adapted to your unique style of practice and the individualized needs of your clients.

SUGGESTED READINGS

Berman, P. S. (1997). *Case conceptualization and treatment planning: Exercises for integrating theory with clinical practice.* Thousand Oaks, CA: Sage Publications.

Bohart, A. C., & Tallman, K. (1999). *How clients make therapy work.* Washington, DC: American Psychological Association.

Corey, G. (2000). *Theory and practice of counseling and psychotherapy* (6th ed.). Pacific Grove, CA: Brooks/Cole.

Egan, G. (1998). *The skilled helper: A systematic approach to effective helping* (6th ed.). Pacific Grove, CA: Brooks/Cole.

Hubble, M. A., Duncan, B. L., & Miller, S. D. (1999). *The heart and soul of change.* Washington, DC: American Psychological Association.

Kottler, J. A. (1991). *The compleat therapist.* San Francisco: Jossey-Bass.

Preston, J. (1999). *Integrative brief therapy: Cognitive, psychodynamic, humanistic, and neurobehavioral approaches.* New York: Impact Publishers.

Prochaska, J. O., & Norcross, J. C. (1999). *Systems of psychotherapy: A transtheoretical approach* (4th ed.). Pacific Grove, CA: Brooks/Cole.

Santostefano, S. (1998). *A primer on integrating psychotherapies for children and adolescents.* New York: Jason Aronson.

Wachtel, P. L. (1997). *Psychoanalysis, behavior therapy, and the relational world.* Washington, DC: American Psychological Association.

CHAPTER 12

PERSONALIZING AND CUSTOMIZING THEORY FOR CLIENTS AND SETTINGS

Lord Chesterfield, the seventeenth-century English statesman, claimed that the world can never be known by a theory. It provides the beginner with a general map with which to navigate through "mazes, windings, and turnings." It distills the wisdom of experienced travelers into a coherent model that can be used as a guide. But it is *only* a guide. Just that. Nothing more.

You will recall that Carl Jung, one of the earliest rebels to secede from the orthodoxy of Freud's psychoanalytic theory, went on to establish his own school of thought that has grown in influence. Yet Jung saw the limits of theory without personalizing it to the demands of a clinical situation and the needs of a client. Furthermore, theories can even insulate you from the uniquely magical encounter that often happens during therapeutic sessions. "Learn your theories as well as you can," Jung advised, "but put them aside when you the touch the miracle of the living soul."

A CUSTOM FIT

Theories are not like ready-to-wear clothes but rather outfits that must be custom made. Depending on your size, build, posture, and preferences, the clothes must be taken in a little here, let out a little there, and shaped to fit your form and preferences. It is the same with theories. You can pick one off the rack that fits you pretty closely, but you will still need to make some alterations in order to have a proper fit.

It is also crucial to remember that these theories not only need to be customized for your unique personality and interaction style but also for the individualized background of each client. Just imagine how

273

differently you would need to adapt your favored approach to the specific needs of the following clients:

1. An African American corporate executive who has pulled herself out of poverty
2. A homeless man, addicted to crack cocaine and cheap wine, who once enjoyed the privileges of wealth until his company folded and son died of leukemia
3. A Native American teenage girl who struggles between the pull of her white boyfriend who wants her to be more like his friends, and the influence of her parents and culture
4. A Vietnam veteran who lost most of his sexual functioning in a battle wound and has been unable, ever since, to enjoy any sort of intimacy with a woman
5. A Mexican American family with a history of depression that is currently being manifested in the withdrawal of two of their children
6. A racially mixed lesbian couple that experiences disapproval from both of their families and discrimination from many other sources
7. A Japanese exchange student who has become so Americanized during his stay that he can't picture himself ever fitting in again back home

■ ■ ■ ■ ■

FOR A CLASS ACTIVITY

In small work groups, select two different theories with which you are fairly familiar. Make sure one approach is somewhat insight oriented and the other is more action focused.

Review each of the seven cases that have been listed, talking about the ways you may need to adjust your style of practice and approach according to the unique backgrounds of these clients.

No doubt, with each of these clients, you would approach matters with respect, compassion, and empathy. You would also most likely follow the usual process with which you are most comfortable and experienced to assess presenting problems and formulate a treatment plan. But remember how important it is to form diagnostic impressions not only according to standard practices but also by taking into consideration the cultural backgrounds of the cases. Moreover, the specific way that you would apply your preferred theory would depend on how the specific client sees things.

Clients Have Theories, Too

This is a book primarily about the theories of counselors and therapists. What about those of our clients? After all, they come to us with their own strong convictions about how change should and does take place (Wile, 1977).

Unless you are prepared to hear, understand, and honor the client's theory, instead of insisting your own view is correct, you are likely to be fired. The challenge is to negotiate with clients so that your preferred theory of change becomes acceptable to them, or adopting a more personalized approach, you agree to work within the parameters of their perceived reality.

Every person who comes to see you has a fairly definite idea of:

- what the problem is
- what needs to be done to fix it
- what you can do to be of service

Of course, most of the time there is no way you could ever subscribe to the client's framework, especially when the most common theory presented is something such as:

- "The problem is my spouse/parent/boss. It's not my fault."
- "What I want you to do is to get others off my back, let me talk a lot and don't interrupt me, and don't nag me about my drinking."
- "You should agree with me, and tell others that I am right and they are wrong."

As part of your initial assessment, you must find out the client's theory by asking how the client believes that change will occur. Such a dialogue sounds something like this:

Therapist: So you've been saying that you've been depressed for quite a long time, ever since you can remember.

Client: Well, maybe not always, but on and off for a while.

Therapist: How and when did this all begin?

Client: I think it started when I spent so much time sick in the hospital. I was just out of it for a long time.

Therapist: You were pretty immobilized and helpless, depending on almost everyone else to take care of you.

Client: That's for sure. I've just never been the same since then, I don't think.

Therapist: Say some more about how you are aware your life changed.

In this preliminary exploration, the therapist is helping the client to articulate when the symptoms first began. Next, time can be spent finding out when and where the depression is better or worse, what seems to help and what doesn't, and what has already been tried before to make things better. Just as importantly, the therapist needs to find out more about the client's expectations for what will help. If you don't discover those expectations and address them, you can do what you think is the best job in the world but it will all be useless if the client doesn't feel like a satisfied customer.

> **Therapist:**   You've talked a lot about those times when you've felt more in control than others, and especially when you start to fall apart. Maybe you could tell me what you'd like from me. What are you hoping that I can do to help?
>
> **Client:**   [Laughs] You don't have a magic wand or something, do you?
>
> **Therapist:**   Wish I did. But I've got the next best thing.
>
> **Client:**   What's that?
>
> **Therapist:**   Oh, lots of good strategies to help you to combat your depression and feel more in control. But before I tell you about that, I'd like to know more about what *you* think will help most.
>
> **Client:**   I guess it would help if you'd hear me out. Most people in my life are sick of listening to me. They say I whine too much and feel sorry for myself.
>
> **Therapist:**   What do *you* think?
>
> **Client:**   Maybe so, I guess. But I think that people just don't understand what I'm going through.
>
> **Therapist:**   So, you are hoping that I'll understand in ways that others never have. And then maybe help you to understand better as well.
>
> **Client:**   Sure. But most of all, I think I've just got this disease still in me from when I was sick a long time ago, and it just won't let go.

The client's theory is beginning to be teased out. Although it sounds like he wants an exorcist rather than a therapist, it isn't at all unusual that expectations would be different from what the therapist hopes to deliver. Still, with depression, it is always a good idea to rule out physical maladies that could be contributing to the problem. In many cases, such as the diagnosis of an endogenous or long-term depression (as in this instance), it is generally advisable to have a psychiatric evaluation to see if medication might be useful as an adjunct to therapy. But all of that is further down the line; for now, your job is to help the client to speak as frankly as possible about how the problem is conceived and how it is best resolved.

During this process of negotiation in the initial phase, keep in mind the following principles:

1. Ask the client how he or she believes change will occur.
2. Don't argue or disagree too much in the beginning, or your client won't return.
3. Avoid imposing your alternative theory on the client without respecting the person's worldview, cultural values, and expectations.
4. No matter which theory you favor, remember that it must be adapted to fit the unique context of each client.
5. Speak in the client's language instead of professional jargon.
6. Negotiate with the client to find a common ground that you can both live with, one that is consistent with your professional strategy as well as the client's values.

Generic Practice of Therapy

The boundaries between theories are becoming blurred. Therapists who were once avid behaviorists later merged with cognitive theory to call themselves cognitive-behavior therapists. Then they embraced constructivism and decided to include themselves as part of that school of thought. This same process of affiliation and integration is happening within other theoretical families as well.

Quite often, beginners to the field are introduced to the theory and research in the profession. You are required to learn the history and the major concepts. Then you are tested on the material and asked to write papers demonstrating your mastery of the material. Your head becomes full of content to the point it sometimes feels like it will burst.

Your first client walks in for help. Quick, what do you do?

The simple answer to this question is that you do whatever you can. You size up the situation as best you can. With only a second or two between verbalizations, there is really no time to think much; you must react on instinct and training. Much of this preparation comes not only from your theory courses but also from the instruction in core therapeutic skills.

Although from this class you might have gotten the distinct impression that therapists and counselors don't agree on very much, that is really not the case at all. There might be variations in one's preferred conceptual framework but very little variation exists in the skills that are used in session. By skills, I am referring to the specific therapist behaviors that are used to respond and intervene in session.

If you would watch live or videotaped sessions of therapists from different theoretical orientations, you would actually notice remarkable similarity in the skills they used. You would hear and see them asking questions and responding to client statements with what sounds like re-statements or at least rephrasing what clients said. You would notice the use of summary statements occasionally in which the therapist ties together several ideas. You would witness some interpretations in which the therapist introduces alternative ways of looking at things. Meanwhile, you would observe lots of head nodding, "uh huhs," and non-verbal behavior to communicate that the therapist is listening intently. You would also hear the therapist probe and explore certain issues by framing questions in particular ways. You would see other skills as well that are virtually universal: confronting clients by pointing out discrepancies, setting goals, role-playing, and structuring therapeutic tasks.

When it comes time to personalize the way you do therapy, this won't come about on a conceptual level alone but also the way you practice in terms of your basic skills and therapeutic behaviors. I remember in my first course we actually sat and practiced for a whole class period how to sit with a client—leaning forward, making easy eye contact, learning attending behaviors. I thought this was silly at the time, but it is an example of the kinds of habits you will be taught to develop.

It is interesting the way different therapist training and counselor preparation programs handle these generic skills. You may already have taken a course in counseling techniques or therapeutic skills before this one. In other curricula, theory is offered first and then skills follow. In one program that I have been involved with, theory, skills, and practice are all integrated into one unit. This is more consistent with Hawaiian culture where the training is offered because it does not make sense in this setting to break up learning into discrete units. Instead, students first learn a theory. Next, they practice the skills and techniques that come from that theory (reflective listening as part of client-centered theory or goal setting as part of behavioral theory). Finally, they apply the theory and skills with clients in the field. Then we move on to the next approach.

Regardless of which sequence you are following, whether you have already had a skills class, are taking it at the same time as this course, or will take it next, you should know that it is at this level that you will end up personalizing your practice the most. You may get drilled in the "correct" way to ask open-ended questions or the most opportune way to confront people without eliciting defensiveness. This is consistent with the way any new skills are taught, whether it is the proper grip for holding a backhand in tennis, the prescribed position of your knees when making a snowplow turn in skiing, or the proper breath control needed to hold a long note in an operatic aria.

Soon after you commit these skills and behaviors to memory and habitual responding, you will begin to adapt them to fit your unique interpersonal style. This is actually a very important stage in your evolution as a clinician, that which makes you come across as natural and comfortable rather than wooden and stiff.

Recently, I did a demonstration of cognitive therapy for an organizational affiliate of an international organization devoted to this theory. This group of psychologists in Iceland had been learning and practicing cognitive therapy for some time but wanted to see how an American would do it. I warned them that it had been many years since I identified exclusively with this orientation, but I would give it a try. On the inside, I was thinking and feeling very much like I was doing cognitive therapy with my client: I purposely stuck with that framework as much as possible for the sake of my audience. On the outside, however, I didn't look much like I was using the theory and skills that they had been learning. They noticed me using a lot of reflections of feeling and paraphrasing. I inserted a few interpretations and connected what the client was saying to other themes. I offered lots of reassurance and came across as very warm and kind.

When we discussed the session afterward, I realized just how much I have personalized these cognitive skills and theory over the years, just as I have with other approaches. Your job will be to do the same thing: to take the generic therapeutic behaviors that are considered somewhat universal and to integrate them into your unique style of communication. There are several texts that train you in these therapist behaviors (Cormier & Cormier, 1998; Egan, 1998; Kottler, 2000), and even one that is programmed as a form of self-instruction (Evans, Hearn, Uhlemann, & Ivey, 1998).

DECIDING ON A STARTING POINT

In many cases, you won't have a choice about which theory you use in your practicum, internship, or first job—your supervisors may require you to follow a particular framework that they believe is best suited for beginners, most appropriate for the setting, or simply their most favored model. At some point in your career, however, you will have the chance to pick the theory you like the best and then later to adapt or integrate it with other things you learn.

In making your choice, you may wish to consider the following questions:

1. *What are your personal strengths and how do they fit best with a theory that seems well suited to your style?* If you are basically low key, nurturing, and warm, you might select an approach that is different from someone who is more flamboyant, provocative, and confrontive. You have read about theories in which the therapist's role is to be a teacher/coach as opposed to a parent/mentor, consultant/tutor, or provocateur. Start with a framework that seems most natural to you.

■ ■ ■ ■ ■

FOR PERSONAL APPLICATION

In your journal or on separate sheets of paper, answer the questions about your core beliefs and values. This will give you the basic workings of a personal theory in development.

2. *What are your beliefs about how change takes place?* Do you think that real change takes a long time or that it can occur very quickly? How important do you think the past is in dealing with present problems? How much responsibility should the client have in the relationship as compared to that of the therapist? Does change take place most effectively at the level of feelings, thoughts, or behavior? Each of these questions signals a distinct preference you might have to choose one theory over another. If you haven't yet made up your mind in these areas (which is entirely appropriate), you might wish to pick a framework that allows for maximum flexibility.

3. *What sort of work will you be doing?* Depending on where you will be working and whom you will be helping, you will find some approaches better than others. You wouldn't want to use a psychoanalytic or other long-term approach if you working with substance abusers or in a crisis intervention clinic. You also would not want to use a complex, intellectual approach with hospitalized schizophrenics or elementary school kids, nor would you attempt a form of brief therapy with someone who has major depression or a personality disorder.

4. *Which approaches that you studied appeal to you most?* You must have some strong reactions, one way or the other, to the ideas you read about. Which ones speak to you? Which ones feel compatible with the way you live your life? A theory should feel like "home," a comfortable place for you to sort things out.

5. *Once you settle on one theory as a starting point, how will you need to personalize it in such a way that it becomes part of your own style?* Don't think of your choice of therapeutic approach as the end of your search but as the beginning. A theory is a tool, just like a computer. You acquire it in its generic form, with the all settings arranged according to the preferences of the orig-

inal programmer. Then it's up to you to customize the instrument so that it fits your needs and responds to your most frequent commands.

6. *Which dimensions of a few other therapeutic approaches might you like to blend into your primary framework?* Once you have picked a central theory, that does not mean you must exclude the attractive features of other approaches you have studied. As you were surveying each of the options available, you probably kept inventory (in the form of mental or written notes) of ideas that you found especially useful. You will find ways to include many of these strategies in your chosen framework after you make the adjustments that are more consistent with the model. If you were existentially inclined, for instance, you would not want to simply start adding goal setting to your therapy without first thinking through how this structure contributes to your overall treatment objectives.

7. *Whom might you consult for supervision and additional training in your preferred model?* It can easily take a lifetime or two to master the intricacies of any single theoretical framework. Every year there are new refinements in the basic ideas, as well as innovations in research, technique, and applications. You can't learn this stuff by reading alone. You must practice the model with a variety of clients, reflect on your relative effectiveness, and get lots of feedback from more experienced practitioners about ways you could improve.

LIMITATIONS OF THEORY

In this text you have learned about the major theoretical frameworks currently in use by therapists. All of them are built on the assumption that understanding change is knowable. Therapists and counselors, as a group, share the strong belief that it is possible to figure out why people do the things they do. More to the point, we believe that it is feasible to (a) guide people in desired directions, then (b) come up with a reasonable and accurate explanation for why and how it happened, and (c) how this can be replicated in the future. In the previous statement, although it is entirely possible that (a) and (c) can be attained most of the time, I don't believe that is the case with (b)—that any theory currently in use can really explain comprehensively and accurately what happened and why.

■ ■ ■ ■ ■

FOR PERSONAL REFLECTION

Think about phenomena in our world that are explained by theories that you consider inadequate. For example, meteorologists apply all that is scientifically known about weather patterns to try and predict what will occur several days in the future. They collect extensive data on wind, atmospheric conditions, and every possible variable. They rely on historical patterns that have been collected over the past century. They use the fastest supercomputers to collate all the information, examine patterns, and forecast what is on its way. Yet with all this know-how, technology, and data available, they are still wrong a significant number of times. Several times a year, they fail to predict a storm that takes everyone by surprise. They miss developing hurricanes. They say it will be a nice day and then it rains. Clearly, their theories of weather forecasting are missing some crucial elements.

What are some other aspects of daily life that also have limited theories to explain things?

In physics and the physical sciences, there are theories that can be empirically tested in such a way that almost all variables can be controlled. Outcomes can be predicted time after time with almost perfect accuracy. This is not nearly the case with the practice of theory. First of all, human behavior is far too complex to ever be truly understood. Second, even if we had a theory that consistently and completely explained why people have personal problems and what could be done to resolve them, the human practitioners could never apply it consistently in such a way that it would always produce the same outcome.

As you know, there are medical specialists who also treat emotional problems with medications and other surgical procedures. These psychiatrists and neurologists have been achieving rather successful outcomes prescribing psychoactive drugs to treat depression, panic disorder, and other severe mental disorders. Electroconvulsive therapy, better known as shock treatment or ECT, has demonstrated even more dramatic benefits, achieving a success rate approaching 80% to 90% with chronic depression (Fischer, 2000). As impressive as the results might be of these medical treatments, most physicians still don't have very good theories to explain how and why they work. Saying that it is the rapid firing of neurons in the brain that recalibrates the neurological system is not entirely satisfactory. Yet we can't argue with success.

I leave you with the humbling thought that the theories you have read about in this text and others you will most likely study in your lifetime represent only approximations of truth. They don't really explain the way people function, nor do they describe all that comprehensively how therapy works. Nevertheless, they are the best models we have at the time, and they are always getting better.

The next step belongs to you. One of the exciting aspects of our young field is that there is still so much more room for growth and development. Your responsibility as a practitioner does not end with only helping your clients; you also have a professional obligation to further the advance of knowledge. You may decide not to publish your ideas and innovations in journals or present them at conferences (although I would strongly urge you to do so), but you are highly likely to discover things about therapeutic practice that have never been known before. Of course, you may not realize this at the time, or maybe ever, unless you decide to share your experiences with others.

A FINAL ASSIGNMENT

Rather than the end of your study of theory, this is just the beginning. A course such as this represents a conceptual foundation that you will need to understand the basic principles of helping others from multiple frames of reference.

If you have not already begun a journal in which to record your thoughts, reflections, insights, struggles, and confusions as a beginning practitioner, now is the time to do so. Once the formal requirements of this class are over and the assignments, papers, and tests are completed, you can concentrate more fully on your own personal and professional development as a therapist.

Make it a habit to write to yourself on a regular basis about the current status of your theory development and practice. Focus on areas that perplex you the most. Highlight the things you read, hear, and see that don't make sense to you. Talk to trusted colleagues about your struggles and invite them to do the same.

Who knows? Perhaps a few decades from now, it will be *your* theory that is profiled in a text like this.

REFERENCES

Abraham, D. F., & Gilgen, A. R. (Eds.). (1995). *Chaos theory in psychology*. Westport, CT: Praeger.

Ackerman, N. W. (1937). *The psychodynamics of family life*. New York: Basic Books.

Adler, A. (1931). *Guiding the child*. New York: Greenberg.

American Association for Marriage and Family Therapy. (1998). *Code of ethics*. Washington, DC: Author.

American Counseling Association. (1995). *Code of ethics and standards of practice*. Alexandria, VA: Author.

American Psychological Association. (1995). *Ethical principles of psychologists and code of conduct*. Washington, DC: Author.

American Psychological Association Task Force on Promotion and Dissemination of Psychological Procedures. (1995). Training and dissemination of empirically-validated psychological treatments: Report and recommendations. *The Clinical Psychologist, 48*, 3–23.

Anderson, W. T. (1990). *Reality isn't what it used to be*. San Francisco: HarperCollins.

Ansbacher, H. L., & Ansbacher, R. R. (Eds.). (1956). *The individual psychology of Alfred Adler*. New York: Basic Books.

Appelbaum, S. A. (1995). *Effecting change in psychotherapy*. Northvale, NJ: Jason Aronson.

Asay, T. P., & Lambert, M. J. (1999). The empirical case for the common factors in therapy: Quantitative findings. In M. A. Hubble, B. L. Duncan, & S. D. Miller (Eds.), *The heart and soul of change*. Washington, DC: American Psychological Association.

Bandler, R., & Grinder, J. (1975). *The structure of magic*. Palo Alto, CA: Science and Behavior Books.

Bandura, A. (1969). *Principles of behavior modification*. New York: Holt, Rinehart, and Winston.

Barber, J. P. (1994). Efficacy of short-term dynamic psychotherapy. *Journal of Psychotherapy Practice and Research, 3*, 108–121.

Baruth, L. G., & Manning, M. L. (1999). *Multicultural counseling and psychotherapy: A life perspective*. Upper Saddle River, NJ: Merrill.

Bateson, G. (1979). *Mind and nature: A necessary unity*. New York: Dutton.

Bateson, G., Jackson, D. D., Haley, J., & Weakland, J. H. (1956). Toward a theory of schizophrenia. *Behavioral Science, 1*, 251–264.

Bateson, M. S. (1984). *With a daughter's eye: A memoir of Margaret Mead and Gregory Bateson*. New York: William Morrow.

Barrett-Lennard, G. T. (1999). *Carl Rogers' helping system: Journey and substance*. London: Sage.

Beck, A. (1967). *Depression: Clinical, experimental, and theoretical aspects*. New York: Harper and Row.

Beck, A. (1997). Cognitive therapy: Reflections. In J. Zeig (Ed.), *Evolution of psychotherapy: The third conference*. New York: Brunner/Mazel.

Beck, A. T. (1999). *Prisoners of hate: The cognitive basis of anger, hostility, and violence*. New York: HarperCollins.

Beck, A., & Emery, G. (1985). *Anxiety disorders and phobias*. New York: Basic Books.

Beck, A., & Young, J. E. (1985). Cognitive therapy of depression. In D. Barlow (Ed.), *Clinical handbook of psychological disorders*. New York: Guilford.

Beck, A., and Associates (1990). *Cognitive therapy of personality disorders*. New York: Guilford.

Becvar, D. S., & Becvar, R. J. (1999). *Family therapy: A systemic integration*. Boston: Allyn and Bacon.

Belenky, M. F., Clinchy, B. M., Goldberger, N. P., & Tarull, J. M. (1986). *Women's ways of knowing: The development of self, voice, and mind.* New York: Basic Books.

Bellak, L. (1992). *Handbook of intensive brief and emergency psychotherapy.* Larchmont, NY: C.P.S.

Bernard, M. E. (2001). *Rational-emotive therapy with children and adolescents: Theory, preventive methods, treatment strategies.* New York: Wiley.

Blatner, A. (1997). *The art of play therapy.* New York: Brunner/Mazel.

Bloom, B. L. (1997). *Planned short-term psychotherapy: A clinical handbook.* Boston: Allyn and Bacon.

Bohart, A. (1993). Experiencing: The basis of psychotherapy. *Journal of Psychotherapy Integration, 3,* 51–67.

Bohart, A., & Tallman, K. (1999). *How clients make therapy work: The process of active self-healing.* Washington, DC: American Psychological Association.

Book, H. E. (1998). *How to practice brief psychodynamic psychotherapy.* Washington, DC: American Psychological Association.

Boorstein, D. J. (1983). *The discoverers: A history of man's search to know his world and himself.* New York: Random House.

Boorstein, D. J. (1992). *The creators: A history of heroes of the imagination.* New York: Random House.

Borden, W. (Ed.). (1999). *Comparative approaches in brief dynamic psychotherapy.* New York: Haworth Press.

Bowen, M. (1966). The use of family theory in clinical practice. *Comprehensive Psychiatry, 7,* 345–374.

Boy, A. V., & Pine, G. J. (1999). *A person-centered foundation for counseling and psychotherapy* (2nd ed.). Springfield, IL: C. C. Thomas.

Brack, C. J., Brack, G., & Zucker, A. (1995). How chaos and complexity theory can help counselors to be more effective. *Counseling and Values, 39,* 200–208.

Breger, L. (2000). *Freud: Darkness in the midst of vision.* New York: Wiley.

Breuer, G. (1982). *Sociobiology and the human dimension.* New York: Cambridge University Press.

Brock, G. W., & Barnard, C. P. (1999). *Procedures in marriage and family therapy* (3rd ed.). Boston: Allyn and Bacon.

Brodsky, A. M., & Hare-Mustin, A. (Eds.). (1980). *Women and psychotherapy.* New York: Guilford.

Brothers, B. J. (Ed.). (1999). *Couples therapy in managed care: Facing the crisis.* New York: Haworth.

Budman, S. H., & Gurman, A. (1988). *Theory and practice of brief therapy.* New York: Guilford.

Bugental, J. F. T. (1965). *The search for existential identity.* New York: Holt, Rinehart and Winston.

Bugental, J. F. T. (1967). *Challenges of humanistic psychology.* New York: McGraw-Hill.

Bugental, J. F. T. (1991). Outcomes of an existential-humanistic psychotherapy. *Humanistic Psychologist, 19,* 2–9.

Bugental, J. F. T. (1992). *The art of psychotherapy.* New York: W. W. Norton.

Buirski, P. (1994). Nine analysts in search of a character. In P. Buirski (Ed.), *Comparing schools of analytic therapy.* Northvale, NJ: Jason Aronson.

Burlew, L. D., & Roland, C. B. (1999). Eastern theories. In D. Capuzzi & D. R. Gross (Eds.), *Counseling and psychotherapy: Theories and interventions.* Upper Saddle River, NJ: Merrill.

Burr, V. (1995). *An introduction to social constructionism.* London: Routledge.

Buss, D. M. (1999). *Evolutionary psychology: The new science of the mind.* Boston: Allyn and Bacon.

Cade, B., & O'Hanlon, W. H. (1993). *A brief guide to brief therapy.* New York: W. W. Norton.

Capra, F. (1975). *The Tao of physics.* Berkeley, CA: Shambhala.

Capuzzi, D., & Gross, D. R. (1999). *Counseling and psychotherapy: Theories and interventions* (2nd ed.). Upper Saddle River, NJ: Merrill.

Carkhuff, R. R., & Berenson, B. G. (1967). *Beyond counseling and psychotherapy.* New York: Holt, Rinehart and Winston.

Carlson, J. (1991). On beyond Adler. *Individual Psychology, 47,* 2.

Carlson, J., & Slavik, S. (Eds.). (1997). *Techniques in Adlerian psychology.* Philadelphia: Accelerated Development.

Chadla, Y. (1999). *Gandhi: A life.* New York: Wiley.

Chambliss, C. H. (2000). *Psychotherapy and managed care: Reconciling research and reality.* Boston: Allyn and Bacon.

Chambliss, C. H., & Hollon, S. (1998). Defining empirically supported therapies. *Journal of Consulting and Clinical Psychology, 66,* 7–18.

Chaplin, J. (1988). *Feminist counselling in action.* London: Sage.

Chesterfield, Lord (1774/1901). *Letters of the Earl of Chesterfield to his son.* Vol. 1, No. 190. London: Charles Strachey.

Cheston, S. E. (2000). A new paradigm for teaching counseling theory and practice. *Counselor Education and Supervision, 39,* 254–269.

Chevalier, A. (1995). *On the client's path: A manual for the practice of solution-focused therapy.* Oakland, CA: New Harbinger.

Clark, A. J. (1998). *Defense mechanisms in the counseling process.* Thousand Oaks, CA: Sage.

Clark, D. W., Beck, A. T., & Alford, B. A. (1999). *Scientific foundation of cognitive theory and therapy of depression.* New York: Wiley.

Clark, R. W. (1971). *Einstein: His life and times.* New York: World.

Cohen, E. D., & Cohen, G. S. (1999). *The virtuous therapist.* Pacific Grove, CA: Brooks/Cole.

Cohen, J., & Stewart, I. (1994). *The collapse of chaos: Discovering simplicity in a complex world.* New York: Viking.

Corey, G., Corey, M., & Callanan, P. (1998). *Issues and ethics in the helping professions.* Pacific Grove, CA: Brooks/Cole.

Cormier, W. H., & Cormier, L. S. (1998). *Interviewing strategies for helpers* (4th ed.). Pacific Grove, CA: Brooks/Cole.

Cottone, R. R., & Tarvydas, V. M. (1998). *Ethical and professional issues in counseling.* New York: Merrill.

Coveny, P., & Highfield, R. (1995). *Frontiers of complexity: The search for order in a chaotic world.* New York: Fawcett Columbine.

Csikszentmihalyi, M. (1975). *Beyond boredom and anxiety.* San Francisco: Jossey-Bass.

Csikszentmihalyi, M. (1998). *Finding flow: The psychology of engagement in everyday life.* New York: Basic Books.

Csikszentmihalyi, M. (1999). If we are so rich, why aren't we happy? *American Psychologist, 10,* 821–827.

Darwin, C. (1859). *The origin of species.* London: Murray.

Darwin, F. (Ed.). (1888/1969). *Life and letters of Charles Darwin.* New York: Johnson.

Davanloo, H. (1980). *Short-term dynamic psychotherapy.* New York: Jason Aronson.

de Shazer, S. (1985). *Keys to solutions in brief therapy.* New York: W. W. Norton.

de Shazer, S. (1991). *Putting difference to work.* New York: W. W. Norton.

Dinkmeyer, D., & Sperry, L. (2000). *Counseling and psychotherapy: An integrated, individual psychology approach* (3rd ed.). Upper Saddle River, NJ: Merrill.

Dollard, J., & Miller, N. E. (1950). *Personality and psychotherapy.* New York: McGraw-Hill.

Dosamantes, E. (1990). Movement and psychodynamic pattern changes in long-term dance/movement therapy groups. *American Journal of Dance Therapy, 12,* 27–44.

Dreikurs, R. (1967). *Psychodynamics, psychotherapy, and counseling: Collected papers.* Chicago: Alfred Adler Institute.

Dryden, W. (1995). *Brief rational emotive behaviour therapy.* London: Wiley.

Dugatkin, L. (1999). *Cheating monkeys and citizen bees.* New York: The Free Press.

Duncan, B., Miller, S., & Sparks, J. (2000). Exposing the mythmakers. *Family Therapy Networker,* March/April, 24–33.

Egan, G. (1998). *The skilled helper* (6th ed.). Pacific Grove, CA: Brooks/Cole.

Ellis, A. (1962). *Reason and emotion in psychotherapy.* Secaucus, NJ: Citadel.

Ellis, A. (1996). *Better, deeper, and more enduring brief therapy.* New York: Brunner/Mazel.

Ellis, A. (1997). The evolution of Albert Ellis and Rational Emotive Behavior Therapy. In J. Zeig (Ed.), *Evolution of psychotherapy: The third conference.* New York: Brunner/Mazel.

Ellis, A., & MacLaren, C. (1998). *Rational emotive behavior therapy: A therapist's guide.* San Luis Obispo, CA: Impact Publishers.

Ellis, A. (2001). *Overcoming destructive beliefs, feelings, and behaviors: New directions for rational emotive behavior therapy.* New York: Prometheus.

Enns, C. Z. (1997). *Feminist theories and feminist psychotherapies.* New York: Harrington Park Press.

Erickson, M. (1954). Special techniques of brief hypnotherapy. *Journal of Clinical and Experimental Hypnosis, 2,* 109–129.

Erickson, M. (1964). The confusion technique in hypnosis. *American Journal of Clinical Hypnosis, 6,* 183–207.

Erikson, E. (1969). *Gandhi's truth.* New York: W. W. Norton.

Eron, J. B., & Lund, T. W. (1998). *Narrative solutions in brief therapy.* New York: Guilford.

Evans, D. R., Hearn, M. T., Uhlemann, M. R., & Ivey, A. E. (1998). *Essential interviewing* (4th ed.). Pacific Grove, CA: Brooks/Cole.

Eysenck, H. (1952). The effects of psychotherapy: An evaluation. *Journal of Consulting and Clinical Psychology, 16,* 319–324.

Feldman, L. (1992). *Integrating individual and family therapy.* New York: Brunner/Mazel.

Fisch, R. (1982). Erickson's impact on brief psychotherapy. In J. K. Zeig (Ed.), *Ericksonian approaches to hypnosis and psychotherapy.* New York: Brunner/Mazel.

Fisch, R., Weakland, J. H., & Segal, L. (1982). *The tactics of change: Doing therapy briefly.* San Francisco: Jossey-Bass.

Fischer, J. S. (2000). Taking the shock out of electroshock. *U.S. News and World Report,* Jan. 24, 46.

Fish, J. M. (1973). *Placebo therapy.* San Francisco: Jossey-Bass.

Fishman, D. B., & Franks, C. M. (1997). The conceptual evolution of behavior therapy. In P. L. Wachtel & S. B. Messer (Eds.), *Theories of psychotherapy: Origins and evolution.* Washington, DC: American Psychological Association.

Folsing, A. (1998). *Albert Einstein: A biography.* New York: Penguin.

Frager, S. (2000). *Managing managed care: Secrets from a former case manager.* New York: Wiley.

Framo, J. L. (1992). *Family-of-origin therapy: An intergenerational approach.* New York: Brunner/Mazel.

Frank, J. D. (1973). *Persuasion and healing.* Baltimore: Johns Hopkins University Press.

Frank, K. A. (1992). Combining action techniques with psychoanalytic therapy. *International Review of Psychoanalysis, 19,* 51–79.

Frankl, V. (1962). *Man's search for meaning.* New York: Washington Square.

Frankl, V. (1978). *The unheard cry for meaning.* New York: Simon & Schuster.

Frankl, V. (1997). *Victor Frankl recollections: An autobiography.* New York: Perseus Books.

Fredericks, J. (1999). *Psychodynamic psychotherapy: Learning to listen from multiple perspectives.* New York: Brunner/Mazel.

Freeman, A. (1993). A psychological approach for conceptualizing schematic development for cognitive therapy. In K. T. Kuehlwein & H. Rosen (Eds.), *Cognitive therapy in action.* San Francisco: Jossey-Bass.

French, T. M. (1933). Interrelations between psychoanalysis and the experimental work of Pavlov. *American Journal of Psychiatry, 89,* 1165–1203.

Freud, S. (1915/1953). The dynamics of the transference. In *Collected Papers*. London: Hogarth Press.

Fujita, C. (1986). *Morita therapy: Psychotherapeutic system for neurosis*. Tokyo: Igaku-Schoin.

Gardner, H. (1993). *Creating minds*. New York: Basic Books.

Garfield, S. L., & Bergin, A. E. (1994). Introduction and historical overview. In A. E. Bergin & S. L. Garfield (Eds.), *Handbook of psychotherapy and behavior change* (4th ed.) New York: Wiley.

Gay, P. (1998). *Freud: A life for our time*. New York: W. W. Norton.

Gelso, C. J., & Carter, J. A. (1994). Components of the psychotherapy relationship: Their interaction and unfolding during treatment. *Journal of Counseling Psychology, 41,* 296–306.

Gendlin, E. (1962). *Experiencing and the creation of meaning*. New York: Free Press.

Gendlin, E. (1981). *Focusing*. New York: Guilford.

Gendlin, E. (1995). *The focusing approach: Experiential psychotherapy*. New York: Guilford.

Gendlin, E. (1997). The use of focusing in therapy. In J. Zeig (Ed.), *Evolution of psychotherapy: The third conference*. New York: Brunner/Mazel.

Gendlin, E. (1988). *Focusing-oriented psychotherapy*. New York: Guilford.

Gerber, S. (1999). *Enhancing counselor intervention strategies*. Philadelphia: Accelerated Development.

Gergen, K. J. (1985). The social constructionist movement in modern psychology. *American Psychologist, 40,* 266–275.

Gerson, B. (Ed.). (1996). *The therapist as a person: Life crises, life choices, life experiences, and their effects on treatment*. New York: Analytic Press.

Gill, M. M. (1984). Psychoanalysis and psychotherapy: A revision. *International Review of Psychoanalysis, 11,* 161–179.

Gilligan, C. (1982). *In a different voice*. Cambridge, MA: Harvard University Press.

Gilligan, S. (1997). Living in a post-Ericksonian world. In W. J. Matthews & J. H. Edgette (Eds.), *Current thinking and research in brief therapy*. New York: Brunner/Mazel.

Gilliland, B. E., & James, R. K. (1998). *Theories and strategies in counseling and psychotherapy* (4th ed.). Boston: Allyn and Bacon.

Gladding, S. T. (1998). *Family therapy: History, theory, and practice* (2nd ed.). Upper Saddle River, NJ: Prentice Hall.

Glantz, K., & Pearce, J. K. (1989). *Exiles from Eden: Psychotherapy from an evolutionary perspective*. New York: W. W. Norton.

Glasser, W. (1965). *Reality therapy: A new approach to psychiatry*. New York: Harper and Row.

Glasser, W. (1969). *Schools without failure*. New York: Harper and Row.

Glasser, W. (1976). *Positive addiction*. New York: HarperCollins.

Glasser, W. (1985). *Control theory: A new explanation of how we control our lives*. New York: Harper and Row.

Glasser, W. (1990). *The quality school*. New York: HarperCollins.

Glasser, W. (1998). *Choice theory: A new psychology of personal freedom*. New York: HarperCollins.

Glasser, W., & Wubbolding, R. E. (1995). Reality therapy. In R. J. Corsini & D. Wedding (Eds.), *Current psychotherapies* (5th ed.). Itasca, IL: F. E. Peacock.

Gleick, J. (1987). *Chaos: Making a new science*. New York: Penguin Books.

Goldenberg, I., & Goldenberg, H. (2001). *Family therapy: An overview* (5th ed.). Pacific Grove, CA: Brooks/Cole.

Goldfried, M. (1980). Toward the delineation of therapeutic change principles. *American Psychologist, 35,* 991–999.

Goldfried, M. (1991). Transtheoretical ingredients in therapeutic change. In R. C. Curtis & G. Stricker (Eds.), *How people change: Inside and outside therapy*. New York: Plenum.

Goodwin, D. K. (1995). *No ordinary time: Franklin and Eleanor Roosevelt*. New York: Simon and Schuster.

Goolishian, H., & Anderson, H. (1987). Language systems and therapy: An evolving idea. *Psychotherapy, 24,* 529–538.

Gordon, T. (1975). *Parent effectiveness training.* New York: New American Library.

Gordon, T. (1986). *Leader effectiveness training.* New York: Bantam.

Gordon, T. (1987). *Teacher effectiveness training.* New York: David McCay.

Greenberg, L. S., & Johnson, S. (1987). *Emotionally focused therapy for couples.* New York: Guilford.

Greenberg, L. S., & Rice, L. N. (1997). Humanistic approaches to psychotherapy. In P. L. Wachtel & S. B. Messer (Eds.), *Theories of psychotherapy: Origins and evolution.* Washington, DC: American Psychological Association.

Greenberg, L. S., Rice, L. N., & Elliott, R. (1993). *Facilitating emotional change: the moment-by-moment process.* New York: Guilford Press.

Greenberg, L. S., & Safran, J. D. (1987). *Emotion in psychotherapy.* New York: Guilford.

Greenson, R. R., & Wexler, M. (1969). The non-transference relationship in the psychoanalytic situation. *International Journal of Psychoanalysis, 50,* 27–39.

Grey, L. (1998). *Alfred Adler: The forgotten prophet.* Westport, CT: Praeger.

Gustafson, J. P. (1986). *The complex secret of brief psychotherapy.* New York: W. W. Norton.

Haas, C. (2000). Entangled in the net. *Counseling Today,* Jan., 27–28.

Hager, D. (1992). Chaos and growth. *Psychotherapy, 29,* 378–384.

Haley, J. (1963). *Strategies of psychotherapy.* New York: Grune & Stratton.

Haley, J. (1967). *Advanced techniques of hypnosis and therapy: Selected papers of Milton H. Erickson.* New York: Grune & Stratton.

Haley, J. (1973). *Uncommon therapy: The psychiatric techniques of Milton H. Erickson.* New York: W. W. Norton.

Haley, J. (1976). *Problem solving therapy.* New York: Harper and Row.

Haley, J. (1984). *Ordeal therapy.* San Francisco: Jossey-Bass.

Haley, J. (1987). *Problem solving therapy* (2nd ed.). San Francisco: Jossey-Bass.

Havighurst, R. (1972). *Developmental tasks and education.* New York: Mackay.

Hill, M., & Rothblum, E. (Eds.). (1999). *Learning from our mistakes: Difficulties and failures in feminist therapy.* New York: Haworth.

Hollender, M. H., & Ford, C. V. (2000). *Dynamic psychotherapy: An introductory approach.* New York: Jason Aronson.

Holt, M. F. (2000). *Some stories are better than others: Doing works in brief therapy and managed care.* New York: Brunner/Mazel.

Horgan, J. (1996). *The end of science.* Reading, MA: Addison-Wesley.

Horowitz, M. (1988). *Introduction to psychodyamics: A new synthesis.* New York: Basic Books.

Hubble, M. A., Duncan, B. L., & Miller, S. D. (1999). *The heart and soul of change.* Washington, DC: American Psychological Association.

Hyde, J. S. (1991). *Half the human experience: The psychology of women* (4th ed.). Lexington, MA: D. C. Heath.

Ibrahim, F. A. (1985). Effective cross-cultural counseling and psychotherapy: A framework. *Counseling Psychologist, 13,* 625–638.

Ivey, A., Ivey, M., & Simek-Morgan, L. (1997). *Counseling and psychotherapy: A multicultural perspective* (4th ed.). Boston: Allyn and Bacon.

Iwakabe, S. (1999). Psychotherapy and chaos theory: The metaphoric relationship between psychodynamic therapy and chaos theory. *Psychotherapy, 36,* 274–286.

Jackson, D. D. (1965). The study of the family. *Family Process, 4*(1), 1–20.

Jensen, J. P., Bergin, A. E., & Greaves, D. W. (1990). The meaning of eclecticism: New survey and analysis of components. *Professional Psychology: Research and Practice, 21,* 124–130.

Johnson, (1995). *Dramatherapy with children and adolescents.* New York: Routledge.

Jones, E. (1961). *The life and work of Sigmund Freud.* New York: Basic Books.

Jung, C. (1926/1954). *Collected works.* Princeton, NJ: Princeton University Press.

Kaplan, H. S. (1974). *The new sex therapy.* New York: Brunner/Mazel.

Karasu, T. B. (1986). The specificity versus nonspecificity dilemma: Toward identifying therapeutic change agents. *American Journal of Psychiatry, 143,* 687–695.

Kernberg O. F. (1975). *Borderline conditions and pathological narcissism.* New York: Jason Aronson.

Kernberg, O. F. (1984). *Severe personality disorders.* New Haven, CT: Yale University Press.

Kernberg, O. F. (1997). Convergences and divergences in contemporary psychoanalytic technique and psychoanalytic psychotherapy. In J. Zeig (Ed.), *Evolution of psychotherapy: The third conference.* New York: Brunner/Mazel.

Kingsolver, B. (1999). *The poisonwood bible.* New York: Harper.

Kohut, H. (1984). *How does psychoanalysis cure?* Chicago: University of Chicago Press.

Kohut, H. (1971). *The analysis of the self.* Madison, CT: International Universities Press.

Kohut, H. (1977). *Restoration of the self.* New York: International Universities Press.

Kottler, J. A. (1991). *The compleat therapist.* San Francisco: Jossey-Bass.

Kottler, J. A. (1992). *Compassionate therapy: Working with difficult clients.* San Francisco: Jossey-Bass.

Kottler, J. A. (1993). *On being a therapist* (rev. ed.). San Francisco: Jossey-Bass.

Kottler, J. A. (1994). *Beyond blame: A new way of resolving conflicts in relationships.* San Francisco: Jossey-Bass.

Kottler, J. A. (1995). *Growing a therapist.* San Francisco: Jossey-Bass.

Kottler, J. A. (1996). *The language of tears.* San Francisco: Jossey-Bass.

Kottler, J. A. (1997). *Travel that can change your life: How to create a transformative experience.* San Francisco: Jossey-Bass.

Kottler, J. A. (2000). *The therapist's workbook.* San Francisco: Jossey-Bass.

Kottler, J. A. (2001). *Making changes last.* Philadelphia: Brunner/Routledge.

Kottler, J. A., & Blau, D. S. (1989). *The imperfect therapist: Learning from failure in therapeutic practice.* San Francisco: Jossey-Bass.

Kottler, J. A., & Brown, R. W. (2000). *Introduction to therapeutic counseling: Voices from the field* (4th ed.). Pacific Grove, CA: Brooks/Cole.

Kottler, J. A., & Hazler, R. (1997). *What you never learned in graduate school.* New York: W. W. Norton.

Kottler, J. A., & Hazler, R. (2001). Therapist as a model of humane values and humanistic behavior. In K. Schneider, J. T. Bugental, & J. F. Pierson (Eds.), *Handbook of humanistic psychology.* Thousand Oaks, CA: Sage.

Kottler, J., Sexton, T., & Whiston, S. (1994). *Heart of healing: Relationships in therapy.* San Francisco: Jossey-Bass.

Krasner, L. (1971). Behavior therapy. In P. H. Mussen (Ed.), *Annual Review of Psychology, 22,* Palo Alto, CA: Annual Reviews.

Kubie, L. S. (1934). Relation of the conditioned reflex to psychoanalytic technique. *Archives of Neurology and Psychiatry, 32,* 1137–1142.

Kwiatkowska, H. (1978). *Family therapy and evaluation throughout.* Springfield, IL: C. C. Thomas.

Lambert, M. J., & Bergin, A. E. (1994). The effectiveness of psychotherapy. In A. E. Bergin & S. L. Garfield (Eds.), *Handbook of psychotherapy and behavior change* (4th ed.). New York: Wiley.

Landy, R. (1993). *Person and performance: The meaning of role in drama, therapy, and everyday life.* New York: Guilford.

Latner, J. (1992). The theory of Gestalt therapy. In E. C. Nevin (Ed.), *Gestalt therapy: Perspectives and applications.* New York: Gardner Press.

Lazarus, A. A. (1971). *Behavior therapy and beyond.* New York: McGraw-Hill.

Lazarus, A. A. (1989). *The practice of multimodal therapy.* Baltimore: Johns Hopkins University Press.

Lazarus, A. A. (1995). Different types of eclecticism and integration: Let's be aware of the dangers. *Journal of Psychotherapy Integration, 5*, 27–39.

Lee, W. M. L. (1996). New directions in multicultural counseling. *Counseling and Human Development, 29*(2), 1–11.

Levenson, H. (1995). *Time-limited dynamic psychotherapy: A guide to clinical practice.* New York: Basic Books.

Levy, F. J. (1988). *Dance/movement therapy: A healing art.* Reston, VA: American Alliance for Health, Physical Education, Recreation, and Dance.

Lewin, R. (2000). *Complexity: Life at the edge of chaos.* Chicago: University of Chicago Press.

Lindley, O. R., Skinner, B. F., & Solomon, H. C. (1953). *Studies in behavior therapy.* Waltham, MA: Metropolitan State Hospital.

Lindsey, C. (1998). *Toward an integration of narrative approaches into therapeutic encounters.* Lubbock, TX: Unpublished manuscript.

Linesch, D. (1993). *Art therapy with families in crisis.* New York: Brunner/Mazel.

Llewelyn, S. P., Elliott, R., Shapiro, D. A., & Hardy, G. (1988). Client perceptions of significant events in prescriptive and exploratory periods of individual therapy. *British Journal of Clinical Psychology, 27*, 105–114.

Lorenz, E. (1996). *The essence of chaos.* Seattle: University of Washington Press.

Lovett, J. (1999). *Small wonders: Healing childhood trauma with EMDR.* New York: Free Press.

Lowen, A. (1958). *The language of the body.* New York: Macmillan.

Lowen, A. (1976). *Bioenergetics.* New York: Penguin.

Lowen, A. (1997). My evolution as a body-mind therapist. In J. Zeig (Ed.), *Evolution of psychotherapy: The third conference.* New York: Brunner/Mazel.

Luborsky, L., & Crits-Christoph, P. (1990). *Understanding transference: The CCRT method.* New York: Basic Books.

Madanes, C. (1981). *Strategic family therapy.* San Francisco: Jossey-Bass.

Madanes, C. (1984). *Behind the one-way mirror: Advances in the practice of strategic therapy.* San Francisco: Jossey-Bass.

Mahoney, M. J. (1995). Theoretical developments in the cognitive and constructive psychotherapies. In M. J. Mahoney (Ed.), *Cognitive and constructive psychotherapies.* New York: Springer.

Mahoney, M. J. (1997). Brief moments and enduring effects: Reflections on time and timing in psychotherapy. In W. J. Matthews et al. (Eds.), *Current thinking and research in brief therapy: Solutions, strategies, narratives.* New York: Brunner/ Mazel.

Mahrer, A. (1986). *Therapeutic experiencing: The process of change.* New York: Morrow.

Mahrer, A. (1996). *The complete guide to experiential psychotherapy.* New York: Wiley.

Malan, D. H. (1976). *The frontier of brief psychotherapy.* New York: Plenum.

Malan, D. H., & Osimo, F. (1992). *Psychodyamics, training, and outcome in brief psychotherapy.* Oxford: Butterworth-Heinemannn.

Mander, G. (2000). *Psychodynamic approach to brief therapy.* Thousand Oaks, CA: Sage.

Mann, J. (1973). *Time-limited psychotherapy.* Cambridge, MA: Harvard University Press.

Mann, J., & Goldman, R. (1982). *A casebook in time-limited psychotherapy.* New York: Mc-Graw-Hill.

Maslow, A. (1954). *Motivation and personality.* New York: Harper.

Maslow, A. (1965). *Toward a psychology of being.* Princeton, NJ: Van Nostrand.

Maslow, A. (1976). *The further reaches of human nature.* New York: Penguin.

Masson, J. (1998). *The assault on truth: Freud's suppression of the seduction theory.* New York: Pocket Books.

May, K. M. (Ed.). (2000). *Feminist family therapy.* Alexandria, VA: American Counseling Association.

May, R. (1958). *Existence: A new dimension in psychiatry and psychology.* New York: Basic Books.

May, R. (1967). *The art of counseling.* Nashville: Abingdon.

May, R. (1981). *Freedom and destiny.* New York: W. W. Norton.

May, R. (1983). *The discovery of being.* New York: W. W. Norton.

May, R., & Yalom, I. (1995). Existential psychotherapy. In R. J. Corsini & D. Wedding (Eds.), *Current psychotherapies* (5th ed.). Itasca, IL: F. E. Peacock.

McAuliffe, G. J., & Eriksen, K. P. (1999). Toward a constructivist and developmental identity for the counseling profession: The context-phase-stage-style model. *Journal of Counseling and Development, 77,* 267–280.

McCullough, L. (1991). Davanloo's short-term dynamic psychotherapy. In R. C. Curtis & G. Stricker (Eds.), *How people change: Inside and outside therapy.* New York: Plenum.

McGoldrick, M., Gerson, R., & Shellenberger, S. (1999). *Genograms: Assessment and intervention* (2nd ed.). New York: W. W. Norton.

McLendon, J. A. (1999). The Satir system in action. In D. J. Weiner (Ed.), *Beyond talk therapy: Using movement and expressive techniques in clinical practice.* Washington, DC: American Psychological Association.

McMullin, R. E. (1999). *The new handbook of cognitive therapy techniques.* New York: W. W. Norton.

Mearns, D., & Thorne, B. (1999). *Person-centered counselling in action.* London: Sage.

Meichenbaum, D. (1977). *Cognitive behavior modification: An integrative approach.* New York: Plenum.

Meichenbaum, D. (1985). *Stress inoculation training.* New York: Pergamon Press.

Meichenbaum, D. (1993). Changing conceptions of cognitive behavior modification: Retrospects and prospects. *Journal of Consulting and Clinical Psychology, 61,* 202–204.

Meichenbaum, D. (1997). The evolution of a cognitive-behavior therapist. In J. Zeig (Ed.), *Evolution of psychotherapy: The third conference.* New York: Brunner/ Mazel.

Menaker, E. (1991). Questioning the sacred cow of transference. In R. C. Curtis & G. Stricker (Eds.), *How people change: Inside and outside therapy.* New York: Plenum.

Messer, S. B., & Warren, C. S. (1995). *Models of brief psychodynamic therapy: A comparative approach.* New York: Guilford.

Messer, S. B., & Wachtel, P. L. (1997). The contemporary psychotherapeutic landscape: Issues and prospects. In P. L. Wachtel & S. B. Messer (Eds.), *Theories of psychotherapy: Origins and evolution.* Washington, DC: American Psychological Association.

Minuchin, S., and Fishman, H. C. (1981). *Family therapy techniques.* Cambridge, MA: Harvard University Press.

Monk, G. (1997). *Contrasting assumptions about mental problems.* Hamilton, N.Z.: Unpublished manuscript.

Monk, G., Winslade, J., Crocket, K., & Epston, D. (1997). *Narrative therapy in practice.* San Francisco: Jossey-Bass.

Moran, M. (1991). Chaos and psychoanalysis: The fluidic nature of mind. *International Review of Psychoanalysis, 18,* 211–221.

Moreno, J. L. (1946). *Psychodrama.* Beacon, NY: Beacon House.

Moreno, Z. T., Blomkvist, L. D., & Rutzel, T. (2000). *Psychodrama, surplus reality, and the art of healing.* Philadelphia: Brunner/Routledge.

Mosak, H. H. (1995). Adlerian psychotherapy. In R. J. Corsini & D. Wedding (Eds.). *Current psychotherapies* (5th ed.). Itasca, IL: F. E. Peacock.

Moss, D. (Ed.). (1999). *Humanistic and transpersonal psychology.* Westport, CT: Greenwood Press.

Moustakas, C. (1961). *Loneliness.* Englewood Cliffs, NJ: Prentice-Hall.

Moustakas, C. (1986). Being in, being for, and being with. *Humanistic Psychologist, 14,* 100–104.

Moustakas, C. (1994). *Existential psychotherapy and interpretation of dreams.* Northvale, NJ: Jason Aronson.

Mueser, K. T., & Glynn, S. M. (1999). *Behavioral family therapy for psychiatric disorders* (2nd ed.). Oakland, CA: New Harbringer Press.

Murphy, P. L., & Abraham, F. D. (1995). Feminist psychology: Prototype of the dynamical revolution in psychology. In F. D. Abraham & A. R. Gilgen (Eds.), *Chaos theory in psychology.* Westport, CT: Praeger.

National Association of Social Workers. (1996). *Code of ethics.* Washington, DC: Author.

Neenan, M., & Dryden, W. (1999). *Rational emotive behaviour therapy: Advances in theory and practice.* London: Whurr Publishers.

Neimeyer, R. A. (1995). An invitation to constructivist psychotherapies. In R. A. Neimeyer & M. J. Mahoney (Eds.), *Constructivism in psychotherapy.* Washington, DC: American Psychological Association.

Nichols, M. P., & Schwartz, R. C. (1998). *Family therapy: Concepts and methods.* Boston: Allyn and Bacon.

Norcross, J. C., & Goldstein, M. R. (Eds.). (1992). *Handbook of psychotherapy integration.* New York: Basic Books.

Norcross, J. C., & Prochaska, J. O. (1988). A study of eclectic (and integrative) views revisited. *Professional Psychology: Research and Practice, 19,* 170–174.

Novotni, M., & Petersen, R. (2000). *What does everybody else know that I don't?* Specialty Press.

Nystul, M. (1999). Problem solving counseling: Integrating Adler's and Glasser's theories. In R. E. Watts & J. Carlson (Eds.), *Interventions and strategies in counseling and psychotherapy.* Philadelphia: Accelerated Development.

O'Donohue, W., & Krasner, L. (1995). *Theories of behavior therapy: Exploring behavior change.* Washington, DC: American Psychological Association.

O'Hanlon, W. H. (1993). *Solution-oriented therapy.* New York: W. W. Norton.

O'Hanlon, W. H., & Hexum, A. L. (1990). *An uncommon casebook: The complete clinical work of Milton H. Erickson.* New York: W. W. Norton.

O'Hanlon, W. H., & Weiner-Davis, M. (1989). *In search of solutions: A new direction in psychotherapy.* New York: W. W. Norton.

Okun, B. F., Fried, J., & Okun, M. L. (1999). *Understanding diversity: A learning-as-practice primer.* Pacific Grove, CA: Brooks/Cole.

Orlinsky, D. E., & Howard, K. I. (1987). A generic model of psychotherapy. *Journal of Integrative and Eclectic Psychotherapy, 6,* 6–27.

Parry, A., & Doan, R. E. (1994). *Story re-visions: Narrative therapy in the postmodern world.* New York: Guilford.

Patterson, C. H. (1986). *Theories of counseling and psychotherapy* (4th ed.). New York: Harper and Row.

Patton, W., & McMahon, M. (1999). *Career development and systems theory.* Pacific Grove, CA: Brooks/Cole.

Perls, F. (1969). *Gestalt therapy verbatim.* Lafayette, CA: Real People Press.

Perna, P. A. (1995). Regression as chaotic uncertainty and transformation. In R. Robterston & A. Combs (Eds.), *Chaos theory in psychology and the life sciences.* Englewood Cliffs, NJ: Lawrence Erlbaum.

Peterson, J. V., & Nisenholz, B. (1999). *Orientation to counseling* (4th ed.). Boston: Allyn and Bacon.

Phillips, J. R. (1984). Influences on personal growth as viewed by former psychotherapy patients. *Dissertation Abstracts International, 44,* 441A.

Pierrakos, J. L. (1987). *Core energetics.* Mendocino, CA: LifeRhythm.

Polster, E., & Polster, M. (1973). *Gestalt therapy integrated.* New York: Vintage.

Potash, H. M. (1994). *Pragmatic-existential psychotherapy with personality disorders.* Madison, NJ: Gordon Handwerk Publishers.

Prigogine, I., & Stengers, I. (1984). *Order out of chaos: Man's new dialogue with nature.* New York: Bantam.

Prochaska, J. O., & DiClemente, C. C. (1982). Transtheoretical therapy: Toward a more integrative model of change. *Psychotherapy: Theory, Research, and Practice, 19,* 276–288.

Prochaska, J. O., & Norcross, J. C. (1999). *Systems of psychotherapy: A transtheoretical approach* (4th ed.). Pacific Grove, CA: Brooks/Cole.

Prouty, G. (1994). *Theoretical evolutions in person-centered/experiential therapy.* Westport, CT: Praeger.

Quick, E. K. (1996). *Doing what works in brief therapy.* New York: Academic Press.

Rand, N., & Torok, M. (1997). *Questions for Freud: The secret history of psychoanalysis.* Cambridge, MA: Harvard University Press.

Reich, W. (1945). *Character analysis.* New York: Farrar, Straus & Giroux.

Rennie, D. L. (1998) *Person-centered counselling.* London: Sage.

Reynolds, D. K. (1980). *The quiet therapies.* Honolulu: University of Hawaii Press.

Rieff, P. (1979). *Freud: The mind of a moralist.* Chicago: University of Chicago Press.

Riley, S. (1994). *Integrated approaches to family art therapy.* Chicago: Magnolia Street Publishers.

Robinson, L. A., Berman, J. S., & Neimeyer, R. A. (1990). Psychotherapy for treatment of depression: A comprehensive review of controlled outcome research. *Psychological Bulletin, 108,* 30–49.

Rogers, C. (1931). *A test of personality adjustment.* New York: Association Press.

Rogers, C. (1939). *The clinical treatment of the problem child.* Boston: Houghton Mifflin.

Rogers, C. (1942). *Counseling and psychotherapy.* Boston: Houghton Mifflin.

Rogers, C. (1957). The necessary and sufficient conditions of therapeutic personality change. *Journal of Consulting Psychology, 21,* 95–103.

Rogers, C. (1980). *A way of being.* Boston: Houghton Mifflin.

Rosenbaum, H. (1999). *Zen and the heart of psychotherapy.* Philadelphia: Brunner/Routledge.

Rosenzweig, S. (1936). Some implicit common factors in diverse methods of psychotherapy. *American Journal of Orthopsychiatry, 6,* 412–415.

Rosewater, L. B., & Walker, L. E. (1985). *Handbook of feminist therapy.* New York: Springer.

Rubin, J. (1999). *Art therapy: An introduction.* New York: Brunner/Mazel.

Satir, V. (1972). *Peoplemaking.* Palo Alto, CA: Science and Behavior Books.

Satir, V. (1988). *The new peoplemaking.* Palo Alto, CA: Science and Behavior Books.

Schneider, K., Bugental, J. T., & Pierson, J. F. (Eds.). (2001). *Handbook of humanistic psychology.* Thousand Oaks, CA: Sage.

Schon, D. A. (1983). *The reflective practitioner.* New York: Basic Books.

Seligman, M. E. (1995). The effectiveness of psychotherapy: The Consumer Reports survey. *American Psychologist, 50,* 965–974.

Shapiro, F. (1989). Eye movement desensitization: A new treatment for post-traumatic stress disorder. *Journal of Behavior Therapy and Experimental Psychiatry, 20,* 211–217.

Shapiro, F. (1995). *Eye movement desensitization and reprocessing: Basic principles, protocols, and procedures.* New York: Guilford.

Shapiro, F. (1997). Eye movement desensitization and reprocessing: Research and clinical significance. In W. J. Matthews & J. H. Edgette (Eds.), *Current thinking and research in brief therapy.* New York: Brunner/Mazel.

Shapiro, F., & Forrest, M. S. (1998). *EMDR: The breakthrough therapy for overcoming anxiety, stress, and trauma.* New York: Basic Books.

Sharf, R. (2000). *Theories of psychotherapy and counseling* (2nd ed.). Belmont, CA: Wadsworth.

Shulman, B. (1973). *Contributions to individual psychology.* Chicago: Alfred Adler Institute.

Sifneos, P. E. (1987). *Short-term dynamic psychotherapy: Evaluation and technique.* New York: Plenum.

Sklare, G. B. (1997). *Brief counseling that works: A solution-focused approach for school counselors.* Thousand Oaks, CA: Corwin Press.

Smith, J. C. (1999). *ABC relaxation training: A practical guide for health professionals.* New York: Springer.

Smith, M. L., Glass, G. V., & Miller, T. (1980). *The benefits of psychotherapy.* Baltimore: Johns Hopkins University Press.

Snyder, C. R., Michael, S. T., & Cheavens, J. S. (1999). Hope as a psychotherapeutic foundation of common factors, placebos, and expectancies. In M. A. Hubble, B. L. Duncan, & S. D. Miller (Eds.), *The heart and soul of change.* Washington, DC: American Psychological Association.

Solomon, M. F. (1989). *Narcissism and intimacy.* New York: W. W. Norton.

Spence, D. P. (1982). *Narrative and historical truth.* New York: W. W. Norton.

Spinelli, E. (1997). *Tales of unknowing: Eight stories of existential therapy.* Washington Square: New York University Press.

Stiles, W. B., Shapiro, D. A., & Elliott, R. (1986). Are all psychotherapies equivalent? *American Psychologist, 41,* 165–180.

Strasser, F., & Strasser, A. (1997). *Existential time-limited therapy.* New York: Wiley.

Strupp, H. H., & Binder, J. L. (1984). *Psychotherapy in a new key: A guide to time-limited dynamic psychotherapy.* New York: Basic Books.

Sue, W. S., Ivey, A. E., & Pedersen, P. B. (1996). *A theory of multicultural counseling and therapy.* Pacific Grove, CA: Brooks/Cole.

Sue, D. W., & Sue, S. (1990). *Counseling the culturally different.* New York: Wiley.

Sullivan, H. S. (1953). *The interpersonal theory of psychiatry.* New York: W. W. Norton.

Svartberg, M., & Stiles, T. C. (1994). Therapeutic alliance, therapeutic competence, and client change. *Psychotherapy Research, 4,* 20–33.

Sweeney, T. J. (1998). *Adlerian counseling: A practitioner's approach* (4th ed.). Philadelphia: Accelerated Development.

Tallman, K., & Bohart, A. C. (1999). The client as a common factor: Clients as self-healers. In M. A. Hubble, B. L. Duncan, & S. D. Miller (Eds.), *The heart and soul of change.* Washington, DC: American Psychological Association.

Talmon, M. (1990). *Single-session therapy.* San Francisco: Jossey-Bass.

Task Force on Promotion and Dissemination of Psychological Procedures. (1995). Training in and dissemination of empirically validated psychological treatments: Report and recommendations. *The Clinical Psychologist, 48,* 3–24.

Thomas, L. (1974). *Lives of a cell.* New York: Viking.

Thompson, R. (1996). *Counseling techniques.* Philadelphia: Accelerated Development.

Tobin, D. L. (2000). *Coping strategies therapy for bulimia nervosa.* Washington, DC: American Psychological Association.

Truax, C. B., & Carkhuff, R. R. (1967). *Toward effective counseling and psychotherapy: Training and practice.* Chicago: Aldine.

Unger, R., & Crawford, M. (1996). *Women and gender: A feminist psychology* (2nd ed.). New York: McGraw-Hill.

Vande Kemp, H., & Anderson, T. L. (1999). Feminist psychology and humanistic psychology. In D. Moss (Ed.), *Humanistic and transpersonal psychology.* Westport, CT: Greenwood Press.

Von Bertalanffy, L. (1968). *General systems theory.* New York: George Braziller.

Wachtel, P. L. (1977). *Psychoanalysis and behavior therapy: Toward an integration.* New York: Basic Books.

Wachtel, P. L. (1997). *Psychoanalysis, behavior therapy, and the relational world.* Washington, DC: American Psychological Association.

Waldrop, M. M. (1992). *Complexity: The emerging science at the edge of order and chaos.* New York: Simon & Schuster.

Walen, S., DiGiuseppe, R., & Dryden, W. (1992). *A practitioner's guide to rational-emotive therapy.* New York: Oxford University Press.

Walter, J., & Peller, J. (1994). *Becoming solution-focused in brief therapy.* New York: Brunner/Mazel.

Warshaw, S. L. (1996). In B. Gerson (Ed.), *The therapist as a person*. New York: Analytic Press.

Watson, J. B. (1924) *Behaviorism*. Chicago: University of Chicago Press.

Watts, R. (1999). The vision of Adler: An introduction. In R. E. Watts & J. Carlson (Eds.). *Interventions and strategies in counseling and psychotherapy*. Philadelphia: Accelerated Development.

Watzlawick, P. (1978). *The language of change: Elements of therapeutic communication*. New York: Basic Books.

Watzlawick, P. (1997). Insight may cause blindness. In J. K. Zeig (Ed.), *The evolution of psychotherapy: The third conference*. New York: Brunner/Mazel.

Watzlawick, P., Beavin, J., & Jackson, D. (1967). *Pragmatics of human communication*. New York: W. W. Norton.

Watzlawick, P., Weakland, J., & Fisch, R. (1974). *Change: Principles of problem formation and problem resolution*. New York: W. W. Norton.

Weifel, E. R. (1998). *Ethics in counseling and psychotherapy*. Pacific Grove, CA: Brooks/Cole.

Weiner, D. J. (Ed.). (1999). *Beyond talk therapy: Using movement and expressive techniques in clinical practice*. Washington, DC: American Psychological Association.

Weisgerber, K. (Ed.). (1999). *The traumatic bond between psychotherapists and managed care*. New York: Jason Aronson.

Wheeler, G. (1991). *Gestalt reconsidered*. New York: Gardner Press.

Wheelis, A. (1973). *How people change*. New York: Harper and Row.

White, M., & Epston, D. (1990). *Narrative means to therapeutic ends*. New York: W. W. Norton.

Wiener, N. (1948). Cybernetics. *Scientific American, 179* (5), 14–18.

Wilbur, K. (1981). *No boundary*. Boston: Shambhala.

Wilbur, M. P., Kulikowich, J. M., Roberts-Wilbur, J., & Torres-Rivera, E. (1995). Chaos theory and counselor training. *Counseling and Values, 39*, 129–144.

Wile, D. (1977). Ideological conflicts between clients and psychotherapists. *American Journal of Psychotherapy, 37*, 437–449.

Wilson, E. O. (1975). *Sociobiology: The new synthesis*. Cambridge, MA: Harvard University Press.

Wilson, E. O. (1978). *On human nature*. Cambridge, MA: Harvard University Press.

Winnicott, D. W. (1958). *Through pediatrics to psychoanalysis*. London: Tavistock Publications.

Winslade, J., & Monk, G. (2000). *Narrative mediation: A new approach to conflict resolution*. San Francisco: Jossey-Bass.

Wittine, B. (1989). Basic postulates for a transpersonal psychotherapy. In R. Valle & S. Halling (Eds.), *Existential-phenomenological perspectives in psychology*. New York: Plenum.

Wolberg, L. R. (1980). *Handbook of short-term psychotherapy*. New York: Thieme-Stratton.

Wolfert, R., & Cook, C. A. (1999). Gestalt therapy in action. In D. J. Weiner (Ed.), *Beyond talk therapy: Using movement and expressive techniques in clinical practice*. Washington, DC: American Psychological Association.

Wolfe, J. (1993). *RET resource book for practitioners*. New York: Albert Ellis Institute.

Wolitzky, D. L., & Eagle, M. N. (1997). Psychoanalytic theories of psychotherapy. In P. L. Wachtel & S. B. Messer (Eds.), *Theories of psychotherapy: Origins and evolution*. Washington, DC: American Psychological Association.

Wolpe, J. (1958). *Psychotherapy by reciprocal inhibition*. Stanford, CA: Stanford University Press.

Wolpe, J. (1997). From psychoanalytic to behavioral methods in anxiety disorders: A continuing evolution. In J. K. Zeig (Ed.), *The evolution of psychotherapy: The third conference*. New York: Brunner/Mazel.

Wright, R. (1994). *The moral animal*. New York: Pantheon.

Wubbolding, R. E. (1988). *Using reality therapy*. New York: Harper and Row.

Wubbolding, R. E. (1991). *Understanding reality therapy*. New York: Harper and Row.

Wubbolding, R. E. (2000). *Reality therapy for the 21st century*. New York: Brunner/ Routledge.

Yalom, I. (1980). *Existential psychotherapy*. New York: Basic Books.

Yalom, I. (1980). Introduction. In C. Rogers, *A way of being*. Boston: Houghton Mifflin.

Yalom, I. (1989). *Love's executioner and other tales of psychotherapy*. New York: Basic Books.

Yalom, I. (1995). *The theory and practice of group psychotherapy* (4th ed.). New York: Basic Books.

Yang, D. J. (2000). Craving your next Web fix. *U.S. News and World Report*, Jan. 17, 41.

Zeig, J. K. (Ed.). (1982). *Ericksonian approaches to hypnosis and psychotherapy*. New York: Brunner/Mazel.

Zeig, J. K. (Ed.). (1985). *Ericksonian psychotherapy*. New York: Brunner/Mazel.

Zukav, G. (1979). *The dancing Wu Li masters: An overview of the new physics*. New York: Bantam.

INDEX

DATE DUE

MR 27 08			
9/13/09			